GW00724736

# Islamic Criminal Law in Northern Nigeria

panacea — p-84

Lay out: Gunnar J. Weimann, Zoetermeer.
Cover illustration: View of the city of Kano; Gunnar J. Weimann, Zoetermeer.
Cover design: René Staelenberg, Amsterdam.

ISBN 978 90 5629 655 1
NUR 740

© Gunnar J. Weimann / Vossiuspers UvA – Amsterdam University Press, 2010

All rights reserved. Without limiting the rights under copyright reserved above, no part of this book may be reproduced, stored in or introduced into a retrieval system, or transmitted, in any form or by any means (electronic, mechanical, photocopying, recording or otherwise) without the written permission of both the copyright owner and the author of the book.

# Islamic Criminal Law in Northern Nigeria

## Politics, Religion, Judicial Practice

ACADEMISCH PROEFSCHRIFT

ter verkrijging van de graad van doctor
aan de Universiteit van Amsterdam
op gezag van de Rector Magnificus
prof. dr. D.C. van den Boom
ten overstaan van een door het college voor promoties
ingestelde commissie,
in het openbaar te verdedigen in de Agnietenkapel
op woensdag 15 december 2010, te 10.00 uur

door


Gunnar Jochen Weimann

geboren te München, Duitsland

*Promotiecommissie*

Promotor: Prof. dr. mr. R. Peters

Overige leden: Prof. dr. mr. C.W. Maris
Prof. dr. A.C.A.E. Moors
Prof. dr. S. Reichmuth
Dr. B.F. Soares
Prof. dr. G.A. Wiegers

Faculteit der Geesteswetenschappen

# Table of Contents

# Acknowledgments

Four chapters of this book have been published previously and are reprinted with permission from Brill Academic Publishers.

Chapter One was published as "Judicial Practice in Islamic Criminal Law in Nigeria—A tentative overview," *Islamic Law and Society*, 14:2 (2007), 240-86.

Chapter Two was published as "Divine Law and Local Custom in Northern Nigerian *zinā* Trials," *Die Welt des Islams*, 49:3-4 (2009), 429-65.

Chapter Three was published as "Islamic Law and Muslim Governance in Northern Nigeria: crimes against life, limb and property in *sharīʿa* judicial practice," *Islamic Law and Society*, 17:3-4 (2010).

Chapter Four was published as "An Alternative Vision of Shariʿa Application in Northern Nigeria: Ibrahim Salih's *Hadd Offences in the Shariʿa*," *Journal of Religion in Africa*, 40:2 (2010), 192-221.

Many are those who have encouraged and supported me during my time in Nigeria and my subsequent research. First and foremost, thanks are due to Prof. Dr. Rudolph Peters for readily accepting me as a PhD candidate after we had shaken hands on one or two occasions in Nigeria. Next is Dr. Philip Ostien for his untiring support, his friendship and advice. I also thank Dr. Franz Kogelmann for the same motives. I have learnt a lot from the editorial comments and stylistic observations of Prof. David S. Powers and Prof. Stefan Reichmuth and the content-related suggestions of the anonymous referees. Final responsibility for the contents rests with me.

My stay in Nigeria from 2002 to 2004 provided me with valuable insights in Nigerian affairs. While in Nigeria, I received support from a great number of people. I am particularly grateful to my former colleagues at the Embassy of the Federal Republic of Germany in Abuja, especially to Ambassador Dr. Dietmar Kreusel, under whose supervision I was able to establish valuable contacts and acquire first-hand experience with Nigerian politics and northern Nigerian Islam. Special thanks go to Wolfgang Erdmannsdörfer for his much appreciated help in collecting the available electronic editions of Nigerian newspapers.

I am indebted to many friends and partners in Nigeria, who made my stay in their country pleasant and enriching. Among them were Dr. Jibrin Ibrahim and Charmaine Pereira, Sanusi Lamido Sanusi and Prof. Muhammad Tawfiq Ladan. Special thanks are due to Gisela Seidensticker-Brikay for her invaluable help in establishing contacts in Maiduguri. Many discussions on a personal and professional level have linked me to Jens Paulus of the Konrad Adenauer Foundation, who arrived in Nigeria at a similar time and whose professional interests partially overlapped with mine. I also would like to thank my fellow PhD candidate Olaf Köndgen for his encouragement and advice. Finally, special thanks are due to Randa Kinany.

My wife, Dr. Liliana Patricia Ramírez Ríos, has always accompanied and encouraged me during the sometimes difficult times of writing this thesis. My children, Oscar and Amanda, have no other memory than that of a world in which their father often enough deserted them to write his ominous "English book." To them, I dedicate this work.

# Introduction

On 19 August 2002, Amina Lawal of Kurami village in northern Nigeria's Katsina State, a divorcee of 30 years of age, lost the appeal of her sentence of death by stoning for extramarital sexual intercourse, which had been imposed by a *sharīʿa* court in the town of Bakori in March of the same year on the strength of a pregnancy out of wedlock. The upper *sharīʿa* court that handled the appeal did not accept Lawal's withdrawal of her initial confession and confirmed the verdict of first instance. This was a major setback for Lawal's defence team, which in the interceding months had invested time and resources to build a solid case combining arguments founded in statutory and Islamic law. The 19 August 2002 was my first day in office at the Embassy of the Federal Republic of Germany in the Nigerian capital Abuja on a two-year assignment in the framework of the German Foreign Office's efforts for the promotion of intercultural dialogue.[1] It is not surprising, then, that the implementation of Islamic criminal law became a major focus of my interest in the following two years. The present work is based on the experience and material gathered during this period.

The adoption and enforcement of Islamic criminal legislation in northern Nigeria, which started in 1999 when Nigeria returned to a civilian system of government, raises the question of how Islamic criminal law can be implemented and how Muslims in northern Nigeria think it should be implemented in the present political and social situation. The present research focuses on judicial practice in Islamic criminal law in northern Nigeria after 1999. The different studies try to provide explanations for the observed developments from different perspectives, including regional and historical preferences (Chapter One), cultural factors (Chapter Two), political considerations and strategies (Chapter Three), and the religious doctrine (Chapters Four and Five).

Islamic criminal law is not an unproblematic term. Criminal law, the body of law that regulates the power of the state to inflict punishment on persons in order to enforce compliance with certain rules (Peters 2005: 1), does not have an equivalent in the traditional categories of Islamic law in the sense of a single, unified branch of the law. Offences in the prosecution of which the state is expected to be involved are discussed in three separate chapters (Peters 2005: 7). Firstly, the *ḥadd* (pl.

[1] On the German Foreign Office's activities in the area of intercultural dialogue, see <http://www.diplo.de/diplo/de/Aussenpolitik/KulturDialog/InterkulturellerDialog/Uebersicht.html>. Some conclusions drawn from my time in Nigeria are formulated in Weimann (2004).

*ḥudūd*) offences are those mentioned in the Qur'ān and are considered violations of the claims of God (*ḥuqūq Allāh*). They comprise theft, banditry, unlawful sexual intercourse, the unfounded accusation of unlawful sexual intercourse, drinking alcohol and—according to some schools of jurisprudence—apostasy. Secondly, the prosecution of offences against persons, i.e. homicide and wounding, is subject to the will of the victim or—in case of homicide—the victim's family, who have considerable influence on the punishment, e.g. by demanding or remitting retaliation (*qiṣāṣ*), and are entitled to financial compensation (*diya*). Finally, the courts and the public authorities are empowered to punish at their discretion sinful or forbidden behaviour (*taʿzīr*) or acts endangering public order or state security (*siyāsa*). Thus, Islamic criminal law is a term which combines offences in Islamic law which under a Western legal understanding are regarded as part of criminal law. This composite nature of Islamic criminal law is not only a construct of Western scholarship but is also reflected in the *sharīʿa* penal codes of northern Nigeria, which are divided into "hudud and hudud-related offences," "qisas and qisas-related offences" and "ta'azir offences."[2] Thus, the term symbolises the transformation of Islamic law in the process of its adaptation to legal and constitutional systems based on Western concepts. The questions whether this transformation, which for instance entails the codification of the law, is acceptable and whether the Islamic nature of the law is preserved in this transformation are at the centre of debates about the status of Islam in many countries at the present stage.

On the national and international level, the debate on *sharīʿa* implementation in northern Nigeria has focused on political and ideological arguments. With regard to judicial practice, reference has constantly been made to a small number of iconic cases, in particular those of Safiyya Hussaini and Amina Lawal. Reliable statistical data on judicial practice, which could have helped to objectify the debate, has been missing. Even large-scale research projects, such as the joint University of Jos (Nigeria) and University of Bayreuth (Germany) project led by Franz Kogelmann and Philip Ostien (Ostien, Nasir and Kogelmann 2005; Ostien 2007), have been unable to provide such data. The only way of gathering representative data would have been to visit a fair sample of the *sharīʿa* courts and prisons in northern Nigeria individually to copy their registers. Given the geographical expanse of the twelve northern Nigerian states implementing the *sharīʿa*, the number of *sharīʿa* courts (70 to 80 per state) and prisons and the difficulties of getting access to and inter-

[2] See, e.g., the table of contents of the Harmonised Sharia Penal Code (in Ostien 2007: 4:36-44).

preting the registers, this exceeds the scope or budget of any research project.

The articles which form the body of the present work aim at gathering and analysing publicly available data on judicial practice in Islamic criminal law in northern Nigeria. Information on judicial practice was mainly provided by journalists and civil rights groups. In the absence of more reliable data, this has become the main source of information for the present studies.[3] It is to be noted that such sources do not provide a representative sample but are an illustration of *sharīʿa* judicial practice in northern Nigeria after 1999. The identified trials are listed in the appendix.

In my professional capacity, I had the opportunity to devote much time to establishing and maintaining contacts with Muslim leaders, rights groups and other stakeholders in an effort to understand the history and the dynamics underlying the initiative to introduce and implement legislation inspired by the *sharīʿa*, particularly as regards criminal offences. For reasons of loyalty towards my former employer and towards the people who spoke to me in my capacity as a German diplomat, I cannot refer to the conversations which I entertained with my contacts in Nigeria. Thus, my research has not been based on field work. Instead, I have relied on published sources and information provided by fellow researchers. My selection and use of academic and media sources were informed by the background knowledge I acquired in Nigeria.

My arrival in Nigeria in August 2002 coincided with the climax of the controversy about *sharīʿa* implementation in northern Nigeria. The tensions which had been building up over the two preceding years escalated in the so-called Miss World crisis a few months after my arrival. Even though the aborted 2002 Miss World contest in Nigeria was not directly related to the introduction of Islamic criminal law, it was interpreted on both sides in the context of the deteriorating relations resulting from this introduction between the country's Muslim north and the mainly Christian south.

From a southern perspective, the defiance of northern politicians and religious leaders, the huge crowds cheering at ceremonies marking the introduction of the *sharīʿa* and the implementation of corporal punishments for offences such as drinking alcohol and amputations of hands for theft nurtured the already existing fears of an Islamisation of the Nigerian state. The apparently intransigent reactions even from Muslim umbrella organisations in northern Nigeria suggested a concerted effort to assert Muslim predominance in the country. It was alleged that Islam

[3] For a discussion of the sources used for the analysis of judicial practice in Islamic criminal law, see Chapters One (pp. 23 to 25) and Three (pp. 110 to 111).

*fear of return to dhimmi status*

was rapidly expanding and that Nigeria was at risk of becoming a country dominated by Muslims in which other religions would be relegated to a position of minorities without rights. However, true figures on the number of converts to or from Islam are missing, as are statistics of the overall proportion of Muslims and Christians in the Nigerian population.[4] Instead, the spectre of mass conversions to Islam is used to emphasise the "Muslim threat."[5]

From a northern perspective, the massive support which the proposal of introducing Islamic criminal legislation received almost instantaneously from the northern Muslim population was the result of several factors, one of which was a widespread feeling of political and economic marginalisation of northern Nigeria. This feeling was not entirely unfounded if one compares Nigeria's relatively high per capita income, which mainly results from the export of crude oil, with the dire living conditions and the situation with regard to education, health care and social services of the great majority of people living in northern Nigeria. In 1996, 37 percent of the population in north-west Nigeria were very poor with an additional 40 percent ranked as relatively poor.[6] Only slightly better was the situation in the north-east: here 34 percent were living in great, 36 percent in relative poverty. Thus, only twenty to thirty percent of the people in the area were living in acceptable conditions. Northern Nigeria is not only one of the poorest but also one of the most densely populated areas of sub-Saharan Africa, and the population continues to grow rapidly.[7] In 1999, a woman in the north-west had an average of 6.5 children in the course of her reproductive life, in the north-east even 6.8. Only a minority of the children receive a school education: in the north-west, 32 percent of boys and 24 percent of girls between 6 and 11 years of age attended primary school; in the north-east, these figures were 41 percent for boys and 37 percent for girls. The lack of access to education is reflected in a high rate of illiteracy: in 1999, no more than 40 percent of men and 20 percent of women above the age of 15 in northern Nigeria knew how to read and write, while in southern Nigeria 74 percent of men and 55 to 60 percent of women were literate.

Economic destitution is coupled with political depravation. In a country that over decades has been ranked among the most corrupt world-

*lack of education.*

---

[4] Conventionally, it is said that Muslims make up half of the population, while Christians and followers of African traditional religions account for the other half. National censuses in the past decades eschewed the question of religious affiliation.

[5] See Pérouse de Montclos (2008).

[6] These and the following figures are taken from Hodges (2001).

[7] In light of the progressing desertification, this fact aggravates the already existing tensions between communities, in particular between cattle-raising nomads and sedentary farmers.

wide, military and civilian regimes, which ironically were mainly dominated by northern Muslims, have ruled without responding to the needs or demands of the population and have contributed to the emergence of a political culture based on personal profit and clientelism. Economic and political marginalisation is not restricted to northern Nigeria, as the continuing crisis in the Niger delta shows. In an effort to avoid being challenged and to sustain their power, the Nigerian ruling classes have exploited topics such as the perceived north-south antagonism, which has existed since the colonial days, for rallying support. This has led to the paradox that, whereas Muslim and Christian political leaders in Nigeria are able to cooperate on a pragmatic level for the mutual benefit of maintaining their position of power, they have done little to attenuate ethno-religious tension.

The use of religion for rallying political support has a long tradition in northern Nigeria. For centuries, Islam was a major source of legitimacy for the states in the region. The application of Islamic law by the ruler was the most visible aspect of upholding Islam and, consequently, has become the symbol of northern religious and political autonomy in modern times. After independence in 1960, the feeling of marginalisation in northern Nigeria became identified with the question of the status of Islamic law, particularly its criminal aspects, in the Nigerian state. In the eyes of many Muslims, Islamic criminal law had virtually been abolished. Demands for a reassertion of the Muslim identity of northern Nigeria through an amplification of the application of the *sharīʿa* were blocked in the constituent assemblies held since then.[8]

When general elections were announced after General Abacha's death in 1998, candidates for political office suddenly had to compete for popular support. Some sought to profit from the north-south antagonism, for example by promising to implement the *sharīʿa*, knowing that the population would see this as a new option to re-establish justice where all others had failed (Loimeier 2007: 65). One of the gubernatorial candidates in Zamfara State, Ahmad Sani, promised "religious reforms" and, upon this, was elected governor. Part of the reforms introduced after his victory was the introduction of Islamic criminal law. This triggered a popular movement which forced eleven other state governors to follow Ahmad Sani's example.

The introduction of Islamic criminal law not only surprised the non-Muslims in Nigeria but also overwhelmed the existing Islamic judicial system. This system consisted of area courts, which applied uncodified Islamic law in civil and the Penal Code in criminal cases, and state *sharīʿa*

---

[8] Ostien (2006) believes that had the Christians made concessions with regard to the status of Islamic law, the drive for *sharīʿa* introduction had not acquired such strength.

codified Islamic criminal law

courts of appeal, competent exclusively to hear appeals from area courts in matters of Islamic personal law. Appeals in criminal and other civil cases went from the area courts to the secular state high courts. Most area court judges became judges of the newly established *sharīʿa* courts. They were totally unprepared for and overwhelmed by the new tasks assigned to them, i.e. the administration of codified Islamic criminal law. The hasty and incomplete introduction of the new legislation and pressure exerted by Muslim lobby groups are largely to blame for the bad quality of the sentences passed in the initial phase.

*impact of Shari'a law has been minimal.*

# Chapter One:
# Judicial Practice in Islamic Criminal Law in Nigeria—A Tentative Overview[9]

Abstract: Uniquely, in Nigeria Islamic criminal law was introduced in the framework of a secular federal constitution. In 2000 and 2001, twelve northern states adopted legislation on the *hadd* offences and the Islamic law of homicide and bodily harm. Reliable statistics on the number of cases tried under the new laws are unavailable. Based on information from the media and human rights organisations, I present roughly 125 criminal cases tried before Nigerian *sharīʿa* courts between 2000 and 2004. This sample shows that the *sharīʿa* was particularly enforced in states dominated by the Hausa. In religiously mixed states, the bid to introduce the *sharīʿa* became part of the religious groups' competition for hegemony and access to public resources, with violent consequences. The expectations which many Muslims attached to the introduction of the *sharīʿa* were inflated. Its impact on the security of life and property, the fight against corruption and the promotion of good governance has probably been minimal.

*criminal offences.*

In January 2000, the Northern Nigerian state of Zamfara enacted a *sharīʿa* penal code[10] which "restored" the *hadd* offences[11] and their respective punishments as defined by Islamic tradition and the Islamic law of homicide and bodily harm. Within a short period of time, eleven northern states of the Nigerian federation followed the example of Zamfara. This act of legislation was preceded, accompanied and followed by a controversy in which all parties exhibited equal passion and anger. While supporters of the "re-introduction of the *sharīʿa*" point to their

---

[9] Originally published in *Islamic Law and Society*, 14:2 (2007), 240-86, and reprinted with permission of Brill Academic Publishers. Some minor errors of fact have been rectified.
[10] The spelling used in the code is "Shari'ah." Except in quotations, I will use *sharīʿa* throughout this book.
[11] The *hadd* (arab. lit. "border," plural *hudūd*) offences and their punishments are mainly deduced from the Qurʾān and refined in the *sunna* or prophetic tradition. They are defined as infringements of the right of God (*haqq Allāh*) towards man and prosecuted by public authorities, which in practice makes them comparable to criminal offences in Western legal terminology.

constitutional right to practice their religion,[12] opponents regard some punishments prescribed by the new codes, in particular stoning to death and amputation, as inhuman and degrading, and therefore unconstitutional.[13]

In September 2001, Zamfara State Governor Sani Ahmad Yerima, in an interview with the Nigerian daily *This Day*, described the adoption of the *sharīʿa* by most states in northern Nigeria as politically motivated and intended to allow governors to be re-elected to office. The governor was quoted as saying that only Zamfara and, to some extent, Niger State adopted the *sharīʿa* with purely religious intentions, whereas the other states were motivated by political expediency.[14]

The impression gained from the present overview of judicial practice in criminal trials before *sharīʿa* courts in northern Nigeria is that the Zamfara State governor seems to be right insofar as many of his counterparts in other states were reluctant to follow Zamfara's example in introducing and implementing the *sharīʿa*, in particular as refers to the *ḥadd* punishments. The political motivation for this reluctance is probably fear of the reaction of the international community and the Nigerian federal government, through which—we should not forget—the Nigerian oil revenues are channelled down to the states. In particular, governors belonging to the same political party as then Nigerian President Olusegun Obasanjo, the People's Democratic Party (PDP), such as Umaru Musa Yar'Adua of Katsina State, Rabi'u Musa Kwankwaso of Kano State, Abdulkadir Kure of Niger State, Ahmed Makarfi of Kaduna State, and Ahmadu Adamu Mu'azu of Bauchi State, found themselves caught between their loyalty to the federal government and the pressure mounted by Muslim lobby groups. As we will see, this dilemma seems to have led several of them to introduce Islamic criminal legislation without putting much effort into its implementation. Umaru Musa Yar'Adua of Katsina State was later nominated PDP's presidential candidate and emerged as the winner in the widely criticised April 2007 presidential polls.[15] Being governor of a "*sharīʿa* state" did not harm his political career. The fact that Katsina has one of the highest numbers of reported *sharīʿa* trials, shows,

[12] Section 38 (1) of the 1999 Nigerian Constitution guarantees freedom of religion: "Every person shall be entitled to freedom of thought, conscience and religion, including freedom to change his religion or belief, and freedom (either alone or in community with others, and in public or in private) to manifest and propagate his religion or belief in worship, teaching, practice and observance."

[13] Section 34 (1) of the Constitution prohibits torture and inhuman treatment: "Every individual is entitled to respect for the dignity of his person, and accordingly—(a) no person shall be subject to torture or to inhuman or degrading treatment; [...]."

[14] "Sharia Was Politically Motivated - Ahmed Sani," *This Day*, 01/09/2001, 1 and 4.

[15] After a prolonged illness, President Yar'adua died on 5 May 2010 before the end of his first mandate. He was succeeded by his deputy, Goodluck Jonathan.

if anything, that the political leadership of the states is only one actor among others in the implementation of the *sharīʿa*.

The motivation of the governor of Zamfara State to initiate a movement which was to propagate throughout northern Nigeria, however, can also be described in political terms. In the electoral campaigns of 1999 and 2003, he presented himself as the restorer of the *sharīʿa*, comparing himself implicitly to the founder of the Sokoto Caliphate, Usman ɗan Fodio, who, in the beginning of the nineteenth century AD, united the independent Hausa city-states in what is generally referred to as the Sokoto *jihād*. In both elections, this strategy yielded the expected results. A similar strategy brought victory to Ibrahim Shekarau in Kano State in the 2003 gubernatorial election. After 2003, the topic rapidly lost prominence in the Nigerian public discourse. In the campaigns for the 2007 presidential and gubernatorial elections, the implementation of the *sharīʿa* does not seem to have played any role.

The most prominent cases since the introduction of Islamic criminal law were those of Safiyya Hussaini of Sokoto State and Amina Lawal of Katsina State. Both women were convicted of *zinā* and sentenced to death by stoning, although the sentences were subsequently annulled on appeal. In fact, little is known about the true number of cases tried under Islamic criminal law in northern Nigeria or about regional differences in the application of Islamic criminal law on the state level. In this chapter I present available information on Islamic criminal law cases tried by *sharīʿa* courts in northern Nigeria in the first five years after the enactment of the Zamfara Sharīʿa Penal Code. After a short historical introduction and a description of the offences and punishments defined by the *sharīʿa* penal codes, I will analyse the situation in particular states. The Nigerian situation is unique in that Islamic criminal law was introduced on a state level within the legal framework set by a secular federal constitution. Therefore, I seek to identify differences in the introduction and application of Islamic criminal law in the various states.

## Historical overview

Many northern Nigerian Muslims regard the "re-introduction" of the criminal offences and their respective punishments as defined by traditional Islamic jurisprudence (*fiqh*), as a long-awaited step of decolonisation. Islamic law was applied in both criminal and personal matters in northern Nigeria until the advent of British colonial rule, which was established in the aftermath of Lord Lugard's military victory over the Hausa-Fulani-dominated Sokoto Caliphate in 1902/03.[16] The British co-

[16] For a summary of the history of the Sokoto Caliphate and the prominent role of Islam in it, see Hauck (2001: 98-108).

1960 - independence - federal republic -
3 autonomous entities.

lonial authorities maintained the pre-colonial Islamic justice system, albeit under their supervision, curtailing the application of the law only in areas which they defined as repugnant to "natural justice, equity and good conscience."[17] The British treated Islamic law as a system of customary law applicable to the native population, like customary law systems in other parts of Nigeria during the colonial period.

At independence in 1960, Nigeria became a federal republic composed of three autonomous entities, each dominated by one major ethnic group: the Yoruba in the Western Region; the Igbo in the Eastern Region; and the Hausa-Fulani in the Northern Region, which in itself accounts for more than half of the Nigerian population. While political life in the Northern Region is dominated by the Muslim Hausa-Fulani elite, the area also contains numerous ethnic minorities, in particular small, largely Christian ethnic groups living in the so-called Middle Belt in the southern part of the region, in addition to Muslim ethnic groups, such as the Kanuri in the north-east.

Since 1960, the Northern Region has been divided into ever smaller states on several occasions. By 1996, nineteen different states[18] and the Federal Capital Territory around the new capital Abuja shared the space previously occupied by the Northern Region. Within these new states, the ethnic and religious majorities have been redefined. Some states, such as Katsina, Kebbi, Jigawa, Sokoto and Zamfara, have an almost exclusively Muslim, mainly Hausa-Fulani population. Not surprisingly, the inhabitants of these states identify strongly with the historic model of the Sokoto Caliphate. The same applies in principle to Kano State even though large immigrant communities of different religious and ethnic background live in Kano metropolis, the economic centre of northern Nigeria. The north-eastern states of Borno and Yobe, which are dominated by the Muslim Kanuri, and Hausa-dominated Gombe[19] have important Muslim and non-Muslim minorities. In Niger State, the predominant group is the Muslim Nupe. The remaining ten successor states of the Northern Region are religiously and ethnically divided. Some of these states have been the scene of violent confrontations between supporters and opponents of Islamic criminal law following the adoption of the controversial legislation by Zamfara State. Islamic criminal law was introduced in Bauchi and Kaduna, where hundreds of people were killed in "*sharīʿa* riots." Neighbouring Plateau was also engulfed in violence, at

[17] For the development of the application of the *sharīʿa* in Nigeria, see Peters (2003: 5-12).

[18] These are Adamawa, Bauchi, Benue, Borno, Gombe, Jigawa, Kaduna, Kano, Katsina, Kebbi, Kogi, Kwara, Nassarawa, Niger, Plateau, Sokoto, Taraba, Yobe, and Zamfara.

[19] In the previously published version of this article (Weimann 2007: 244 and 283), Gombe State is described as being dominated by the Kanuri ethnic group. This is incorrect. The majority of Gombe's population are Hausas.

least partly instigated by the introduction of Islamic criminal law in Bauchi.[20] However, Islamic criminal law was not introduced.

The British colonial authorities were aware of the threat to the country's unity posed by dissenting opinions about Islamic criminal law. Before Nigeria was granted independence in 1960, the colonial administration, in an attempt to accommodate the non-Muslim minorities living in northern Nigeria, brokered a compromise with the Muslim elite of the Northern Region which led to the adoption of the 1959 Penal Code for the Northern Region. This Penal Code was based on the Indian (1860) and the Sudanese (1899) Penal Codes, and was essentially an English code. However, here and there special provisions were included based on Islamic criminal law (Peters 2003: 12). The 1959 Penal Code was inherited by all nineteen successor states of the Northern Region.[21]

This compromise has been deemed insufficient by many Muslims in northern Nigeria. Every time the country has embarked on re-defining its constitutional order, Muslim delegates have attempted to strengthen the position of Islamic criminal law. The constituent assemblies of 1977, 1987 and 1994 were split over the issue of the *sharīʿa*. However, in the view of the Nigerian scholar Kyari Mohammed (2002), it was the military, which has governed the country for most of its independence, that ultimately has prevented the status quo from being changed. He explains: *Military – prevented status quo from being changed*

> On all occasions the military government stopped the debate. The inability to [...] thrash out the shari'ah issue comprehensively may have made it an attractive campaign platform for politicians who do not have much to offer their constituents. The military by scuttling the debates, rather than allowing [them] to go to [their] logical conclusion, [has] contributed to making the shari'ah a hot potato.

After his victory in the 1999 gubernatorial elections, Zamfara State Governor Sani Ahmad began to act on his pre-election promise that he would "re-introduce the *sharīʿa*." This move may be seen as the abolition of a legal system that was imposed on northern Nigerian Muslims by the British colonial power. For many Muslims the slogan of "re-introducing the *sharīʿa*" had became linked to the hope of building a just, equitable and democratic society. Muhammed Tabi'u (2004: 119), Professor of Law at Bayero University in Kano, explains that in "a gradual process of transformation and subjugation" the British colonial authorities in-

---

[20] On the 2001 violence in Plateau State, see Human Rights Watch (2001).
[21] The laws of the original regions or states were continued in force in and became the laws of the new states carved out of them (Ostien 2006: 221-55).

de-secularise the legal system

tended to secularise the legal system in northern Nigeria, a process Muslims have tried to reverse since independence by "remov[ing] restrictions that impede the administration of the Shari'a." He points out:

> There was considerable expectation that a new legal order would ensue [from the restoration of Islamic criminal law] that would guarantee security for life and property, fight corruption and promote good governance, including better government commitment to the welfare of the people. The restoration of Shari'a was largely seen as a means of gaining access to much sought after but very elusive dividends of democracy.

This intention to restore the *sharīʿa* in northern Nigeria notwithstanding, the application of Islamic criminal law in twelve northern Nigerian states differs in important ways from the way in which it was administered in pre-colonial times. The 1999 Nigerian Constitution, while empowering states to introduce legislation on criminal matters,[22] demands that criminal offences and their punishments be specified in a written law enacted by the federal parliament or a state parliament.[23] To be applicable within the legal framework set by the Nigerian Constitution, Islamic criminal law therefore needed to be codified.[24]

Islamic criminal law was introduced in Zamfara and most other states by establishing *sharīʿa* courts competent to hear both civil and criminal cases involving Muslims and those non-Muslims who choose to be tried by them. At the same time, a corresponding legislation has been enacted, in particular a *sharīʿa* penal code that replaced the 1959 Penal Code for the Northern Region in the *sharīʿa* courts. Non-Muslims in these states continue to be tried by magistrate courts that apply the old Penal Code. In Niger State, the changes were introduced by amending the existing Penal Code. Here, the amendments have introduced additional

---

[22] Criminal offences remain unmentioned both in Part I (Exclusive Legislative List of the Federal Government) and Part II (Concurrent Legislative List) of the Second Schedule (Legislative Powers) of the Nigerian Constitution. Thus, legislation on criminal offences is the sole responsibility of the states.

[23] Section 36 (12) of the 1999 Constitution: "Subject as otherwise provided by this Constitution, a person shall not be convicted of a criminal offence unless that offence is defined and the penalty therefor is prescribed in a written law, and in this subsection, a written law refers to an Act of the National Assembly or a Law of a State, any subsidiary legislation or instrument under the provisions of a law."

[24] In some states, cases of Islamic criminal law were tried and sentences executed even before a *sharīʿa* penal code came into force (see Peters 2003: 13). On the other hand, one important ground of appeal against the stoning sentence inflicted on Safiyya Hussaini was the retroactive application of the Sokoto State Sharīʿa Penal Code, since she had been arraigned before the bill was signed into law. It, therefore, appears that a continued application of uncodified Islamic criminal law would have been contested on constitutional grounds.

*Codifying* — base judgements on the letter of the codes.

punishments applicable to Muslims with regard to offences like homicide, theft, adultery, defamation, intoxication, rape and causing bodily harm (Ladan 2004: 82f). As long as the Penal Code was the only criminal law applied in the nineteen successor states of the Northern Region there was, in essence, legal uniformity across the region. With the introduction of Islamic criminal legislation on the state level, however, this uniformity was compromised. Nevertheless, most differences between the codes are minor and concern the punishments defined for specific offences.

Codifying Islamic criminal law has changed the way in which justice is administered. Instead of relying on their knowledge of the classical works of Mālikī *fiqh*, the advice of the *'ulamā'* or Muslim scholars, and other instruments of Islamic law, judges in *sharī'a* courts are now required to base their judgments on the letter of the codes. Previously, most *sharī'a* judges exercised their profession in the former area courts, where they administered the *sharī'a* as an un-codified "customary" law in matters of personal and family law and applied the Penal Code in criminal matters. In the lower instances, in particular, they seem to have lacked the training and experience to implement the new codified legislation. Ruud Peters (2003: 17) reports from his 2001 field trip to Nigeria:

> We heard many complaints that the changes [in the judiciary] were not properly introduced. The judges of the new Shari'a Courts were the same judges who had sat in the area courts, but they had not been prepared nor trained to apply the changes in the legal system. Ignorance of the law of procedure, we were told, seriously hampered the course of justice.

This fact, together with the absence of *sharī'a* criminal procedure codes in several states during the first years after the introduction of Islamic criminal law,[25] no doubt accounts for the high number of sentences under Islamic criminal law, in particular in the initial period, which ignored procedural guarantees and evidentiary restrictions defined by Mālikī law.

## Islamic criminal offences and punishments in Nigeria

The *sharī'a* penal codes provide for offences and punishments applicable to Muslims and to non-Muslims who voluntarily consent to being tried before a *sharī'a* court (Ladan 2004: 80). The codes maintain the provisions of the 1959 Penal Code under the heading of *ta'zīr*, or discretionary punishment, to which are added chapters defining the *hadd* offences and the

---

[25] Muhammad Tawfiq Ladan (2004: 82) mentions three states (Katsina, Borno, Bauchi) which by August 2003 had only draft bills of *sharī'a* criminal procedure codes.

Zina – death by stoning

Islamic law of homicide and bodily harm. In addition, the number of offences punishable by corporal punishments (caning or flogging) has been increased (Peters 2006: 223). The rules with regard to *ḥadd* offences largely follow the classical Mālikī doctrine (Peters 2003: 18; for a comparative analysis of the codes, see ibid.: 17-30).

*Zinā*, or unlawful sexual intercourse, is punishable by death by stoning, if the offender is currently married or has been married in the past. Otherwise the penalty is 100 lashes. In addition, men are imprisoned for one year. The same punishments are prescribed for rape, sodomy and incest, except that in cases of rape, the male offender is also required to pay the proper bride price (*ṣadāq al-mithl*).[26]

*Qadhf*, or false accusation of *zinā*, is punishable by eighty lashes.

*Shurb al-khamr*, or drinking alcohol or any intoxicant voluntarily, is punishable by eighty lashes, according to most codes.

*Sariqa*, or theft, is punishable by amputation of the right hand from the wrist for first offenders. The definition of *sariqa* respects many of the classical restrictions on the application of the *ḥadd* punishment for theft. In particular the stolen property must have a minimum value (*niṣāb*) and must have been kept in a safe place (*ḥirz*).[27] However, the codes fail to define the exact monetary value of the *niṣāb*. Some codes specify cases in which, in accordance with classical Mālikī law, the application of the penalty of amputation for theft is precluded (Peters 2003: 22).

The punishment for *ḥirāba*, or armed robbery, depends on the gravity of the damage caused. Most codes make it punishable by life imprisonment, if neither property nor life was taken; by amputation of the right hand and the left foot, if property was stolen; and by death, if murder was committed. Some codes prescribe crucifixion as punishment for armed robbery if property and lives were taken.[28]

The most important difference between the provisions regarding homicide and bodily harm found in the Islamic criminal codes and the classical Islamic doctrine is the fact that it is now the state prosecutor who brings the accused to trial, not the victim or the victim's next of

---

[26] See, e.g., Zamfara State Sharīʿa Penal Code, Section 129(c). The proper brideprice (also *mahr al-mithl*), which according to the classical doctrine is to be paid in cases of unlawful intercourse in which the woman is unmarried, is the average bride-price that a woman of the same age and social status would receive upon marriage in that region (Peters 2005: 59).

[27] Zamfara State Sharīʿa Penal Code, Section 144: "The offence of Theft shall be deemed to have been committed by a person who covertly, dishonestly and without consent, takes any lawful and movable property belonging to another, out of its place of custody (*hirz*) and valued not less than the minimum stipulated value (*nisab*) without any justification."

[28] E.g. Zamfara State Sharīʿa Penal Code, Section 153 (d). However, the punishment of crucifixion is not defined, which is a serious omission since the matter is controversial in classical Mālikī doctrine (Peters 2003: 24).

kin. However, the basic principle of retaliation (*qiṣāṣ*) is respected. This means that, once the court has convicted a defendant of intentional homicide, punishment can be death, if the victim's next of kin demand it. The method of execution is the same as that used by the offender on his victim. In cases of grievous bodily harm, the victim can demand retaliation, i.e. that the convict suffer the same injury as the victim. In most cases, the plaintiffs have the possibility to remit the *qiṣāṣ* punishment and accept monetary compensation (*diya*) instead.

If they remit both, the murderer receives a corporal punishment and/or imprisonment, depending on the *sharīʿa* penal code applicable. In cases of unintentional homicide or wounding, the perpetrator must pay *diya*. The codes, however, do not clearly define the size of *diya*, setting it variously at "one thousand dinars, or twelve thousand dirhams or 100 camels."[29]

The chapter on *taʿzīr* of the *sharīʿa* penal codes contains the same offences listed in the 1959 Penal Code. In particular, it includes provisions regarding offences committed by or relating to public servants.[30] In defiance of the classical doctrine, Kano State considers embezzlement of public funds a special form of *sariqa* which is punishable by amputation of the right hand and not less than five years' imprisonment.[31] These provisions aim at fighting the rampant corruption, an evil for which the introduction of Islamic criminal law promised to bring a rapid remedy.

Rudolph Peters (2003: 14) notes that the *sharīʿa* penal codes seem to have been drafted in great haste, which "explains the poor legislative quality of the codes with lapses such as faulty, sometimes even incomprehensible wording, incorrect cross references, omissions and contradictions." After drafting the 2000 Zamfara Sharīʿa Penal Code, the Centre for Islamic Legal Studies at Ahmadu Bello University in Zaria has produced both a Harmonised Sharīʿa Penal Code and a Harmonised Sharīʿa Criminal Procedure Code, which were submitted to the twelve northern Nigerian *sharīʿa* states. At least Zamfara State has adopted the harmonised codes in late 2005.[32]

## Reporting on cases tried under Islamic criminal law

To comprehensively assess Islamic criminal law court practice in northern Nigeria after the introduction of *sharīʿa* penal codes, a broader foundation is needed than the few internationally known cases. Although

[29] E.g. Zamfara State Sharīʿa Penal Code, Section 59.
[30] E.g. Zamfara State Sharīʿa Penal Code, Sections 288-304: "Offences by or Relating to Public Servants."
[31] Kano State Sharīʿa Penal Code, Section 134B.
[32] Personal communication by Philip Ostien in April 2007.

media - owned / based in South - hostile to Shari'a -

official statistics on judicial cases in Nigeria remain unobtainable,[33] the relatively free and diverse Nigerian print media and reports by nongovernmental organisations are important sources of information on the judicial practice in criminal trials before *sharīʿa* courts in Northern Nigeria. This valuable source of information calls for careful analysis: Nigerian journalists do not always have expert knowledge of Islamic criminal law, and most of the print media in Nigeria are based in the south and owned by either the *sharīʿa*-hostile federal government or by non-Muslim private owners, most of whom are critical of the "*sharīʿa* project of the north." This is likely to impact on the way they report on cases under Islamic criminal law in the northern states. Nevertheless, the facts contained in these media reports can provide a general, albeit often enough incomplete, picture of the reported cases.

The present survey is based on news articles found in the Nigerian print media (or on their respective websites)[34] and a limited number of non-Nigerian news providers: BBC World News, Agence France Presse (AFP)[35] and the United Nations Integrated Regional Information Networks (IRIN).[36] This information is complemented by reports issued by non-governmental organisations (NGO), in particular Human Rights Watch (HRW) and the Lagos-based BAOBAB for Women's Human Rights. The information retrieved often remains fragmentary. Frequently, the history and the final outcome of a case remain unknown. This is probably due to the thin media coverage of events taking place in northern Nigeria, in particular on the regional and local level. It may be assumed that the cases reported in the press represent only a small fraction of all criminal cases tried before *sharīʿa* courts in northern Nigeria. In addition, many cases tried before *sharīʿa* courts involved offences already defined in the 1959 Penal Code, which were taken up by the *sharīʿa* penal codes under the heading of *taʿzīr*. As such, although technically trials under the new Islamic criminal codes, they did not constitute anything novel and, therefore, were not reported individually in the media.

---

[33] The lack of official data has been repeatedly noted, e.g. Human Rights Watch (2004).

[34] Articles were mainly taken from the following Nigerian newspapers: *This Day* (Lagos, private), *Daily Trust* and its weekly counterpart *Weekly Trust* (Abuja, private), *The Guardian* (Lagos, private), *Vanguard* (Lagos, private), *New Nigerian Newspaper* (Kaduna, federal government). Articles, the references of which do not include page numbers, were retrieved from the Internet.

[35] I thank Rudolph Peters for putting at my disposal AFP reports from September 2000 to May 2002.

[36] These foreign news providers were chosen because they have their own network of correspondents on the ground and do not rely on media or news agencies whose information they might not be able to verify. IRIN, however, seems at times to rely on reports from other news providers.

The abovementioned NGOs report on some cases that are not mentioned in the media. Many of these cases come to the attention of these groups when their members or lawyers engaged by them visit prisons to talk to defendants in unrelated cases. It seems that many people are charged and imprisoned on remand while awaiting trial, or sentenced and kept in prison waiting for their sentence to be implemented, without the media taking notice of them. For certain types of cases, i.e. cases whose political sensitivity awakens the media's interest, it can be assumed that the picture drawn by the media is not too distant from reality. Case numbers should be reasonably reliable (a) in cases of *zinā*, or illicit sexual relations, at least those cases which have been appealed, because these trials have become the symbol, for *sharīʿa* critics, of the incompatibility of Islamic criminal law and the individual rights guaranteed by the Nigerian constitution, and (b) in cases involving public servants and politicians, because the issue of corruption and the accountability of state representatives arouses great interest in the Nigerian media, irrespective of the *sharīʿa* question.

## *Regional distribution of cases*

Since the beginning of 2000, twelve northern Nigerian states have introduced new punishments for violations of Islamic criminal law.[37] In this section, I will give a tentative overview of how this new legislation was introduced and applied on the state level between 2000 and 2004. In three states (Borno, Gombe, Yobe), no court cases under Islamic criminal law were reported during this period.[38] From Niger, Kaduna, and Kebbi only two, three, and eight cases respectively were reported in this period. This means that almost 90% of the roughly 125 cases identified[39] took place in six of the twelve states, i.e. Bauchi, Jigawa, Kano, Katsina,

---

[37] On the introduction of the new codes and changes in the judiciary, see Peters (2003: 13f) and Ladan (2004).

[38] This finding was confirmed to me by Philip Ostien in a personal communication in May 2006.

[39] The exact number of cases is not entirely clear because in some instances the reports do not specify if prison inmates were tried summarily or separately. The problem of the number of trials has led to some inconsistencies between the different chapters. In the overview provided in the appendix, I specify 137 cases, as opposed to 125 in this chapter, published as Weimann (2007). Here, I only considered cases between 2000 and 2004 reported in the media or by NGOs with explicit reference to a court trial. Excluded were trials after 2004 and prison inmates mentioned by NGOs without explicit reference to a trial in court. In later chapters, I found that these limitations unnecessarily restricted the number of cases in specific crime areas, in particular with regard to theft. Therefore, I decided to include also cases after 2004 and all prison inmates mentioned by NGOs. The change in methodology does not affect my conclusions, since these are not based on a statistical analysis. The trials described only serve as an illustration of judicial practice.

Sokoto, and Zamfara. The last three states alone account for 60% of all cases.

The general trend for all states except Bauchi is that the highest number of new cases reported is found shortly after the introduction of the respective Islamic criminal code. Over time, the number of cases reported decreases, until 2004, when no more than seven cases were reported, two in Zamfara and five in Bauchi. One explanation for this trend is that the attention paid to Islamic criminal law by the media has decreased over time. However, developments in the application of Islamic criminal law seem to be subject to dynamics on the state level. In order to demonstrate how judicial practice in Islamic criminal law is shaped by the particular circumstances in individual states, I will outline in brief the nature of Islamic criminal cases reported from each of the twelve "*sharīʿa* states," beginning with Zamfara and proceeding from there to predominantly Muslim states in the north-west, then in the north-east of the country. Finally, the religiously mixed states of Kaduna and Bauchi will be discussed.

### Zamfara

As the first state of the Nigerian federation, Zamfara put into force a new Islamic criminal code on 27 January 2000, although *sharīʿa* courts had been established earlier (Peters 2003: 13). In 2003, Zamfara State reportedly enacted a law establishing a state-controlled *sharīʿa* enforcement group, or *ḥisba*, responsible for arresting violators of *sharīʿa* regulations and handing them over to police (Garba 2006).

The pioneer state of Islamic criminal law in Nigeria accounts for roughly one-third of all cases, i.e. forty of the approximately 125 cases identified in this survey. Of these forty cases, sixteen were brought before a *sharīʿa* court in 2000, six in 2001, seven in 2002, nine in 2003 and two in 2004. This number, however, is probably only the tip of the iceberg. According to a press report, 5,287 criminal cases were treated by *sharīʿa* courts in Zamfara in 2002 alone.[40]

The most frequent indictment in the Zamfara cases is *sariqa* (theft), with eleven cases involving thirteen defendants.[41] In none of the re-

---

[40] "Sharia implementation: Are Muslims better off?", *Weekly Trust*, 18-24/01/2003, 1-2. The article does not specify the source of this information.

[41] These are the cases of Buba Bello Jangebe (amputation sentence in February 2000); Kabiru Salisu (sentenced in September 2000); Musa Gummi (amputation sentence in September 2000); Lawali "Inchi Tara" Isah (amputation sentence in December 2000); Lawali Dan Mango Dadin (amputation sentence in April 2001); Musa Shu'aibu (amputation sentence in September 2001); Abdullahi Abubakar (amputation sentence) and Mustapha Ibrahim (February 2002); Ibrahim Sulaiman (amputation sentence in January 2003); Abubakar Yusuf (amputation sentence in April 2003); Sirajo Mohammed (amputa-

ported cases was the defendant acquitted. Eleven defendants were sentenced to amputation. Only two defendants were reported to have received another form of punishment.[42] Two amputation sentences, handed down in 2000 and 2001, were carried out. These were the cases of Buba Bello Jangebe, sentenced in February 2000, amputated on 22 March 2000; and Lawali "Inchi Tara" Isah, sentenced in December 2000, amputated on 3 May 2001. After these two amputations, the state governor seemed reluctant to approve further amputations. Persons sentenced to amputation remained in prison. In June 2003, seven persons were reported awaiting amputation.[43] Human Rights Watch (2004: 39) gives the figure for early 2004 as twelve.

The only indictment for bodily harm in Zamfara State was reported as early as February 2000. A *sharīʿa* court in the state capital Gusau ordered Dantanim Tsafe to pay 157,933.70 Naira (1,500 US$)[44] for knocking out his wife's teeth in a quarrel. The media reports do not specify who would receive the money. Section 59 of the Zamfara State Sharīʿa Penal Code stipulates that *diya* is to be paid to the victim. However, one report mentions that Tsafe's wife pleaded for the "fine" to be set aside, as her husband was incapable of paying. The judge then reduced the fine to 50,000 Naira (470 US$).[45] If unable to pay, Tsafe would have to "submit his teeth for forceful removal." As Peters (2003: 28) points out, the *sharīʿa* penal codes, unlike classical doctrine, regard *diya* as a punishment, not as compensation for a civil liability. In the present case, this confusion may have been at the root of the wife's plea for a compensation to be set aside which she was entitled to receive.

With regard to *zinā* and related offences, no stoning sentence was reported from Zamfara between 2000 and 2004. The defendants in four *zinā* cases involving six persons,[46] one case of sodomy[47] and one of rape[48] all

---

tion sentence in April 2003); and Abubakar Lawali and Lawali Na Umma (both sentenced to amputation in May 2003).

[42] On 22 September 2000, Kabiru Sule was sentenced to six months in prison and 50 strokes of the cane for stealing a shirt valued 400 Naira (4 US$). See "Two men flogged publicly in Nigeria for drinking, stealing," AFP, 25/09/2000. Probably, the value of the stolen good was not regarded exceeding the *niṣāb*. In February 2002, Mustapha Ibrahim was sentenced to six months in prison and thirty lashes, while his accomplice Abdullah Abubakar received an amputation sentence (Human Rights Watch 2004: 56).

[43] "Sharia: Seven on Wrist Amputation List," *This Day*, 19/06/2003; and "Kano Sharia court orders amputation of two men for theft," *The Guardian* (Nigeria), 24/06/2003, 3.

[44] Conversion of Nigerian Naira amounts into US$ throughout this book is approximate, based on the contemporary exchange rate.

[45] "Zamfara amputation: Raising the stakes of Sharia implementation," *The Guardian* (Nigeria), 29/02/2000, 8. See also "Sharia: Farmer fined N158,000 for beating wife," *The Comet*, 15/02/2000, print edition.

[46] These were Zuweira Aliyu and Sani Mamman (February 2000); Bariya Ibrahim Maguza (September 2000); Amina Abdullahi (August 2001); Zuwayra Shinkafi and Sani Yahaya

received corporal punishments. Four *qadhf* cases ended in corporal punishment for five defendants.[49] In one case, it is not clear if the defendant was indicted.[50]

Other cases dealt with immoral behaviour, problems between co-wives, and criminal trespass.[51] Apparently, all defendants in these cases received corporal punishments. In September 2000, militant Islamic preacher Mohammadu Sani Julijoka was indicted for inciting violence and sentenced to one year in prison after he urged people to protest against the "lenient way" in which the *sharīʿa* is implemented in the state.[52]

Two further cases of interest in Zamfara State involved public servants. In November 2001, State House of Assembly Member Abdulsalami Ahmed Asha was indicted for selling his official car.[53] In October 2003, four members of the governor's re-election campaign committee were accused of diverting 374 motorcycles meant for the state's poverty alleviation programme.[54] No sentence has been reported in either case.

In addition to the *sharīʿa* penal code, the Zamfara government enacted legislation designed to impose Islamic conduct. In August 2000, 200 commercial motorcycle riders were arrested for carrying women under a newly passed law prohibiting the transport of passengers of the opposite sex on one motorcycle, if driver and passenger are not married. At

---

(March 2003). However, it cannot be excluded that this last case is identical with the first one. With exception of the year stated by HRW, there are striking similarities not only in the names but also in the facts reported.

[47] Abdullahi Abubakar Barkeji (February 2002).

[48] Tukur Aliyu (October 2003).

[49] An unidentified jealous husband (June 2000); Aishat and Haruna Dutsi (September 2000); Gado Maradun (2000); Ibrahim Na-Wurno (April 2001).

[50] In January 2004, Hafsi Bakura, chairperson of the ANPP governing party in Zamfara State, was reported to court for having accused the ANPP chairperson in Gusau Local Government Area of extramarital relations. It is unclear if the tribunal admitted the complaint for trial. See "ANPP chieftains in Sharia court for alleged adultery," *Daily Independent*, 05/01/2004.

[51] Garuba Bagobiri-Umguwar and Mohammadu Danige, accused of gambling (September 2000); Nagogo Kakumi, accused of marrying more than four wives (November 2001; however, it is unclear if this was treated as criminal case); Hawa Yahaya, Umar Garba and Yaro, accused of conspiracy to robbery (February 2002); Luba Mainasara, accused of beating her fellow wife with a pestle (April 2002); four accused of criminal trespass (January 2003); Shafaiatu Tukur, accused of burning down her fellow wife's home (September 2003); and a wedding party comprising eight individuals, accused of immoral acts (December 2004).

[52] "Islamic scholar jailed for preaching violence in Nigeria," AFP, 28/09/2000.

[53] "Sharia court orders amputation of hands, legs in Sokoto," *The Guardian* (Nigeria), 20/12/2001, print edition.

[54] "Sharia: Zamfara gov's campaign manager docked over theft," *Daily Independent*, 31/10/2003.

least two men, identified as Jafaru Isa and Maniru Abdullahi, were sentenced to twenty lashes.[55]

It seems that corporal punishments are carried out on a daily basis in the state. Human Rights Watch (2004: 58), relying on information provided by local sources in August 2003, reports that "floggings sometimes took place twenty times a week." In light of this, the five court cases for *shurb al-khamr* (consumption of alcohol) must be considered a small fraction of the real figure.[56]

Even though *ridda* (apostasy) is not defined as a crime in any of the *sharīʿa* penal codes in force in northern Nigeria, in a case reported from Zamfara State two former Muslims who allegedly converted to Christianity were brought before a *sharīʿa* court in April 2002. The case was dismissed (Human Rights Watch 2004: 82). This is the only case involving an accusation of *ridda* reported in Nigeria in the period under review.

## Katsina

Under strong pressure from pro-*sharīʿa* activists,[57] the Katsina State Government, then headed by Umaru Musa Yar'Adua (PDP), enacted a law establishing *sharīʿa* courts which commenced adjudicating on *sharīʿa*-related matters on 1 August 2000. Pressure on the government to implement the *sharīʿa* seems to have been maintained thereafter. Repeatedly, an independent committee on the implementation of the *sharīʿa*, headed by Aminu Maigari, accused the government of impeding the implementation of the *sharīʿa* in the state and threatened it with creating chaos if it failed to carry out the wish of the people.[58] Among the accusations levelled against the state government was the allegation that it issued a directive to the *sharīʿa* courts not to accept any more cases brought before them by independent, i.e. not state-controlled, *sharīʿa* monitoring groups (*ḥisba*).[59] Indeed, implementation of Islamic law does not appear to have been a priority for the state government. A prominent member of the state's official *sharīʿa* commission alleged in July 2003 that of eighty-six judges who were heading the state's *sharīʿa* courts, only two were competent.[60] Despite this reluctance, Katsina has

---

[55] "Sharia beating for motorcyclists," BBC News, 10/08/2000.

[56] Dahiru Sule (February 2000); Hassan Umoru (September 2000); Lawali Jekada (September 2000); *sharīʿa* court judge Muhammadu Na'ila (January 2001); Garba Aliyu (July 2003).

[57] "Katsina begins Sharia on August 1," *The Guardian* (Nigeria), 08/07/2000, 3.

[58] "Sharia: Katsina Muslims Accuse Governor of Paying Lip service to Implementation," *This Day*, 30/03/2001; and "Committee accuses Katsina govt of sabotaging Sharia," *Vanguard*, 01/08/2001, 10.

[59] "Sharia implementation in Katsina, the journey so far," *Weekly Trust*, 26/07-01/08/2003, 8. To my knowledge, Katsina State has not adopted legislation on the creation of a state-controlled *ḥisba*.

[60] Ibid.

one of the highest numbers of reported trials. Of seventeen criminal cases brought before the *sharīʿa* courts until the end of 2004, three were initiated between August and the end of 2000, nine took place in 2001, and three each took place in 2002 and 2003. By contrast, in January 2003, a press report stated that 7,491 cases under Islamic criminal law had been handled by the *sharīʿa* courts in Katsina State.[61] However, the report does not specify the period of time during which the trials had taken place.

The Katsina State Sharīʿa Penal Code was promulgated in August 2001.[62] Previously, several local government areas had put into force by-laws prohibiting the sale and consumption of alcoholic beverages, prostitution and related matters. Thus, it is not always possible to determine the legal basis of the sentence pronounced in cases reported from the state prior to the enactment of the *sharīʿa* penal code. Nevertheless, serious offences such as theft, bodily harm and *zinā* are exclusively defined by the *sharīʿa* penal code. At least four cases involving one of these offences were tried by *sharīʿa* courts in the state before codified Islamic criminal law was in place.[63]

Two cases tried in Katsina State attracted widespread attention. The first was the death sentence against Sani Yakubu Rodi for homicide in November 2001. Rodi was convicted of brutally stabbing to death the wife of a high-ranking security officer and their two children while attempting to rob their house. The victims' next of kin demanded retaliation (*qiṣāṣ*), and the court therefore ruled that Rodi should be stabbed to death with the same knife used in his crime.[64] The method of execution was later changed, reportedly to avert riots.[65] He was hanged on 3 January 2001. This is the only publicly acknowledged execution in Nigeria since the transition to a civilian government in May 1999. It is also the only reported execution pronounced under Islamic criminal law in the period under review.

The second internationally known case was the one of Amina Lawal Kurami, who, after giving birth to an illegitimate baby in November 2001, was sentenced to death by stoning for *zinā* in March 2002 on the

---

[61] "Sharia implementation: Are Muslims better off?" *Weekly Trust*, 18-24/01/2003, 1-2.

[62] "State-related materials acquired by state as of 4 April 2003" (henceforth SIDP), unpublished list of official reports related to Islamic criminal law and Islamic criminal legislation collected by the Shari'a Implementation Documentation Project of Jos (Nigeria) and Bayreuth (Germany) Universities.

[63] These are Nasiru Abba, accused of theft (August 2000); Attine Tanko and Lawal Sada, accused of *zinā* (November 2000); Isiyaku Sanni and Suleman Abdullahi, accused of theft (January 2001); and Ahmed Tijjani, accused of bodily harm (May 2001).

[64] "Sharia court sentences man to death by knifing," *The Guardian* (Nigeria), 15/11/2001, print edition.

[65] "First Nigerian executed under Sharia laws," BBC News, 04/01/2002.

Transition to civilian government in 1999.

basis of her confession.[66] The man she said was responsible for her pregnancy, Yahaya Mohammed, was acquitted after swearing by the Qur'ān that he was not the father of the child.[67] The first appeal against the verdict failed in August 2002, when the court did not accept Lawal's withdrawal of her confession. However, a second appeal, before the Katsina Sharīʿa Court of Appeal, resulted in quashing the death sentence. By a majority of four to one, the judges agreed that the two lower courts made a mistake of law by failing to carry out a proper investigation into the allegations against Lawal. Instead, the judges pointed out, "the prosecution of the case, when it began, was based on rumour."[68] The appeals court accepted Lawal's withdrawal of her confession. It also accepted the argument that there was a possibility for the child to be fathered by her former husband due to a delayed pregnancy ("sleeping embryo").[69] The presiding judge was quoted as saying that, although Amina previously had acknowledged the charge, it was clear that she was misled into confessing her guilt.[70] Lawal had not been told about the gravity of the punishment for the offence.

The remaining fifteen cases reported from the state received considerably less media coverage. In another *qiṣāṣ* case in May 2001, the victim asked for the removal of Ahmed Tijjani's right eye in retaliation for the loss of his own eye in a fight with the defendant. The judge ruled that Tijjani should have either one of his eyes removed or pay a compensation of 50 camels.[71] The plaintiff insisted on retaliation.[72] The execution of the sentence was not reported.

Regarding sex crimes, in addition to the case of Amina Lawal, one more *zinā* case was reported. In November 2000, Attine Tanko and Lawal Sada were sentenced to corporal punishment in combination, for the

[66] According to one source ("... As another woman gets stoning sentence in Katsina," *The Triumph*, 26/03/2002), the case had been before the court of first instance for at least ten months before judgment was passed. In this case, she must have been brought before the court while still pregnant. Another report ("Nigerian woman who faced stoning to death is acquitted," AFP, 25/03/2002) claims Lawal was arrested by people of her village of Kurami on 4 March 2002.

[67] "Sharia: Woman to Die by Stoning," *This Day*, 20/08/2002, 1 and 6.

[68] "Sharia court quashes sentence, frees Amina Lawal," *The Guardian* (Nigeria), 26/09/2003.

[69] In Mālikī law, a pregnancy can last up to a maximum of five to seven years, depending on the source. The claim by the defendant that her pregnancy goes back to a former husband produces *shubha*, which in itself should be enough for the *ḥadd* punishment not to be applicable (Peters 2006: 236f).

[70] "Adultery: Sharia Appeal Court frees Amina," *New Nigerian Newspaper*, 26/09/2003, 1 and 2.

[71] "In Katsina, it's an eye for an eye," *The Guardian* (Nigeria), 26/05/2001, 1 and 2.

[72] "Plaintiff asks Nigerian Islamic court to pluck out a man's eye," AFP, 26/05/2001.

male defendant, with a prison term.[73] In January 2003, Ibrahim Ayuba and Mohammed Ibrahim were indicted for rape of a 3.5 and a 4-year-old girl, respectively.[74] No sentence was reported.

Four cases of *sariqa* involving seven defendants were reported, one per year between 2000 and 2003.[75] Six of the defendants were sentenced to amputation of the right hand, and no sentence has been reported for the remaining defendant. No execution of an amputation sentence was reported from the state.

In three trials, a total of five men reportedly were convicted of drinking alcohol and given between eighty and ninety lashes.[76] Here again, it can be assumed that the real figure is higher. One man was flogged and jailed for indecent behaviour in 2003,[77] whereas in September 2002 seven women were given 15 strokes of the cane each in Funtua for "loitering." They had been accused of being prostitutes.[78]

Initially, the government-appointed Katsina State Sharīʿa Commission had banned public musical performances as un-Islamic. In fact, two court cases against musicians were reported in April 2001. In Funtua, Dauda Maroki and Gambo Maibishi, two traditional Hausa praise singers, were given ten strokes of the cane in public.[79] In the second case, traditional Hausa musician Sirajo Ashanlenle was pardoned after he promised never to play at weddings again.[80] In August 2001, however, the Sharīʿa Commission lifted the ban on performing music. The commission directed "that singing and drumming [are] desirable at wedding, Id

---

[73] "Second teen mum in Nigeria awaits flogging for pre-marital sex," AFP, 11/01/2001.
[74] "Two Charged with Raping Minors," *This Day*, 27/01/2003.
[75] Nasiru Abba (August 2000); Isiyaku Sanni and Suleman Abdullahi (amputation sentences in January 2001); two bull thieves (amputation sentences in 2002, reportedly appealed); and Abubakar Sani and Masaudu Ibrahim (amputation sentences in October 2003).
[76] Sule Sale (August 2000); Umaru Bubeh (March 2001). Kabiru Yusuf, Salisu Danjuma and Rabiu Mohammed were sentenced to eighty lashes each for drinking alcohol in contravention of a Funtua bye-law in May 2001. Three other men were discharged and acquitted from the same offence. See "3 old men receive 80 lashes each for consuming alcohol," *Vanguard*, 12/05/2001, 2.
[77] In June 2003, Abdu Rabe was found guilty of having entered in a female students' hostel, where he indecently touched a student. He was sentenced to two years' imprisonment and 20 strokes of the cane. See "Sharia court jails 45-yr-old man," *Daily Trust*, 24/06/2003, print edition.
[78] "Kebbi sacks Sharia court judge over financial scam," *The Guardian* (Nigeria), 10/09/2002, print edition.
[79] "Sharia strokes for musicians," *The Comet*, 24/04/2001, print edition; and "Sharia: Musicians Caned for Playing at Wedding," *This Day*, 27/04/2001.
[80] Ibid.

prayers and circumcision ceremonies, and [can] also take place during wars or while welcoming a fellow Moslem from a trip."[81]

In the only reported case of public officers being tried for abuse of authority, two policemen received 100 strokes of the cane in Funtua in 2001 following their conviction by a *sharīʿa* court for illegal confiscation of petrol from fuel vendors.[82]

## Sokoto

The legal basis for *sharīʿa* courts in Sokoto State was created in February 2000 with the promulgation of the Sharīʿa Courts Law.[83] These courts commenced their activities on 2 August 2000 (Peters 2003: 58). The Sokoto State Sharīʿa Penal Code came into force on 31 January 2001 (ibid.: 53). Fifteen trials reportedly took place in 2001 and four in 2002. Here again, the identified cases appear to be only a small fraction of the total number of cases.[84]

The Sokoto State Government was criticised for not giving statutory backing to a *sharīʿa* enforcement group or *ḥisba*. In an interview with the Nigerian weekly *Weekly Trust* in July 2003, the director of a local Islamic organisation said that the government's failure to introduce a state-controlled *ḥisba* weakened the administration of the *sharīʿa*. He added that there was a "group that is 'flogging' those who commit adultery or [are] found drinking alcohol," but this was insufficient.[85]

As in Zamfara, the indictment most frequently found in Sokoto State is *sariqa*. Seven cases involving eight defendants indicted for theft and one accomplice led to four amputation sentences.[86] One of the amputation sentences was executed: the right hand of Umaru Aliyu, sentenced in April 2001, was amputated in July 2001. Three defendants were sen-

[81] "Katsina Sharia panel okays singing, drumming," *The Guardian* (Nigeria), 10/08/2001, print edition.
[82] "Sharia court orders amputation of hands, legs in Sokoto," *The Guardian* (Nigeria), 20/12/2001, print edition.
[83] See SIDP.
[84] "In Sokoto, between May 2000 and September 2002, a total of 1,262 criminal cases was received out of which 1,024 have been disposed of with 248 pending" ("Sharia implementation: Are Muslims better off?" *Weekly Trust*, 18-24/01/2003, 1-2). The article does not specify the source of this information.
[85] "Poor sharia monitoring in Sokoto - Sheikh Isah," *Weekly Trust*, 26/07-01/08/2003, 7.
[86] Lawali Bello and Sani Mohammed (April 2001); Umaru Aliyu (amputation sentence in April 2001); Lawali Garba (amputation sentence in July 2001); Mohammed Ali (November 2001); Aminu Bello (amputation) and his accomplice Salisu Abdullahi (December 2001); Bello Garba (amputation sentence in January 2002); and Mustapha Abubakar (August 2002). An appeal was filed at least for the amputation sentences of Aminu Bello and Bello Garba. In the case of Mustapha Abubakar, the sentence has not been reported.

tenced to imprisonment and corporal punishment because the value of the stolen goods did not exceed the *niṣāb*.[87]

Two more amputation sentences were pronounced in connection with the only *ḥirāba* (armed robbery) case reported from northern Nigeria between 2000 and 2004. The two defendants, Garba Dandare and Sani Shehu, were charged with stealing goods and cash. In December 2001, they were sentenced to have their right hand and left foot amputated.[88] They declared they would not appeal the judgment. The execution of the sentence has not been reported. Apart from these cases, many more unreported amputation sentences seem to have been pronounced in the state. As early as December 2002, twelve people were in jail awaiting amputation.[89] Human Rights Watch (2004: 57) mentions around ten prisoners awaiting amputation in Sokoto prison in 2003, the majority of whom were under the age of eighteen.

Of the six identified *zinā* cases in the state, which involved eight defendants,[90] the most prominent was the trial of Safiyya Yakubu Hussaini, a divorcee who was indicted in October 2001 after being found pregnant out of wedlock.[91] Yakubu Abubakar, who she claimed was the father of her child, was acquitted due to lack of evidence.[92] Hussaini was sentenced to death by stoning on the strength of her confession, which she withdrew on appeal. The defence then argued that a child may be attributed to a woman's former husband for seven years after the divorce, and that the alleged offence had taken place before the enactment of the *sharīʿa* penal code. In March 2002, Hussaini was discharged and acquitted on procedural grounds. This was the only stoning-to-death sentence reported from the state.

Another noteworthy *zinā* trial was that of Abubakar Aliyu in July 2001. He was indicted for committing adultery with a mentally deranged

---

[87] Mohammed Ali, Lawali Bello and Sani Mohammed.

[88] "2 robbers face amputation in Sokoto," *Daily Trust*, 20/12/2001, 1; and "Sharia court orders amputation of hands, legs in Sokoto," *The Guardian* (Nigeria), 20/12/2001, print edition.

[89] "Eyewitness: Nigeria's Sharia amputees," BBC News, 19/12/2002.

[90] Hawa'u Garba and Hussaini Mamman (June 2001); Abubakar Aliyu (July 2001); Safiyya Yakubu Hussaini and Yakubu Abubakar (October 2001); Aisha Musa (2001); Hafsatu Abubakar and Umaru Shehu (January 2002); and Maryam Abubakar Bodinga (October 2002). The trials of Hafsatu Abubakar and Umaru Shehu, as well as Maryam Abubakar Bodingo ended with the defendants being discharged and acquitted. Aisha Musa filed an appeal after being sentenced to corporal punishment. For Hawa'u Garba and Hussaini Mamman, no sentence was reported.

[91] For a detailed discussion of this case, see Peters (2006).

[92] A confession allegedly made to police, in which he admitted having sexual relations with Hussaini, was dismissed by the judge "because, under Sharia law, four witnesses are required in a case of this nature" ("Nigerian appeals Sharia sentence," BBC News, 19/10/2001).

woman and sentenced to 100 strokes of the cane in addition to one year's imprisonment.[93] No mention is made of the woman's fate. According to Islamic law, an insane person has no criminal responsibility, making this one of the rare *zinā* trials in which only the man is indicted. After 2002, no new cases of *zinā* or a related offence were reported. But this does not necessarily reflect the reality: in January 2002, a number of young nursing mothers were being kept in Sokoto prison.[94] It is likely that some of these women were imprisoned, with or without trial, after they gave birth to children out of wedlock.

One indictment of a single defendant for *shurb al-khamr* was reported in April 2001,[95] and one trial of smoking Marihuana involving four Muslims was reported in July 2001.[96] All defendants were punished with lashing. As in other states, this is probably just the tip of the iceberg.

Another case tried in a *sharīʿa* court involved a man accused of selling carrion.[97] Mohammed Jobi and Issa Abdullahi, two officials of the state's branch of the National Orientation Agency, were accused of embezzling the cash gratuity meant for a man who was about to retire. They were sentenced in August 2001 to corporal punishment and fine, in one of the few successful trials of public servants under the *sharīʿa* legal system.[98]

Finally, Emmanuel Oye and Femi Lasisi, born Christians, reportedly insisted that they be tried before a *sharīʿa* court. They had been charged with "idleness" and "belonging to a group of thieves."[99] Possibly, they reckoned that the punishment awaiting them under Islamic criminal law would be less severe than under the secular Penal Code.

### Jigawa

In Jigawa State, the *sharīʿa* courts took up their activities on 2 August 2000. A *sharīʿa* penal code was submitted by the state government to the State House of Assembly as early as 27 November 2000.[100] However, the law was only enacted on 18 December 2001.[101]

---

[93] "Man Sentenced for Committing Adultery with Lunatic," *This Day*, 14/07/2001.

[94] "Hafsatu still in detention, says counsel," *The Guardian* (Nigeria), 17/01/2002, print edition.

[95] Umar Mohammed. See "Two Kids Share 40 Lashes for Goat Theft," *This Day*, 25/04/2001.

[96] "Sharia Court Convicts Two Christians," *This Day*, 01/08/2001.

[97] Sani Mamman (July 2001). See "Sharia Court Jails Man for Selling Dead Animal's Meat," *This Day*, 20/07/2001, 5.

[98] "Nigeria civil servants flogged under Sharia," BBC News, 15/08/2001; and "NOA Director, Accountant Get 80 Lashes for Cheating," *This Day*, 17/08/2001.

[99] "Sharia Court Convicts Two Christians," *This Day*, 01/08/2001.

[100] "Panel Submits Sharia Legal Code to Jigawa Assembly," *Post Express*, 28/11/2000, 4.

[101] See SIDP.

A total of ten cases tried in *sharīʿa* courts until the end of 2004 have been reported: two in 2001, eight in 2002 and one in 2003. By contrast, the state's Chief Judge, Justice Tijjani Abubakar, announced that, in the legal year 2002, 3,144 criminal cases[102] and, in the legal year 2004, 4,642 criminal cases had been tried in the state, most of which were handled by *sharīʿa* courts.[103] These figures, even if they are exaggerated, indicate that a very large number of criminal cases tried in *sharīʿa* courts remain unreported.

There were four indictments for intoxication: five persons, among them the only woman convicted of the offence, were sentenced to eighty strokes each, all in 2002.[104] In one case, the Emir of Dutse stripped the culprit, Abdulkadir Garba, of his traditional title of Sarkin Fulani for being a bad example to the people.[105] In another case, Abba Bashir, son of a senior member of the Dutse Emirate Council, was flogged twice for drunkenness by the same *sharīʿa* court in December 2002 and January 2003. In response to this, the emirate council accused the local *ḥisba* group of publicising the case with the intent to embarrass the emirate. After relations worsened, the emirate council dissolved the executive committee of the *ḥisba* and set up a commission to select a new one.[106] Another traditional ruler, Abba Ajiya, was found guilty of living with a woman to whom he was not married. In November 2001, he, his companion and an accomplice were sentenced to 40 strokes of the cane and one year's imprisonment.[107]

Umaru Musa and Usman Shehu were brought before a *sharīʿa* court in the only indictment for *sariqa* identified in Jigawa State. The trial started in March 2002, but no sentence has been reported.[108]

The trial which received the greatest media attention in Jigawa State was the case of Sarimu Muhammad of Baranda village. In May 2002, he was sentenced to death by stoning for raping a nine-year-old girl. After a prolonged appeal, he was acquitted in August 2003 on grounds of insan-

---

102 "Jigawa sets up c'ttee to review courts' performance," *Daily Trust*, 13/01/2003, 18. Furthermore, on page 2 of its 18-24 January 2003 edition, *Weekly Trust* mentions, without specifying a period of time, 2,858 cases under Islamic criminal law registered in Jigawa State, of which 2,575 had been treated.

103 "Jigawa Justice Reforms Cottee Gets N46.6m Counterpart Funding," *This Day*, 02/10/2004.

104 Bello Abdulkadir (February 2002); Abdulkadir Garba (September 2002); Abdulsalam Garba and his girl friend Ladi Muhammad (September 2002); and Abba Bashir (on two counts in December 2002 and January 2003).

105 "Village Head, Tutor, Girlfriend Caned 240 Lashes," *This Day*, 25/09/2002.

106 "Emirate Council Dissolves Sharia Committee," *This Day*, 21/02/2003.

107 "Sharia: FG, Sokoto Fight Over Safiya," *This Day*, 18/11/2001, 1 and 4.

108 "Sharia court adjourns for suspects to reconsider confession," *Daily Trust*, 27/03/2002, print edition.

ity.[109] In September 2002, while Babaji's trial was still pending, five men who were accused of raping an eleven-year-old girl were sentenced to five months in prison.[110] In November 2003, twenty-year-old Umaru Zurena was indicted for incest after raping and impregnating his seventeen-year-old niece.[111] No sentence has been reported. Already in August 2001, Yunusa Yargaba was charged with attempted rape of a blind woman and sentenced to 100 strokes of the cane.[112]

In April 2004, a criminal suit against the governor of Jigawa State, Saminu Turaki, over the disbursement of a 30 billion Naira allocation (150 million US$) to local governments in the state was dismissed by a *sharīʿa* court in Dutse for formal defects.[113] The judge, however, stated that the immunity of the governor, as guaranteed by Section 308 (3) of the 1999 Nigerian Constitution, is not applicable in *sharīʿa* courts.

The conflict between the local *ḥisba* and the emirate council was created by the Jigawa State government's approach to *sharīʿa* implementation.[114] Supporters of the state government's position responded to allegations of lack of resolve with the argument that Jigawa had opted for a gradual introduction of the *sharīʿa*, focussing in an initial phase on the collection and distribution of *zakāt*, or religiously proscribed alms, and education.[115]

### Kebbi

Kebbi State introduced a *sharīʿa* penal code, which entered into force beginning on 1 December 2000 (Peters 2003: 58). As in other states, in the initial phase after the introduction of Islamic criminal law, public floggings seem to have been used to change public behaviour. Relying on local sources, Human Rights Watch (2004: 58) reports that after the introduction of Islamic criminal law in Kebbi State, floggings took place on average once a week in the state capital of Birnin Kebbi. By the end of 2003, the number had decreased to one per month. Sometimes these floggings seem to have taken the character of mass trials, such as, e.g., in Gwandu Local Government Area, where in June 2001 "no fewer than 107 prostitutes" were given twenty lashes of the cane each, on the orders of

[109] "Sharia: Stoning Verdict on Alleged Rapist Quashed," *This Day*, 20/08/2003, 4.
[110] "For rape, sharia court passes death, fines others," *The Guardian* (Nigeria), 03/09/2002, 7.
[111] "Man, 20, in court for impregnating niece," *Weekly Trust*, 22/11/2003.
[112] "Man to Get 100 Lashes for Attempted Rape," *This Day*, 27/08/2001.
[113] "No Immunity Under Sharia, Says Court," *This Day*, 29/04/2004, 1 and 4.
[114] "Jigawa: Effective Zakkat system, poor sharia implementation," *Weekly Trust*, 26/07-01/08/2003, 7.
[115] Ibid.

a *sharīʿa* court in Gwandu, for idleness and wandering.[116] In 2003 the only identified trial for intoxication, which led to the flogging of the culprit in Birnin Kebbi (Human Rights Watch 2004: 61), is surely only one of a much higher number of cases.

Apart from public order issues, a small number of important cases have been reported from Kebbi State. After having been indicted for sodomy, Attahiru Umar was sentenced to death by stoning in September 2001 for sexual abuse of a seven-year-old boy.[117] However, the execution of the sentence has not been reported. Human Rights Watch (2004: 40) mentions a total of five cases of *sariqa* brought before a *sharīʿa* court in the state between July 2001 and November 2002.[118] Six alleged thieves were sentenced to amputation, while two accomplices were flogged and jailed. The authors of the report found the convicts in prison in December 2003, awaiting the execution of their sentences.

One case in Kebbi State deserves particular attention: in 2002, Yahaya Kakali was sentenced to amputation of the right hand for theft.[119] After a first appeal was rejected, a second appeal was filed on his behalf at the Federal Court of Appeal in Kaduna, making Kakale's case the first in Nigeria to reach the level of federal courts. This could open the way for probing the constitutionality of the state's Islamic criminal legislation before the Nigerian Supreme Court. But the Nigerian print media has essentially ignored this case, despite its precedential potential.

### Kano

Kano, the capital of Kano State, is the most populous city and the economic centre of northern Nigeria. It has a large non-Muslim population. Kano State started implementing Islamic criminal law beginning on 26 November 2000, or 1 Ramadan 1421 AH, only one day after the Sharīʿa Courts Law and the Sharīʿa Penal Code were put into force.[120]

The state government was accused of yielding to public pressure and not being sincere about the implementation of the *sharīʿa*. The government insisted that the implementation of the *sharīʿa* in Kano must be

---

[116] "107 prostitutes, 20 gamblers caned in Kebbi," *Vanguard*, 16/06/2001, 3.
[117] "Obasanjo visits Zamfara, cautions on Sharia," *The Guardian* (Nigeria), 14/09/2001, print edition; "Sharia Court Sentences Man to Death by Stoning," *This Day*, 14/09/2001; and "Nigerian sentenced to stoning," BBC News, 14/09/2001.
[118] Abubakar Aliyu (amputation sentence) and two accomplices (July 2001); Altine Mohammed (amputation sentence in July 2001); Abubakar Mohammed (amputation sentence in September 2001); Bello Mohammed and Mohammed Mansir (amputation sentences in November 2001); and Abubakar Hamid (amputation sentence in October 2002).
[119] In Weimann (2007: 267), I described Kakale's offence as armed robbery (*ḥirāba*). It is more likely that the charge was theft (*sariqa*), as the sentence reported was amputation of the right hand. The punishment for *ḥirāba* would have been cross-amputation.
[120] See SIDP.

gradual due to the cosmopolitan makeup of the population.[121] In defiance of a standing statutory *sharīʿa* implementation committee, Islamic scholars favourable to the full implementation of the *sharīʿa* set up an independent *sharīʿa* implementation committee, which in turn established a *ḥisba* group charged with ensuring compliance with Islamic injunctions in the state. On several occasions, this religious non-governmental body clashed with police forces.[122] In 2003, no doubt in response to this escalation, Kano State enacted a law establishing a state-controlled *ḥisba* board (Garba 2006).

The topic of *sharīʿa* implementation dominated the electoral campaign that preceded the 19 April 2003 gubernatorial elections. Governor Rabi'u Musa Kwankwaso, a member of PDP, lost in the polls and was succeeded by Ibrahim Shekarau of the All Nigerian People's Party (ANPP). Shekarau's main pre-election promise had been to implement the *sharīʿa* effectively in the state. The fact that the only three cases of sex crimes reported from the state took place after the change in government may not be unconnected to this power change. Be it as it may, the global figures of cases under Islamic criminal law in Kano are not significantly different from other states: mass trials against alleged prostitutes and their clients took place following the enactment of Islamic criminal legislation. In one instance, more than forty-five women were apprehended by police in late 2000 and subsequently arraigned before *sharīʿa* courts for prostitution.[123] In January 2001, police reportedly arrested sixty people, including eleven suspected prostitutes. One of the women arrested died in prison, another gave birth in detention while awaiting trial. At the end of the trial, ten women were sentenced to two weeks' imprisonment, while twenty-six men received one month's imprisonment for participating in an "immoral gathering."[124]

Human Rights Watch (2004: 37) reports that, at the end of 2003, floggings were carried out in Kano State at an average of three cases a month, most of them cases of alcohol consumption. But only three trials for *shurb al-khamr* were identified over the five-year period. In July 2000, i.e. four months before the Sharīʿa Penal Code entered into force, Nasiru Mohammed was sentenced to flogging and imprisonment for "drunkenness and intentional insult of an innocent citizen under the influence of

[121] "Two years of Sharia in Kano: Shekarau's Humanist Approach," *Weekly Trust*, 26/07-01/08/2003, 4.
[122] Ibid.
[123] "45 Prostitutes Face Kano Sharia Courts," *Post Express*, 16/12/2000, 94.
[124] "Sharia Court Jails 10 Women in Kano," *This Day*, 16/02/2001; and "Sharia: Suspected prostitute dies in detention," *The Guardian* (Nigeria), 17/02/2001, 48.

alcohol."[125] Three other men convicted of intoxication were reportedly flogged.[126]

Three sex crimes cases have been identified in Kano State in 2003 and 2004 respectively. In one case, Hafsatu Idris stated to the police that she had been raped by Ahmadu Haruna. When they appeared in court in May 2004, the police report accused her, together with Ahmadu Haruna, of committing *zinā*. The state's attorney-general was to assume her defence in court, but a sentence has not been reported.[127] In August 2003, Hamisu Suleiman was convicted of rape and sentenced to eighteen months' imprisonment with the option of a fine, for being a first-time offender.[128] Also in 2003, the alleged rape of a four-year-old girl by Saminu Abbas was interpreted by the court as "gross indecency."[129]

The most frequent indictment reported from Kano State, however, is *sariqa*. At least seven court cases involving ten defendants have been identified, two in 2001, three in 2002, and two in 2003, i.e. after the change in government.[130] Nine amputation sentences were handed down. Appeals were filed against a minimum of four amputation sentences.[131] While none of the sentences has been annulled, a number of convicts were released on bail after spending some time in prison (see, e.g., Human Rights Watch 2004: 40). In December 2003, eighteen alleged cattle thieves were put on trial, seven of whom were remanded in prison custody, but no sentence was reported.[132]

## Niger

Niger State announced the introduction of the *sharīʿa* for mid-January 2000.[133] Niger State did not introduce a new *sharīʿa* penal code but amended the existing Penal Code to include punishments for offences

[125] "Kano man to get 80 strokes for drinking alcohol," *The Guardian* (Nigeria), 05/07/2000, print edition.
[126] Nuhu Abdullahi and Sa'adu Aminu (January 2001); and Mudansiru Abdulmumini (June 2003).
[127] "Rape victim's father accuses police of changing FIR," *Daily Trust*, 24/03/2004, 29.
[128] "Rape suspect bags 18 months jail term," *Daily Trust*, 21/08/2003, 23.
[129] "Man in Sharia court for raping 4-year-old girl," *Daily Trust*, 26/05/2003, 23.
[130] A certain Adamu (indicted in January 2001); Danladi Dahiru (amputation sentence in August 2001); Abubakar Mohammed and Mohammed Bala (amputation sentences in January 2002); Ali Liman, Aminu Ahmed, and Haruna Musa (amputation sentences in January and February 2002); Haruna Bayero (amputation sentence in April 2002); and Hassan Ibrahim and Hamza Abdullahi (amputation sentences in June 2003).
[131] These are the sentences of Haruna Bayero, Mohammed Bala, Hassan Ibrahim and Hamza Abdullahi.
[132] "Cattle rustlers arraigned before Sharia court," *Daily Trust*, 10/12/2003.
[133] "Niger opts for modified Sharia," *The Guardian* (Nigeria), 22/12/1999, print edition.

under Islamic criminal law applicable to Muslims. The amendments to the Penal Code became enforceable on 4 May 2000 (Peters 2003: 52).

As in other states, when Islamic criminal legislation was first introduced public floggings were frequent. Human Rights Watch (2004: 58f), relying on a local source, mentions the figure of ten to a maximum of twenty floggings per month in Niger State in 2000 and early 2001. By mid-2003, their number had declined to one or two per month.

One trial of a rape case was reported in November 2002: Aminu Ruwa was sentenced to 100 lashes and required to pay the medical bill of the six-year-old girl with whom he had forceful intercourse.[134] The report does not mention whether or not the defendant was required to pay the proper bride price (*ṣadāq al-mithl*) to the victim.

Niger State has been in the focus of attention for one particular *zinā* trial: in August 2002, Fatima Usman and Ahmadu Ibrahim were sentenced to imprisonment with the option of a fine, on the basis of the old version of the Penal Code. Three weeks later, this sentence was changed into stoning to death without retrial, even without informing the defendants, who were already serving their prison terms. The change was in line with the amended Penal Code. An appeal against the sentence was still pending in 2004 (Human Rights Watch 2004: 25). There are indications that more death sentences for *zinā* offences were pronounced in Niger State than reported.[135]

### Yobe

In Yobe, the *sharīʿa* became enforceable beginning on 1 October 2000. At that date, however, *sharīʿa* courts had not taken up their activities.[136] A *sharīʿa* penal code was only assented to by the governor on 9 March 2001.[137]

In June 2000, Yobe State Governor Bukar Abba Ibrahim (ANPP) announced that he would introduce a version of the *sharīʿa* acceptable to both Muslims and Christians.[138] In an interview with the Nigerian news magazine *Tell*, a special assistant to the governor said that the *sharīʿa* is purely a religious affair that does not affect non-Muslims in the state.[139] No case under Islamic criminal law has been identified during the period under review.

---

[134] "Man gets 100 strokes for indecency," *The Comet*, 20/11/2002, 6.

[135] Philip Ostien estimates that there are four or five cases of death sentences for illegal intercourse in Niger State (personal communication in May 2006).

[136] "Sharia Without Tears," *Tell*, 30/10/2000, 37.

[137] See SIDP.

[138] "Yobe plans modified Sharia," *The Comet*, 06/06/2000, 7.

[139] "Sharia Without Tears," *Tell*, 30/10/2000, 37.

### Borno

In Borno State, the "adoption of the *sharīʿa*" was announced on 1 June 2001.[140] This date apparently marked the beginning of enforcement of a law prohibiting prostitution, lesbianism, homosexuality and the operation of brothels, which was signed by Governor Mala Kachallah on 10 December 2000.[141] However, the draft Borno State Sharīʿa Penal Code 2000 was signed into law only on 3 March 2003.[142]

In April 2001, the Borno State Committee for the Implementation of Sharīʿa recommended a "gradual and multi-dimensional approach to the implementation" of the Islamic criminal legislation.[143] This statement, together with the lengthy legislative process, betrays a general reluctance on the part of the government of this state in the north-eastern corner of Nigeria to follow the example set by the north-western states, such as Zamfara, Katsina, or Sokoto. The sources available to me do not mention any court case tried under Islamic criminal law in the state. Philip Ostien, reader in Law at the University of Jos (Nigeria), confirmed to me that in Borno State the Islamic criminal legislation has remained a dead letter.[144]

Borno, alongside Kano, was one of two northern Nigerian states which changed government as a result of the 19 April 2003 gubernatorial elections. The transfer of power from Mala Kachallah, who left the ANPP and joined the Alliance for Democracy (AD) in late 2002, to Ali Modu Sherrif (ANPP), however, apparently did not have any effect on the implementation of Islamic criminal law. In stark contrast to Kano State, where the *sharīʿa* was the predominant topic of the 2003 electoral campaign, it was hardly an issue in Borno State.

### Gombe

As the last of the twelve "*sharīʿa* states," Gombe put into force legislation establishing *sharīʿa* and customary courts on 14 December 2001.[145] In late 2001, a *sharīʿa* penal code law and a customary code law were enacted to complement the existing Penal Code (Ladan 2004: 76). By providing for a tripartite legal system consisting of *sharīʿa* courts, customary courts and magistrate courts, the state government sought to ease the apprehensions of non-Muslims about an alleged attempt to Islamise the state, a solution conceived earlier in Kaduna (see below). In fact, the introduc-

---

[140] "Borno adopts Sharia today," *The Guardian* (Nigeria), 01/06/2001, 64.

[141] See SIDP.

[142] Information gratefully received from Philip Ostien in August 2006.

[143] "Sharia implementation takes off in Borno June 1," *Daily Times*, 10/04/2001, print edition.

[144] Personal communication, May 2006.

[145] "Gombe Adopts Sharia at Last," *This Day*, 18/12/2001.

tion of Islamic criminal legislation was controversial in Gombe State. As other states in Northern Nigeria enacted *sharīʿa* penal codes, tensions between Muslims and Christians were mounting, at times culminating in violent confrontations. In September 2000, ten people were killed in inter-religious clashes in the state.[146] In May 2001, 25 people were injured after a group of Muslims confronted three Christians who were carrying a picket bearing the words "No Sharia."[147]

Between 2002 and 2004, no court case under Islamic criminal law was reported from the state. Gombe State Governor Abubakar Habu Hashidu (ANPP) tried to resist pressure from Muslim activists to introduce Islamic criminal law in the first place,[148] and it is reasonable to assume that he did not make it a priority of his government after its enactment. In the 19 April 2003 gubernatorial elections, Hashidu lost his post to the PDP candidate Mohammed Danjuma Goje, but this does not seem to have changed the government's attitude towards the *sharīʿa*.

### Kaduna

Kaduna embarked on the implementation of Islamic law on 2 November 2001,[149] twenty-one months after Zamfara State started the process. On this date, the newly constituted *sharīʿa* and customary courts commenced their activities, but a *sharīʿa* penal code was promulgated only in June 2002.[150] The late enactment of Islamic criminal law in Kaduna State was a consequence of the so-called *sharīʿa* riots in late February 2000, when in response to the introduction of Islamic criminal law in Zamfara State a wave of religious violence engulfed Kaduna metropolis and environs.[151]

Kaduna State contains a mixture of Muslims and non-Muslims. The north, where the university town of Zaria is the regional centre, is predominantly Muslim, whereas Christians make up the majority of the population in the south. Kaduna metropolis was founded by the British colonial power, which established its administrative and military headquarters in the new settlement in 1917. As a result, no ethnic or religious group in the city can claim "indigenity."[152] The city is said to be almost evenly split between Christians and Muslims. Other regions in northern Nigeria are clearly dominated by the Muslim majority of the population,

---

146 "Religious clashes in Nigeria kill ten," BBC News, 09/09/2000.
147 "NIGERIA: Religious clash in Gombe State," IRIN, 23/05/2001.
148 "Gombe Adopts Sharia at Last," *This Day*, 18/12/2001.
149 "Uneasy Calm as Kaduna Implements Sharia," *This Day*, 03/11/2001.
150 See SIDP.
151 "Uneasy Calm as Kaduna Implements Sharia," *This Day*, 03/11/2001.
152 For the importance of the word pair "indigenous"—"settler" in the Nigerian context, see International Crisis Group (2006: 24).

whereas the mainly non-indigenous non-Muslim communities accept their minority status. In "neutral" Kaduna, by contrast, inter-religious violence has been a frequent occurrence over the last decades.[153] As a result of this explosive situation, the implementation of Islamic criminal law in Kaduna State has taken a different form from other "*sharīʿa* states." After State House of Assembly Members from the southern (mainly non-Muslim) part of the state threatened to secede if Islamic criminal law were to be implemented across the state, the state government proposed a tripartite court system to accommodate all sections of the population.[154] Area courts were abolished. They were replaced by customary courts in predominantly non-Muslim areas, and by *sharīʿa* courts in predominantly Muslim areas. The magistrate courts continued to exist. In the mixed parts of Kaduna city and other principal towns, the implementation of any form of religious laws was explicitly foreclosed.[155]

Only a small number of court cases tried under Islamic criminal law were reported in the three years following the introduction of the *sharīʿa*. In November 2003, the state's Grand Qāḍī announced that two men, convicted by a *sharīʿa* court in Zaria, were to have their right hand amputated soon.[156] Between August and September 2003, the Zaria Upper Sharīʿa Court convicted six men charged with "shop lifting, thefts of provisions, textile materials, a cow and a motorcycle and house breaking"[157] and sentenced them to amputation of the right hand. After one year in prison waiting for their judgments to be signed by the governor, their cases were made public by human rights activists, who claimed that the convicts had been tried and sentenced in one day and were not given the opportunity to engage the services of legal counsel.[158] An appeal was filed on behalf of the "Zaria Six." The amputation sentences were set aside in May 2005. The men were released from prison on the grounds that the two years that they had already spent in prison were sufficient punishment.[159]

Two other criminal cases were tried before the same *sharīʿa* court in the Magajin Gari area of Kaduna city during the same period. In May

[153] More recent examples of inter-religious violent conflicts were the "Miss World riots" in September 2002, and the violent spill-overs of the crisis in Plateau State in May 2004.
[154] "Shari'a: Kaduna opts for tripartite legal system," *The Guardian* (Nigeria), 22/07/2000, 2.
[155] "Kaduna signs bills setting up customary, Sharia courts," *The Comet*, 03/05/2001, 2.
[156] "Sharia: Two Convicts to Be Amputated," *This Day*, 10/11/2003, 4; and "Two Sharia convicts face amputation in Kaduna," *The Guardian* (Nigeria), 10/11/2003.
[157] "Sharia appeal court to review conviction of six men," *Vanguard*, 17/08/2004.
[158] "Sharia : 6 Await Amputation," *This Day*, 12/08/2004.
[159] "Sharia court grants bail to six convicts," *The Guardian* (Nigeria), 18/05/2005, 7; and *The Guardian* (Nigeria), 28/05/2005, 4. I thank Philip Ostien for providing me with information on the outcome of this case.

2002, Halima Abdulkarim was accused by her husband of committing *qadhf*. She was said to have accused him of having an affair with his mother. In court, Abdulkarim denied having made such an allegation against her husband.[160] In June 2002, bus driver Tasi'u Saidu was charged with injuring two women, one of whom was pregnant, by pushing them out of his moving bus after an argument, in which he accused them of being prostitutes.[161] No judgment was reported in either case.

### Bauchi

The last state to be examined in this regional overview is Bauchi. Situated in the Middle Belt, this state has a predominantly Muslim population, but with significant Christian minorities and some pockets of animists.[162] As in Kaduna State, the introduction of Islamic criminal law in Bauchi State led to violent conflicts between the religious communities. Shortly after the introduction of the *sharīʿa* in June 2001, several mosques were destroyed in riots that began after a bus driver asked Christian passengers to sit gender-segregated. In July 2001, ethnic and religious clashes killed many dozens of people and forced thousands to flee. Christian minorities in the state felt threatened by the introduction of the *sharīʿa* (Peters 2003: 54). These violent clashes prefigured the riots of September 2001 in Bauchi's southern neighbour, Plateau State. In both states the introduction of the *sharīʿa* was a controversial topic. However, whereas Bauchi State enacted a *sharīʿa* penal code, the government of Plateau State, under the Christian state governor Joshua Dariye (PDP), did not introduce Islamic criminal legislation. In neither case, a tripartite system as in Kaduna seems not to have been envisaged.

In Bauchi State, the application of the *sharīʿa* commenced on 1 June 2001 (Peters 2003: 54). A *sharīʿa* penal code was enacted in the same year.[163] The Bauchi State Sharīʿa Commission Law 2001 provides for the establishment of a *ḥisba* under the supervision of the *sharīʿa* commission (Garba 2006). One court case was reported in 2001, four in 2002, three in 2003 and five in 2004.

One trial for drinking alcohol was identified in late 2004.[164] Two cases of grievous bodily harm were reported: in March 2004, a gang member named Sabo Sarki was arrested and tried. He was accused of having forcefully removed the eyes of a teenage boy to sell them to another

---

160 "Woman Docked for Accusing Husband of Having an Affair with his Mother," *This Day*, 24/05/2002.
161 "Man Remanded for Assault on Pregnant Woman," *This Day*, 07/06/2002.
162 Reliable figures on the percentage of non-Muslims in the population are unavailable.
163 See SIDP.
164 "Alcohol: Sharia Court Orders Man Caned 80 Strokes," *This Day*, 01/02/2005. The arrest of the culprit, Ibrahim Musa, took place in November 2004.

man who intended to use them in a ritual. Sarki was sentenced to pay compensation of 5.5 million Naira (27,500 US$). However, the victim rejected the compensation and insisted on retaliation.[165] The second case of grievous bodily harm involved a jealous husband who cut off his wife's right leg with a machete. The wife demanded *qiṣāṣ*. In January 2003, after a trial that lasted several months, Adamu Hussaini Maidoya was sentenced to have his right leg amputated under the knee without anaesthesia. The judge pointed out that Maidoya had to experience the same pain that he had inflicted on his wife.[166] In August 2006, three and a half years after the verdict of first instance, the Bauchi State Sharīʿa Court of Appeal rejected Maidoya's appeal. The three *qāḍīs* unanimously argued that the verdict of the Upper Sharīʿa Court was correct since Maidoya had confessed to committing the crime.[167]

Nine of the thirteen reported cases in Bauchi State were indictments for sex crimes: five cases of *zinā*, two for rape, and one each for incest and sodomy. In 2001, Hajo Poki was sentenced to 100 strokes of the cane after she was convicted of *zinā*. She had been found pregnant out of wedlock.[168] The sentence was to be carried out after the delivery of the baby. However, some reports indicate that it was executed while Poki was still pregnant.[169] A similar case is that of Adama Yunusa, who, in early 2002, tried to drag the man who she alleged had impregnated her to court to make him assume his responsibilities as the father of her child. When she failed to prove her case, she was sentenced to 100 strokes of the cane and banned from the area. The judgment was confirmed by an appeals court, which, however, revoked the banishment.[170]

In June 2002, Yunusa Rafin Chiyawa was sentenced to death by stoning for having sexual relations with the wife of a neighbour, after he declined repeated opportunities to withdraw his confession to the act.[171] The woman was acquitted after she swore on the Qurʾān that she had been hypnotised by Chiyawa. Human Rights Watch (2004: 32) reports that Chiyawa's sentence was overturned in November 2003. With the exception of the case of Abubakar Aliyu in Sokoto State, this is the only

---

[165] "Shariah court convicts man over ritual," *Daily Trust*, 30/03/2004, 5; and "Boy turns down N6m compensation for eyes," *Daily Trust*, 13/05/2004. The reports do not mention if the victim's request for retaliation was granted.

[166] "Man loses limb for amputating wife's leg," *New Nigerian Newspaper*, 06/01/2003, 30. See also "The Justice She Wants," *Newswatch*, 18/11/2002, 48-9.

[167] "Sharia Court of Appeal affirms first amputation in Bauchi," *Daily Trust*, 21/08/2006.

[168] "Sharia court orders amputation of hands, legs in Sokoto," *The Guardian* (Nigeria), 20/12/2001, print edition.

[169] "Niger sharia court sentences two to death by stoning," *The Guardian* (Nigeria), 29/08/2002, 1-2.

[170] "Sharia: Woman Gets 100 Strokes over Pregnancy," *This Day*, 06/05/2002.

[171] "Nigerian man faces death for adultery," BBC News, 27/06/2002.

known case in which a man was convicted and the woman was discharged and acquitted.

No new *zinā* cases were reported in 2003, although the year witnessed three other trials for sexual offences: in September 2003, Jibrin Babaji was sentenced to death by stoning after he was found guilty of sodomy with three boys between the ages of ten and thirteen years.[172] The boys were given six strokes of the cane each, allegedly for accepting ten Naira (seven US cent) for their sexual services. The stoning-to-death sentence was overturned on appeal in March 2004 on the grounds of procedural shortcomings at the initial trial. The lower court judge was ordered to tender an unreserved apology to the three boys and pay them compensation.[173]

In October 2003, Adamu Jugga was dragged before a *sharīʿa* court by a woman who accused him of raping her.[174] The outcome of the trial has not been reported.

In late December 2003, the Alkalere Upper Sharīʿa Court sentenced Umaru Tori to death by stoning and his fifteen-year-old step-daughter Altine Tori to 100 strokes of the cane, to be administered after the delivery of the child she was carrying at the time of the trial.[175] They were convicted of incest.[176] Umaru Tori confessed to the offence,[177] and a police officer testified in court that Altine Tori tried to resist her stepfather when he had forceful sexual intercourse with her.[178] It appears, however, that this testimony was not interpreted in Altine's favour. The sentence was appealed in January 2004. Altine Tori's defence counsel argued that the court should have taken into account that Altine had been forced to commit adultery, that she was a minor at the time of the offence, and that there was no definitive proof of the offence as required by Islamic law.[179] Umaru Tori's appeal was upheld on 24 May 2005 by the Bauchi State Sharīʿa Court of Appeal, which ordered that the case be retried before the Upper Sharīʿa Court in Kobi.[180] This trial exemplifies

---

[172] "Sodomy: Sharia court sentences man to death by stoning," *Daily Trust*, 25/09/2003.

[173] "Sodomy: Judge to pay N3000 for wrongful conviction," *Daily Trust*, 23/03/2004, 5; and "Wrongful conviction: Lower Sharia court judge ordered to apologise," *New Nigerian Newspaper*, 24/03/2004, 21.

[174] "Alleged rape victim, 35, offers to swear by Qur'an," *Weekly Trust*, 04-10/10/2003, 17.

[175] "NIGERIA: Man sentenced to stoning for sex with step-daughter," IRIN, 06/01/2004.

[176] "Incest: Sharia Court sentences man to death by stoning," *Daily Trust*, 06/01/2004, 1-2.

[177] "Sharia: Man to die by stoning for impregnating step-daughter in Bauchi," *The Guardian* (Nigeria), 06/01/2004.

[178] "Incest: Sharia Court sentences man to death by stoning," *Daily Trust*, 06/01/2004, 1-2.

[179] "Shariah Court Entertains 11-Month-Old Appeal," *Weekly Trust*, 30/11/2004. The final hearing was slated for 7 December 2004. However, the outcome of the appeal could not be established. It is not clear if Altine and Umaru Tori filed their appeal together.

[180] Amnesty International Annual Report 2006.

the vulnerability of women in rape cases, in which the burden of proof rests on the victim due to the fact that consensual intercourse out of wedlock is a criminal offence (*zinā*).[181]

In 2004, three more trials for sexual offences were reported from Bauchi State. Not much information is available on the stoning-to-death sentence against Selah Dabo for rape in September 2004.[182] Two women were sentenced to death by stoning by a court of first instance in September and October 2004, respectively. Their sentences were overturned on appeal: Daso Adamu was acquitted in December 2004 on the grounds of the possibility that her pregnancy was caused by her former husband.[183] In addition, the appeal judge held that the initial trial was improper because the defendant had been dragged to court and tried against her wishes. Nineteen-year-old Hajara Ibrahim was initially sentenced to stoning to death and 100 strokes of the cane after she confessed to having intercourse with a man she said had promised to marry her.[184] Apparently, the lower court learnt of Ibrahim's pregnancy when her father attempted to drag her fiancé to court in connection with his daughter's pregnancy.[185] The latter, however, was discharged and acquitted due to lack of evidence.[186] The sentence was annulled in November 2004 due to procedural flaws in the initial trial. The trials of Daso Adamu and Hajara Ibrahim were the latest cases of stoning-to-death sentences for *zinā* which were reported in the first five years of the implementation of Islamic criminal law in northern Nigeria.

Among criminal cases from Bauchi State, sex crimes are predominant. In the only case of *sariqa* that was reported in the media, Abdul Jolly Hassan was convicted, in June 2002, of stealing eighteen sheep, worth 50,000 Naira (360 US$). He was sentenced to one year's imprisonment and forty strokes of the cane. The *ḥadd* punishment of amputation for theft was not applied because the animals were not kept in a cage and, therefore, the requirement of *ḥirz* was not met.[187]

However, a considerable number of amputation sentences—for indictments of *sariqa* or as a result of *qiṣāṣ*—apparently were handed down in Bauchi without attracting the media's attention. If the figures provided are accurate, media reports illustrate well the problem, already

---

[181] See also Peters (2003: 19).

[182] Amnesty International Annual Report 2005; and "Sharia : Legal Aid Council to appeal against 30 convictions," *Vanguard*, 17/11/2004.

[183] "Sharia Court Nullifies Death Penalty On Woman," *Vanguard*, 11/12/2004.

[184] "Sharia: Woman to Die for Adultery," *Daily Trust*, 13/10/2004.

[185] "Upper Sharia Court to rule in Hajara's appeal November 10," *Vanguard*, 28/10/2004.

[186] "Sharia: Another woman faces death by stoning in Bauchi," *Daily Independent*, 13/10/2004.

[187] "Man Escapes Amputation over Theft of 18 Sheep," *This Day*, 24/06/2002.

highlighted in other states: defendants sentenced to amputation or stoning to death are remanded in prison for an undetermined period awaiting the execution of the punishment. In June 2003, twelve people were waiting to be stoned to death or have a limb amputated. The sentences required endorsement by Bauchi State Governor Ahmadu Adamu Mu'azu (PDP).[188] In January 2004, twenty-two persons were waiting for the governor to assent to their amputation sentences, while two people, Chiyawa and Jibrin Babaji, were awaiting the execution of their stoning sentences.[189] By October 2004, the number of amputation sentences had risen to twenty-three, while the total number of stoning-to-death sentences imposed in the state was five.[190] In November 2004, the number of convicts awaiting amputation was twenty-eight.[191] By December 2004, the number of people awaiting execution of their stoning sentence had possibly decreased to two, after four stoning sentences—those of Rafin Chiyawa, Jibrin Babaji, Hajara Ibrahim and Daso Adamu—were quashed on appeal.[192] This unsatisfactory situation has prompted reactions from different quarters. Governor Mu'azu has come under pressure from human rights groups[193] and Muslim groups[194] to set aside or implement amputation sentences, respectively.

It cannot be excluded, on the basis of the fragmentary data available, that other northern Nigerian states have experienced a similar development in the numbers of amputation sentences to be executed. Nevertheless, the situation in Bauchi appears to be unique in that it is the only state in which the number of newly reported cases has increased over time. This may be explained by more intensive media coverage in the state. However, it is remarkable that in the great urban centres in north-

[188] "Kano Sharia court orders amputation of two men for theft," *The Guardian* (Nigeria), 24/06/2003, 3. The verdicts included the stoning-to-death sentence against Yunusa Rafin Chiyawa and the retaliation sentence against Adamu Hussaini Maidoya.
[189] "Sharia: Man to die by stoning for impregnating step-daughter in Bauchi," *The Guardian* (Nigeria), 06/01/2004; and "Man, 45, sentenced to death by stoning," *New Nigerian Newspaper*, 07/01/2004, 28. This again included the retaliation sentence against Maidoya.
[190] "Sharia court sentences woman to death by stoning," *Daily Trust*, 13/10/2004.
[191] "Sharia: Legal Aid Council to appeal against 30 convictions," *Vanguard*, 17/11/2004.
[192] In May 2006, Philip Ostien mentioned to me that a woman was sentenced to death for witchcraft in Bauchi State. However, I have not found more information on this case.
[193] The Legal Aid Council, a Nigerian federal agency which provides legal representation for indigent accused in serious cases, declared that it would file appeals against the conviction of 30 persons by *sharīʿa* courts in Bauchi State, who were in prison awaiting the execution of their sentence. See ibid.
[194] During a courtesy visit by the 'Yan Izala movement, Governor Mu'azu had to exonerate himself over allegations that he was reluctant to implement the judgments, explaining that he had delegated the responsibility of overseeing the implementation of the courts' verdicts to the *sharīʿa* commission. See "Sharia court sentences woman to death by stoning," *Daily Trust*, 13/10/2004.

ern Nigeria, such as Kano and Kaduna, where media presence presumably is higher than in the remote Bauchi State, and even in states such as Zamfara, Sokoto and Katsina, which present high numbers of cases reported, numbers of identified cases decrease over time. Thus, the increase of cases, with a predominance of sex crimes, in Bauchi State calls for an explanation.

As mentioned, Bauchi is a religiously mixed state. For this reason, missionary groups, like the 'Yan Izala movement,[195] regard it as an area of propagation of Islam. Shortly after the re-election of Governor Mu'azu in 2003, delegations of the 'Yan Izala movement visited him on two occasions to commend him on the introduction of Islamic criminal law.[196] Even before this, Governor Mu'azu was aware of the danger posed by overzealous *sharīʿa* partisans. In an unprecedented move in December 2002, he publicly advised *sharīʿa* judges in the state not to rush to judgment of women accused of adultery on the basis of pregnancy out of wedlock and thus threatened with death by stoning. He said, with reference to the legal concept of the "sleeping embryo," that a pregnancy manifesting itself up to five years after a divorce may be attributed to the former husband.[197] The fact that no such case had been reported from Bauchi State at that time lends greater significance to this announcement. It is possible that the 'Yan Izala and other groups that seek to enforce an Islamic way of life are pressuring *sharīʿa* judges, in particular on lower—thus more accessible—levels, to accept charges of *zinā* brought before them. As mentioned above, the only two stoning-to-death sentences for *zinā* reported in northern Nigeria in 2004 were pronounced by lower *sharīʿa* courts in Bauchi State. Both verdicts were annulled on appeal.

## Conclusion

Since the interpretation of Islamic criminal law is discussed in greater detail in subsequent chapters, I limit myself here to the political and

[195] The *Jamāʿat Izālat al-Bidʿa wa-Iqāmat al-Sunna*, or 'Yan Izala in short, is a Muslim anti-establishment movement, which traces its origins to the conflict of Sheikh Abubakar Gumi, former Grand Qāḍī of the Northern Region of Nigeria and founding member of the Muslim World League, and the traditional Nigerian Sufi brotherhoods (Loimeier 1993a). On Gumi's view on the emergence of the Izala movement, see Gumi (1994: 155f). Christian fundamentalist movements also appear to be active in Bauchi State. They sometimes even claim that Christians make up more than half of the population of the state, which is hardly believable.

[196] See "Mu'azu Restates Commitment to Sharia," *This Day*, 06/06/2003; and "Ulamas Hail Muazu over Sharia," *This Day*, 14/07/2003.

[197] "Mu'azu cautions sharia judges," *Vanguard*, 18/12/2002, 10.

socio-political aspects of the introduction of Islamic criminal law in northern Nigeria.

The debate triggered by the efforts to introduce an Islamic criminal law in northern Nigeria touched on the question of identity and the future of the Nigerian nation, as outlined by the northern Nigerian political scientist and human rights activist Jibrin Ibrahim (2003):

> For the pro-Shari'a group, democracy is meaningless without religious freedom, the most important aspect of which is the right to exercise their religion fully, which is impossible without the full implementation of the Shari'a. For the anti-Shari'a group, the full implementation of the Shari'a is a political transformation indicating the establishment of an Islamic state and the persecution of non-Muslims.

The reintroduction of the *sharīʿa*, in particular the imposition of strict sexual morals, serves as an identity marker among Muslims by creating the impression that corruption and decadence are the result of a loss of Muslim values. Hence the emphasis on sexual morality. The popular support that has resulted from this identity building has, at least in the initial phase, spread throughout northern Nigeria. It can be assumed that religious lobby groups have played a role in this rapid propagation. However, northern Nigeria is not a homogeneous entity and populations in different parts of the region have shown varying levels of dedication to the project heralded by Zamfara State, a fact which also seems to have influenced judicial practice in criminal cases in *sharīʿa* courts. This is best illustrated by the differences in case numbers reported from the north-west and the north-east of the country. In the Hausa states of the north-west, such as Zamfara, Kebbi, Sokoto, Katsina, Jigawa and Kano, where identification with the historic precedent of the Sokoto Caliphate is strongest, the number of cases identified is high. This may be linked to the activities of state-controlled or independent *sharīʿa* enforcement groups, which bring infringements of the Islamic rules of conduct to the attention of *sharīʿa* courts. By contrast, in the north-eastern states, such as Borno and Yobe, where the majority of the population belongs to the Kanuri ethno-linguistic group, the introduction of the *sharīʿa* in the Zamfara style was widely perceived as a Hausa project. The Islamic identity in these states is shaped by the historical experience of the much older Muslim Kanuri kingdom of Kanem-Borno and its more introspective Islamic tradition. "It is for this reason, and coming from such a historical background," writes political scientist and Kanuri intellectual Kyari Tijani (2002: 31), "that neither the people of Borno nor their leaders or *ulama* ever understood the *furore*, now raging over the *Shari'a* in Nigeria."

It is in religiously mixed states, however, that the symbolic, and therefore political, value of the *sharīʿa* has had the most devastating consequences. Here, it is less the number of cases that is of importance than the fact that one religious community is able to prevail over the other by either introducing or preventing the *sharīʿa*. Jibrin Ibrahim (2003) argues that the creation of ever smaller states in Nigeria since independence has led to the redefinition of new (ethnic or religious) majorities and minorities on the state level. These groups compete for hegemony and access to public resources. As the 1991 census, and again the 2006 census, did not pose the question of religious affiliation, it is not known which of the two major religions, Islam or Christianity, is the majority in these states: "Political entrepreneurs use religious mobilisation to enhance their legitimacy at the local and national level." Consequently, in states such as Kaduna, Plateau, and Bauchi, where there is no common assessment as to which community holds the majority of the population, violent confrontations between Muslims and Christians over the introduction of the *sharīʿa* have broken out. In Kaduna, the state government found a compromise aiming at accommodating the divergent interests in an attempt to limit the tensions. In Plateau State, the government, under the Christian Joshua Dariye, did not introduce the *sharīʿa* at all. The most interesting state in this regard, however, is Bauchi, which usually receives little attention outside its own borders. As in neighbouring Plateau State, so too in Bauchi, Christian and Muslim missionaries compete for influence over the population. Both communities claim to be the majority. Thus, in the struggle for political influence, it is essential for Islamic lobbies to establish that Bauchi is a true "*sharīʿa* state." We can assume that some of their members are motivated to "promote" Islamic criminal law by dragging presumed offenders—here again emphasis is obviously placed on sexual offenders—to court or by exerting leverage on judges to obtain the desired sentence. In addition, the improper implementation of the changes in the judiciary and the lack of training for *sharīʿa* judges leave the courts vulnerable to external pressure.

Has the introduction of Islamic criminal law had an impact on the living conditions in the affected states?

In early 2004, Auwalu Hamisu Yadudu, Professor of Law at the Bayero University in Kano stated that "sufficient time has not elapsed from the first gale of the adoption of *shari'ah*, which commenced late in 1999, to the present, to lead to the emergence of any discernible trend or pattern."[198] Yadudu may be right that judicial practice will develop over time and that certain trends or patterns will become clearer. For the

[198] Quoted in Ostien et al. (2005: 140f).

time being, I will content myself with identifying the expected results which have not yet materialised. As pointed out in the beginning of this chapter, it was expected that the introduction of the *sharīʿa* would guarantee security for life and property, reduce corruption and promote good governance.

With regard to security for life, only six cases of homicide and bodily harm tried before *sharīʿa* courts have been identified across the twelve states over a period of five years.[199] This figure is numerically and statistically insignificant. As for security of property, I have identified at least thirty-eight trials for theft and robbery and forty-two people who were sentenced to amputation of the right hand.[200] Many more amputation sentences are probably unreported. Three amputations were carried out, in 2000 and 2001. Since 2001, the governors have been reluctant to approve amputation sentences. Some people sentenced to amputation have been released after being remanded to prison for a prolonged period. In practice, this means that they suffered a punishment different from their sentence. To date, no one has raised the question if amputation sentences are to be pronounced and carried out in the future. The answer to this question will probably depend on the political climate and, therefore, on the activities of religious groups. The danger that any decision in this field will spark violent reactions should not be underestimated.

Finally, the promotion of good governance falls into the realm of the *taʿzīr* legislation, which covers offences committed by public servants. However, only four indictments of a total of ten public servants have come to light. In two cases, no sentence was reported. The indictment of the governor of Jigawa State was dismissed. Since indictments of representatives of public authorities generally attract high attention in the Nigerian media, it is unlikely that the number of indictments of public servants is much higher than this. The low number of cases suggests that the introduction of Islamic criminal law has not had a great impact on public service in the states implementing it. A handful of cases against low and medium-ranking officials cannot be considered a strong deterrent, which is the main goal of Islamic criminal law.

Clearly, the expectations about the benefits that would accrue from the implementation of the *sharīʿa* were inflated. The resulting disillusionment, however, may motivate northern Nigerian politicians to create more realistic policies, as pointed out by Philip Ostien (2002):

---

[199] Chapter Three (p. 104-110) mentions one homicide case and seven cases of bodily harm.

[200] By contrast, the analysis of judicial practice in theft cases (Chapter Three, p. 110-116) is based on the analysis of 51 trials for theft with 52 amputation sentences.

> The expected benefits are those associated in many religions with return by the people to conformity with the will of God. But quite probably, notwithstanding the implementation of *shari'a*, the world will wag on much as it always has, and the governments of the implementing states will find that they still have a great deal to do to trim bloated bureaucracies, reform education, fight crime and corruption, foster development, encourage investment, and so on and on. The point is that having implemented *shari'a*, having, so to speak, cleared away that issue, they will be free to focus on the more immediate causes of their problems and perhaps to address them more realistically than they have in the past.

This prediction, made at an early stage of the reintroduction of Islamic criminal law in northern Nigeria, seems to be confirmed by the virtual absence of the topic in the campaigns for the presidential and gubernatorial elections in Nigeria in April 2007.

# Chapter Two: Divine Law and Local Custom in Northern Nigerian *Zinā* Trials[201]

Abstract: The introduction of Islamic criminal law in twelve northern states of the Nigerian federation after 1999 was widely perceived as an attempt to Islamise the Nigerian state. In this article it is argued that the "*sharīʿa* project" started as a pre-election promise, but was immediately supported by Muslim reform groups whose aim was not the establishment of an Islamic state but rather the imposition of *sharīʿa*-compliant behaviour on Muslims. Particular emphasis was put on illicit sexual relations (*zinā*). However, Muslim societies of northern Nigeria have a notion of *zinā* which differs in important aspects from the classical doctrine, and certain forms of socially accepted extramarital sexuality still exist. Based on an analysis of a sample of *sharīʿa* court trials for rape, sodomy, incest and *zinā*, it is shown that the judicial practice in *sharīʿa* courts has helped to mitigate the effects of Islamic criminal law on the traditional societies in northern Nigeria. In particular, accusations based on suspicion and pregnancy out of wedlock as proof of *zinā* have been rejected by the courts, thereby confirming the privacy of the family compound and traditional conflict resolution through mediation. At the same time, male control over female sexuality has been strengthened.

Between October 1999 and December 2001, twelve northern states of the Nigerian federation implemented legislation codifying Islamic criminal law and introducing Islamic codes of behaviour, such as the prohibition of alcohol and the segregation of sexes in public transport. These measures were promoted under the slogan of the "restoration of the *sharīʿa*."[202] Two *sharīʿa* court rulings, the stoning-to-death sentences of the unmarried mothers Safiyya Hussaini and Amina Lawal, caused particularly vehement national and international reactions.[203] Both sen-

[201] Originally published in *Die Welt des Islams*, 49:3-4 (2009), 429-65, and reprinted with permission from Brill Academic Publishers.

[202] On the introduction of Islamic criminal law in Nigeria, see Peters (2003).

[203] The records of proceedings and judgments in the two cases, translated into English, along with other information and analysis, are given in Ostien (2007, vol. 5). An analysis

tences were quashed on appeal. To date no stoning-to-death sentence has been executed in Nigeria.[204]

The predominantly Christian south of Nigeria—and the international community—considered the introduction of the *sharīʿa* as a preliminary stage to the proclamation of an Islamic state and, after the first sentences of stoning to death had become publicised, an acute threat to the fundamental rights as stipulated in the 1999 Constitution of the Federal Republic of Nigeria and the international human rights instruments to which Nigeria is a state party.[205] In contrast, many northern Nigerian Muslims expected that the introduction of the *sharīʿa* would improve their security situation and living conditions.[206] Beside material benefits, however, the religious aspect of salvation through a return to a divine code of behaviour in society should not be underestimated. In particular, the issue of strict sexual morals has been perceived—by supporters and critics alike—as a crucial element of the societal changes intended by the introduction of the *sharīʿa* in northern Nigeria. The prominence accorded to sexuality in the Muslim discourse on Islamic law in northern Nigeria can only be explained as an attempt to restore lost virtues in society and to put it back on the straight and narrow.

The question of how and to what extent Islamic law should be applied in the independent Nigerian state has been a recurrent issue in the Nigerian political discourse.[207] Since the introduction of the 1959 Penal Code of the Northern Region, which put an end to the application of uncodified Islamic criminal law, Islamic law gradually became the basic element of the political identity of Muslims in northern Nigeria. It has been propagated as a panacea for all problems of the Nigerian polity, which led to the wide-spread belief that corruption and decadence are the result of a loss of Muslim values caused by external influence or a lack of Islamic education. This perception seems to be shared by a majority of northern Nigerian Muslims, irrespective of the diverging positions they

---

of the case of Safiyya Hussaini is provided in Peters (2006). For accounts of the two cases by one of the lead defence lawyers, see Yawuri (2004).

[204] Thousands of Nigerians lost their lives in outbreaks of inter-confessional or interethnic violence directly or indirectly connected to the introduction of the *sharīʿa*. These seem to have attracted the attention of international and national human-rights organisations to a much lesser extent than the two prominent trials for illicit sexual intercourse (Kogelmann 2006: 257).

[205] A closer look on the reactions of both Muslims and Christians to the introduction of *sharīʿa*, however, reveals that the frontlines especially on the local level were not as clear-cut as it may seem from the outside (Ludwig 2008).

[206] This aspect is discussed in more details in Chapter Three.

[207] For a discussion of the status of Islamic law in Nigeria before 1999, see Abun-Nasr (1988, 1993b).

take with regard to the multi-religious Nigerian state and its secular constitution.[208]

The issue of the application of Islamic law returned to the scene on the advent of civilian rule in 1999 after decades of military dictatorship. Reintroducing the *sharīʿa* was the main campaign promise of the gubernatorial candidate of Zamfara State, Ahmad Sani Yerima. After his victory, he immediately started to act on his pre-election pledge, creating *sharīʿa* courts and introducing Islamic criminal legislation in Zamfara.[209] Governors of eleven other northern Nigerian states followed suit, partly under enormous popular pressure (see Chapter Three).

Notwithstanding the political nature of the initiative, religious movements—in particular the local reform movement, whose main representative is the *Jamāʿat izālat al-bidʿa wa-iqāmat al-sunna* (Society for the removal of innovation and reinstatement of tradition), or 'Yan Izala in short—were quick to espouse the project on the basis of common interests. The 'Yan Izala emerged in the late 1970s in strong opposition to the traditional forms of Islam of the *ṣūfī* orders.[210] Their ideological background has mainly been provided by *salafī* thought and Wahhābī theology.[211] Notwithstanding the conservatism of these sources, the reform movement has been characterised as representing Muslim modernity in the sense that it mediates social change in northern Nigeria (Umar 2001; Kane 2003). This is partly due to the fact that its members have advocated the education of women and challenged the respect which children traditionally owe to their parents in Hausa society. Another central element of the modernist doctrine is that it emphasises the centrality of the *sharīʿa* in Islamic beliefs and practices. This trait is comparable to the emphasis put on legal positivism in modernity in a Western sense (Umar 2001: 132-4).

Members of the reform movement saw the legal reforms as an opportunity to achieve a strict application of Islamic law and to transform Muslim society through the elimination of Western cultural influences and features of the traditional forms of Islam, both of which they considered unlawful innovations (*bidaʿ*) (Sanusi 2004: 81-2). The reasons that led them to support the political initiative of the introduction of Islamic

---

[208] For a discussion of the major trends in northern Nigerian Islam and the relations between them, see Umar (2001).

[209] On the implementation of Islamic criminal law in Zamfara and subsequent developments, see Ostien (2007, 1:vii-xi) and Sada (2007).

[210] The emergence and ideological orientation of the 'Yan Izala has been studied by Loimeier (1997) and Kane (2003).

[211] For the sources referred to by the movement's spiritual mentor Abubakar Gumi in his Hausa translation of the Qur'ān, see Brigaglia (2005: 429). Kane (2003: 123-7) discusses books, mainly authored by Wahhābī scholars, which are used by the 'Yan Izala in proselytising.

criminal law were not primarily linked to Islamising the state, as alleged by many non-Muslim critics. Rather, the reformers saw the introduction of Islamic criminal law as a chance to impose what they perceived as an Islamic way of life by enforcing their interpretation of the *sharīʿa* through the judicial system and thereby deterring Muslims from un-Islamic behaviour.

However, Muslim societies in northern Nigeria have evolved under the influence of Islam for centuries, and local customs have been shaped in interaction with the injunctions of Islamic law. The modernist project challenges behaviour that a majority of the population perceives, if not as Islamic, then at least as acceptable in a Muslim society. Infractions of the newly introduced Islamic criminal legislation are most likely to occur in areas in which the local custom differs from the variant of the divine law codified in the *sharīʿa* penal codes. From the reformers' perspective, the success of the introduction of Islamic criminal law depends on whether judicial practice in cases involving charges of illicit sexual intercourse contradicts or reproduces prevailing sexual habits.

This article contrasts traditional notions of illicit sexual intercourse among the Muslim Hausa with the canonical Islamic law of *zinā* and analyses the effects caused by the conflict of traditional Muslim behaviour in north-western Nigeria and the modernist religious doctrine. The analysis is based on a sample of trials for illicit sexual relations in northern Nigerian *sharīʿa* courts.

## *The northern Nigerian cultural context*

North-western Nigeria has a long history of Islamisation. A *jihād*, waged by the reform movement of Usman ɗan Fodio against the Hausa city states between 1804 and 1812, resulted in the establishment of the Sokoto Caliphate.[212] The Caliphate was divided in largely autonomous emirates, approximately thirty of them by the mid-nineteenth century. John N. Paden points out that the political system of the emirates shaped the societies under their control to an extent that central tendencies of what he calls the emirate civic cultures become identifiable, in particular as regards their orientation to time and destiny, community, authority, civic space, and conflict resolution (Paden 2005: 70-98).[213] Of the currently thirty-six states of the Nigerian federation, fourteen had direct

Sokoto Caliphate

[212] For the history of the *jihād* and its leaders, see Hiskett (1973). For the history of the Sokoto Caliphate, see Last (1967).

[213] Sanusi (2007: 179) goes as far as to talk about "a near-monolithic society in most of northern Nigeria."

experience with the emirate system.[214] The trials of illicit intercourse analysed in this study have taken place in seven of these states.[215]

The culturally dominant group in the region formerly covered by the Sokoto Caliphate are the Hausa.[216] Whereas these are not a homogeneous ethnic group (Barkow 1972: 317-8), certain cultural features seem to have been communally adopted by a majority of the Muslim Hausa.

The Hausa cultures traditionally see legal action before a court of justice as the last resort. On the local level, conflicts usually are resolved informally through mediation by the elders of the community (Paden 2005: 93-4). Only if this mediation fails, the case may eventually be raised to a court. It can be assumed that this applies in particular in cases of extramarital sexual intercourse, which causes considerable embarrassment to the families involved if discussed publicly in court.

In the words of Nigerian-based feminist writer Charmaine Pereira (2005), the introduction and enforcement of Islamic criminal law constitute a radical break with the prevailing heterosexual culture of northern Nigeria. To shed light on the notion of illicit sexual intercourse among the Hausa, it is useful to outline briefly certain aspects of gender relations in the (Muslim) Hausa cultures in general.

In the Hausa-speaking areas of northern Nigeria, gender segregation has taken the form of seclusion, often referred to as *purdah* (or *kulle* in Hausa).[217] The Hausa consider wife seclusion as typically Islamic, in particular because it is not found among the *maguzawa* or Hausa who still adhere to pre-Islamic traditional beliefs (Kleiner-Bossaller 1993: 86). There is a feeling that seclusion is a means to maintain social order in line with Islamic rules, a view expressed in the following quote from northern Nigerian sociologist Yakubu Zakaria (2001: 110):

> With the seclusion of adult women in Hausa society, intrusion into privacy, unwanted pregnancies among adult females and other social vices have been reduced to the barest minimum. For the Muslim Hausa woman the keeping of the rules of purdah and wearing the veil have become symbols of Islamic identity, a sign of

---

[214] The states which were at least partly incorporated in the Sokoto Caliphate are the Hausa-Fulani-dominated states of Sokoto, Kebbi, Zamfara, Katsina, Kano, Jigawa, Bauchi, and Gombe, but also other states such as Niger, Kaduna, Kwara, Kogi, Adamawa and Taraba, which are dominated by other ethnic groups or are composed of a ethnically mixed population (Paden 2005: 63 and 150-1).

[215] Court trials for illicit sexual intercourse have been reported from Bauchi, Jigawa, Kano, Katsina, Niger, Sokoto, and Zamfara (see Chapter One).

[216] Politically, the Sokoto Caliphate was dominated by ethnic Fulani, who by the time of the *jihād* had adopted many aspects of the Hausa culture (Hiskett 1973: 5 and 19).

[217] On the situation of women in the Hausa society, see Kleiner-Bossaller (1993), Werthmann (2000) and Nasir (2007).

> protection and respect rather than of oppression. In Hausa society female seclusion and the wearing of the veil are proofs of the acceptance and practice of Islamic norms and values. Often, they are distinguishing symbols between the Muslim and non-Muslim women.

However, wife seclusion as a predominant practice in Muslim Hausa societies is a rather recent phenomenon.[218] Seclusion became a general practice only after the Second World War. In the 1980s, ninety-five percent of married women in Kano city were living in seclusion (Callaway 1984: 431). Even in rural areas, seclusion appears today to be largely universal among married women regardless of their husband's occupation, status, or wealth of the household (Robson 2000: 185).[219] However, in the rural ambit the rules of seclusion may be handled in a more flexible way, a system called *kullen tsari* (arranged seclusion), due to the necessity for women to work on the fields and perform other tasks outside the house (Imam 1991). In an urban environment, on the other hand, businessmen, executives and academics with Western education nowadays encourage their women and daughters to take up activities outside the house.

Women are not secluded during their entire life. Jerome Barkow (1971: 59) has identified six stages of a Hausa woman's life: *yarinya* or young girl; *bera* or pre-nubile girl; *buduruwa* or girl whose breasts have begun to grow but who is not yet married; *matan aure* or married woman; *bazawara* or woman between marriages; and *tsofuwa* or old (post-menopausal) woman. Only a married woman is expected to observe seclusion fully. Before marriage, girls enjoy great freedom of movement in traditional Hausa society. They serve as their secluded mothers' communication links to the outside world and carry out their commissions. In addition, they usually are in charge of selling their mothers' products on the street (*talla* or hawking). In an urban, more anonymous, environment, hawking can pose a threat to underage girls, e.g. of becoming victims of rape (Kleiner-Bossaller 1993: 85). Northern Nigerian governments have tried in the past to control hawking by young girls, but the practice still persists (Nasir 2007: 81).

In the 1960s, a number of authors still described a form of premarital sexual practice, known in Hausa as *tsarance*, during which several couples consisting of a *buduruwa* and a young man, who might or not be married, spend the night together teasing and petting, usually without

[218] On the development of female seclusion among the Hausa, see Callaway (1984), Imam (1991), Werthmann (1995) and Robson (2000).

[219] Robson conducted her field research in Zarewa village, located in Kano State, north of Zaria, between 1991 and 1993.

actual intromission.[220] By now, *tsarance* seems to have been almost completely abandoned (Pereira 2005). Already in the early 1970s, it had been largely replaced by more individual forms of premarital intimacy (Barkow 1971: 60; and 1972: 319). Already then, for Muslim adolescents, sex-play had to take place surreptitiously, the participants always worried that an adult may come upon them (Barkow 1973: 73). The acceptance of premarital forms of sexuality has certainly decreased in the last thirty years. The number of charges for premarital sex brought before *sharīʿa* courts in northern Nigeria, however, indicates that sexual relations before marriage continue to exist.

Another traditional occasion for young men and women to meet and possibly acquire sexual experience was to attend marriage celebrations out of town which could last several days. This tradition currently seems to be practiced only in remote villages (Pereira 2005). But it may still exist. In December 2004, eight persons, including a newly wed couple, were convicted of "immoral activities" by a *sharīʿa* court in Zamfara State and sentenced to 25 strokes of the cane and a fine of 5,000 Naira (38 US$) each. They had organised a wedding picnic. The judge admonished the people not to indulge in "similar activities" when getting married,[221] possibly a reference to the described traditional practice.

In Hausa society, for both sexes, the first marriage is a *rite de passage* into adulthood. Namely for the woman, in most cases, it means the passage from the freedom of a *buduruwa* to the secluded life of a *matan aure.* Practically all women and men have contracted marriage at least once in their life (Kleiner-Bossaller 1993: 97-8). The age at which the first marriage is contracted, however, is significantly lower for girls than for boys. Early marriage—at the age of eleven to fifteen years—is the rule for women, the exception being girls who have received a formal school education (ibid.).[222] In 2004 the Nigerian federal government reported to the UN Committee on the Rights of the Child that in north-west and north-central Nigeria, i.e. Hausaland, fourteen years is the age of marriage (United Nations 2004). The Nigerian 2003 Child Rights Act (CRA), the domesticated version of the UN Convention on the Rights of the Child (CRC), sets the statutory minimum age of marriage for the whole of Nigeria at eighteen years. This provision is one of the principal reasons for the reluctance of certain state Houses of Assembly, especially in the north, to ratify the CRA (Nasir 2007: 86). By late 2008, the only predominantly Muslim northern state to have passed a law to enforce the CRA was Jigawa. But even this law, adopted in 2007, does not specify an age

[220] See Barkow (1971: 60fn4) for bibliographic references.
[221] "Wedding picnic: Sharia court sentences couples to 25 lashes," *Daily Trust*, 29/12/2004.
[222] For the negative medical consequences of early marriage, see Wall (1998).

limit for marriage, referring only to "puberty" and letting the judge decide. This, according to the state government, was done in a bid to make the law acceptable to the local population. In addition, it will be enforced only once the population has been fully sensitised on its existence.[223]

Most marriages are concluded under Islamic law; no records are kept of such marriages in any government office (Nasir 2007: 84). Polygyny is widespread (ibid.: 86-7). First marriages for girls are typically arranged by their fathers, in some cases without the girl's explicit consent or even against her will. An age difference of twenty or more years between spouses is not uncommon (Kleiner-Bossaller 1993: 99). This may be one reason for the high frequency of divorce in Hausaland. A man can divorce his wife, in line with Islamic law, by simply repudiating her without necessity to give reasons. No official records are kept of such divorces (Nasir 2007: 87). A woman may be married three or more times in the course of her life. For instance, when 30-year-old Amina Lawal was indicted for *zinā*, she already had been divorced twice and had given birth to two children in wedlock, after first marrying at the age of 14. Safiyya Hussaini, who was aged 35 at the time of her trial, had been married three times.

Between two marriages, i.e. in the stage of the *bazawara*, and as a *tsofuwa* after the menopause, a woman may not necessarily live in seclusion. In the early 1980s, Barbara J. Callaway estimated that, in the city of Kano, 10 to 11 percent of adult women are divorced and not married at any given time. However, an individual woman usually will not be out of marriage for more than a few months to a year (Callaway 1984: 443). Most divorced women stay with male relatives. In the 1970s, Jerome Barkow observed that a divorced woman might take lovers discretely, accepting their usually cash gifts and eventually marrying one of them (Barkow 1972: 320). The high number of divorced women tried for illicit sexual intercourse in northern Nigerian *sharīʿa* courts suggests that a whole range of individual practices subsist.

A traditional alternative to remarrying is courtesanship (*karuwanci*). A courtesan (*karuwa*, pl. *karuwai*) is a previously married woman in her reproductive age that lives with other *karuwai* in a *gidan mata* or women's house (Barkow 1971: 65). *Karuwai* can have relations with one or more men, but unlike prostitutes they choose their partners by themselves and relationships often are long-lasting (Kleiner-Bossaller 1993: 91-2). *Karuwanci* is usually only a temporary stage in the life of a woman, since she will probably marry after some time. Some women go back to *karuwanci* after each of their several marriages (Barkow 1971: 70).

[223] "NIGERIA: Early marriage adds to socioeconomic woes, NGOs say," IRIN, 26/11/2008.

After the introduction of the *sharīʿa*, in general, the local *gidan mata*, both in towns and villages, has been closed following pressure exercised by *sharīʿa* enforcement groups, known as *ḥisba*, while *karuwai* continue to exercise their trade in private houses (Last 2008: 52fn). In May 2007, the chairman of the Bauchi State *sharīʿa* commission declared that during the past six years the commission closed down 200 brothels and beer parlours; more than 1,000 "prostitutes" were rehabilitated.[224] An indication that *karuwanci* has not disappeared completely may be the case of a college teacher in Jigawa State who was sentenced—together with his "girl friend"—to 80 lashes each by a *sharīʿa* court in September 2002 for intoxication.[225]

*Karuwanci* could become an accepted part of popular Hausa culture because, traditionally, faithfulness is not expected on the part of the husband. A husband's unfaithfulness is not considered adultery unless it involves a married woman (Barkow 1972: 323-4). Extramarital sexual relations continue to be tolerated by the population in northern Nigeria, certainly in the case of men, but also—provided they take place discretely—for women.

The Hausa have a notion of illicit sexual intercourse, which they call *zinā*. However, the understanding of *zinā* among the Hausa differs from the Islamic legal doctrine. Northern Nigerian Muslims perceive *zinā* as a criminal offence—in the sense that the community, if not the state, takes an interest in prosecuting it—only in cases where an extralegal settlement of the civil aspects between the affected families fails and the conflict becomes a public affair.[226] Adultery might become a criminal case, for example, if the husband of the adulteress threatened to kill or harm the adulterer, or if the family or ward made a big issue of the matter (Paden 2005: 95). Even the offence of rape is seen foremost as a civil issue. It can become a criminal case when the parents of the girl do not accept a settlement, which may include that the rapist is forced to marry the victim (ibid.).

Conflicts arising from sexual relations which exceed the socially accepted norm probably are resolved, first and foremost, through mediation between the parties involved. For a case of illicit intercourse to reach a *sharīʿa* court, it must have escalated in the sense that the families involved were unable to reach an agreement or that it became public for some other reason.

---

[224] "Shari'a commission rehabilitates 1,000 prostitutes in Bauchi," *Daily Trust*, 08/05/2007.

[225] "Village Head, Tutor, Girlfriend Caned 240 Lashes," *This Day*, 25/09/2002. This is the only trial of a woman for intoxication which has come to my knowledge.

[226] Charmaine Pereira (2005) has collected an insightful sample of answers from the grassroots to the question of what constitutes *zinā*.

Since married women live almost invariably in seclusion, they are unlikely to be charged with adultery before a court. Illicit intercourse is more likely to become public knowledge in settings in which unmarried girls or women meet men, be they married or not, outside the close mutual supervision of the family compound. Groups likely to be involved in trials of illicit sexual intercourse, consequently, are girls who move freely without being surveyed by their secluded mothers; young people practicing premarital sex; divorced women who do not conform to a secluded lifestyle; and *karuwai*. Since promiscuity of men is widely accepted, they are less likely to face accusations of *zinā* or may be discharged more easily by judges in male connivance.

## Unlawful sexual intercourse in Mālikī doctrine

The popular understanding of *zinā* among northern Nigerian Muslims differs in important aspects from the Islamic legal doctrine.[227] Under the *sharīʿa*, sexual intercourse is only permitted within marriage or between a slave woman and her master. As slavery has been abolished, in practice, unlawful intercourse nowadays is limited to extramarital sexual relations. There are three different aspects to the offence: firstly, it is an offence punishable at the discretion (*taʿzīr*) of the *qāḍī* in view of its negative impact on society, which is expressed in Qurʾān 17:32: "Do not come near *zinā*, for it is a shameful (deed) and an evil, opening the road (to other evils)" (see Ostien and Umaru 2007: 44). Based on this verse, not only unlawful intercourse itself but also acts which might lead to it, as e.g. private meetings between men and women who are not closely related, may be punished by way of *taʿzīr* (ibid.).

Secondly, a man who engages in unlawful sexual intercourse commits a civil tort against the woman, regardless of whether or not the woman consented. If the woman is not married, the man is liable for the proper brideprice (*mahr al-mithl*, i.e. the average brideprice that a woman of the same age and social status would receive upon marriage in that region), for having enjoyed her sexual services.

Finally, if the strict evidentiary requirements are fulfilled, persons who have had illegal sex can be punished with a *ḥadd* penalty. The *ḥadd* punishment for *zinā*, according to the Mālikī school which is followed in West Africa, is one hundred lashes and, only for male convicts, banishment for one year. For a specific group of people, called *muḥṣan*, capital punishment by stoning applies. A *muḥṣan* is a person who is adult, free, Muslim and has previously enjoyed legitimate sexual relations in a matrimony, regardless of whether the marriage still continues. Adulthood is

[227] For the classical doctrine of *zinā*, see Peters (2005: 14-5 and 59-62).

reached with (physical) puberty. According to the Mālikīs, boys and girls cannot be considered adults under the age of nine; and they cannot be considered minors after the age of eighteen.

In the classical Islamic doctrine, the requirements for proving the *ḥadd* offence of *zinā* are the strictest among the rules of evidence for *ḥadd* offences: a confession by the accused or concurring testimonies of four male eyewitnesses are required. The witnesses must have seen the act in the most intimate details, i.e. the penetration. If the testimonies do not satisfy the requirements, the witnesses can be sentenced to eighty lashes for *qadhf* or false accusation of *zinā*. As the only one of the four canonical schools of Islamic law, however, the Mālikīs allow circumstantial evidence in *zinā* trials: they regard childbirth in the case of an unmarried, or legally divorced, woman as a proof of unlawful sexual intercourse. If in such a case she pleads that she was a victim of rape, she must, in order to corroborate her plea, produce circumstantial evidence. In these cases, the burden of proving her innocence is put on her. According to the other schools, already her claim that she was raped produces *shubha* or uncertainty which should normally prevent the *ḥadd* punishment for *zinā* from being pronounced.

A plea accepted by the Mālikīs that produces *shubha* is the attribution of the pregnancy to a former husband (Peters 2006: 237). According to Mālikī authorities, a pregnancy may last five or even seven years. Therefore, if the child is born within five or seven years after the dissolution of her marriage, it is considered possible that conception occurred during the woman's former marriage. In this case, pregnancy alone cannot be considered sufficient proof of *zinā*.

According to Ibrahim Na'iya Sada, former director of the Centre for Islamic Legal Studies at the Ahmadu Bello University in Zaria, which was tasked to revise the initial draft of the Zamfara Sharīʿa Penal Code, the main aim of the *ḥadd* punishment for *zinā* is the preservation of *nasab* or lineage, one of the purposes of marriage being "to procreate in an organised manner" (2002).[228] Indeed, married women are protected by Islamic law after the sixth month of their marriage. If the husband wants to deny the paternity of a child of whom his wife is pregnant or to whom his wife has given birth, he can resort to the procedure of *liʿān*, which results in the rejection of his paternity and in a divorce, but not in criminal proceedings against the wife (Peters 2005: 193). Thus, while unmarried women—if they are to avoid charges of *zinā*—need to prove that the alleged illicit intercourse took place against their will, the burden of proving that the pregnancy of a married woman is the result of illicit intercourse is placed on the husband.

---

[228] See also Bambale (2003: 38-9).

## *Unlawful sexual intercourse in the* sharīʿa *penal codes*

In the *sharīʿa* penal codes of northern Nigeria,[229] *zinā* is to be punished by death by stoning if the offender is married.[230] In other cases the penalty is one hundred lashes. Men are punished, in addition, by imprisonment for one year. The same punishments are prescribed for the offences of rape,[231] sodomy and, in most codes, incest.[232] Most codes punish lesbianism (*siḥāq*) with 50 lashes and a maximum of six months' imprisonment. In Bauchi, the prison term may extend to up to five years; Kano and Katsina prescribe death by stoning (Ostien 2007: 4:71). Only in cases of rape, the male offender is, in addition, required to pay the victim the proper brideprice (*ṣadāq al-mithl*) (ibid.: 4:69).[233]

Sexual intercourse by a man with his own wife is not regarded to be rape (Ostien 2007: 4:69). Any sexual intercourse, with or without consent, with a girl under fifteen years of age—under the age of maturity (*taklīf*) in Bauchi and Kaduna—or a woman of unsound mind is considered rape (ibid.). The age limit may protect girls under the age of fifteen from being prosecuted for *zinā*, e.g. in cases of rape. However, it does not apply to sexual intercourse within a marriage, which under no circumstances is regarded as rape. In contrast, under the 1959 Penal Code for the Northern Region, which was replaced by the *sharīʿa* penal codes for Muslims but continues to apply to non-Muslims in the *sharīʿa* states, intercourse with wives who have not attained puberty was considered rape (ibid.).

Many codes fail to specify the evidentiary value of pregnancy. Only the Kebbi code mentions pregnancy specifically as proof of *zinā* (Ostien 2007: 4:68). Kano and Niger accept only confession or statements by four male witnesses as proof for *zinā*, thereby precluding the acceptance of pregnancy or childbirth out of wedlock as circumstantial evidence (Peters 2003: 20). Failure to specify the rules of evidence in the northern Nigerian *sharīʿa* penal codes and the *sharīʿa* codes of criminal procedure opens the door for the application of uncodified Mālikī rules of evidence (Peters 2006: 240). In practice, the *sharīʿa* courts have applied Mālikī law

[229] Eleven states enacted separate *sharīʿa* penal codes. Most states followed the model of Zamfara. Niger introduced corresponding amendments to the existing Penal Code. I rely on the comparative edition of the different *sharīʿa* penal codes prepared by Ostien (2007: 4:33-139).

[230] The word "married" used in the codes is an apparently incorrect translation of *muḥṣan*, as already remarked by Peters (2006: 226 fn 15), for the case of Safiyya Hussaini. Judicial practice shows that the courts consistently construe "married" as *muḥṣan*.

[231] Bauchi extends the term of maximum imprisonment to 14 years, Kano and Katsina to life (Ostien 2007: 4:69).

[232] Kano and Katsina omit the offence of incest (ibid., 4:70).

[233] *Ṣadāq al-mithl* is synonymous to *mahr al-mithl*.

of evidence, including the acceptance of pregnancy out of wedlock as circumstantial evidence of *zinā*.[234] As a result, at least in the initial phase, pregnancy or childbirth out of wedlock were the most frequent grounds of indictment for unlawful sexual intercourse, in many cases followed by the woman's confession in court. In such trials, the woman was charged, while the man often were discharged for lack of evidence. In most cases, the circumstantial evidence was rejected by the appellate instances.

## *Judicial practice in* zinā *trials*

Judicial practice in cases involving illicit sexual intercourse is analysed on the basis of a sample of *zinā* trials reported from northern Nigeria between 2000 and 2004[235] and an additional rape case of May 2007. The trials involved charges of rape, sodomy, incest and consensual unlawful intercourse, for which the codes use the term *zinā*.

Many verdicts handed down by lower instances were deficient. All too often the judges administering justice in the *sharīʿa* courts have not been qualified to apply Islamic criminal law and the new legislation codifying it. In addition, they have been exposed to the activities of Muslim pressure groups, a fact which seems to have encouraged disrespect of procedural guarantees.[236]

### Rape

Nine cases of rape with a total of fourteen defendants were identified between 2000 and 2004. An additional trial for rape came to light in May 2007 (see the appendix, p. 173f). Most cases of rape were reported to the courts by members of the community,[237] family members of the victim,[238]

---

[234] On the applicability of uncodified Islamic procedural rules in northern Nigerian *sharīʿa* courts, see Ostien (2007: 4:188-91).

[235] For an overview of the trials identified for the period 2000-2004, see Chapter One.

[236] For example, the 19 August 2002 hearing which saw Amina Lawal's death sentence confirmed was attended by a "group of Muslim radicals numbering about fifty [who] were present to see whether Sharia law would be enforced. [... W]henever the judge made a finding or a ruling which went against Amina Lawal, the group of radicals would chant the *takbir* (*Allahu akbar!* – Allah is the Greatest!). After the judgment the group broke into jubilation, chanting that Islam had overcome *kufr* (unbelief)" (Yawuri 2007: 133-4). Aliyu Musa Yawuri, Amina Lawal's lead lawyer, was accused of betraying his religion (2007: 139).

[237] Ado Baranda was surprised by neighbours in his house, trying to stop the girl from crying after raping her ("All Set for Sarimu's Public Stoning in Jigawa," *This Day*, 02/09/2002). Aminu Ruwa was reported to the police by "one Mohamed Alhaji of Tutjiba area" ("Man gets 100 strokes for indecency," *The Guardian* (Nigeria), 20/11/2002, 16). Mohammed Ibrahim's offence was allegedly reported to the police by a certain Shuaibu Sani ("Two Charged with Raping Minors," *This Day*, 27/01/2003). Tukur Aliyu was handed over to a *ḥisba* group by his neighbours ("Man, 45, gets 40 lashes for raping four-year-old girl", *Daily Independent*, 20/10/2003).

or school authorities.[239] Abubakar Aliyu was caught in the act by police.[240] Only in the trial of Adamu Jugga, it was the victim who brought the case to court. The 35-year-old married woman alleged that 50-year-old Jugga entered her matrimonial home and assaulted her.[241]

At least in five of the ten trials, involving eleven of the fourteen defendants, the victims were eleven years of age or younger, a fact which illustrates the risk incurred by young girls who leave the parental compound without the supervision of their mothers living in seclusion.

The convictions (of first instance) of Ado Baranda, Aminu Ruwa, Hamisu Suleiman, Ibrahim Ayuba and Mohammed Ibrahim, i.e. in more than one third of the known rape trials, were based on confession.[242] Whether Abubakar Aliyu, the only man reported to have been caught in the act, was convicted on the strength of testimonies by the police officers who surprised him remains unclear. There are no reports that men charged with rape were convicted on the grounds of a pregnancy of the victim. In other words, in none of the known *zinā* indictments based on pregnancy out of wedlock the courts received and allowed a claim of forceful intercourse.

Three rapists were sentenced to death by stoning:[243] while not much is known about the circumstances of the trials of Selah Debo and Ade Debo, Ado Baranda of Jigawa State was convicted in May 2002 of raping a four-year-old girl and sentenced to death by stoning, one hundred strokes of the cane and payment of 10,000 Naira (83 US$) brideprice.[244] The trial attracted some media attention, not least because of a public comment by then Jigawa State Governor Ibrahim Turaki. In a reference to Baranda's death penalty, he stated at a 'Yan Izala convention that as a governor he could not stop a divine law from being carried out, in particular in the light of the fact that the convict had pleaded guilty.[245] Initially, Baranda seemed to have accepted the judgment. Nevertheless, an

---

[238] Ibrahim Ayuba was reported to the police by the victim's father, after "it was discovered that one Ibrahim Ayuba was the culprit" ("Two Charged with Raping Minors," *This Day*, 27/01/2003).

[239] The five rapists in Jigawa State were reported to the police by the authorities of the girl's school after she had told her teachers that she had been raped on her way to school ("For rape, sharia court passes death, fines others," *The Guardian* (Nigeria), 03/09/2002, 7). How the courts were informed about the accusations of rape against Hamisu Sulaiman, Selah Debo and Ade Debo has not been reported.

[240] "Man Sentenced for Committing Adultery with Lunatic," *This Day*, 14/07/2001.

[241] "Alleged rape victim, 35, offers to swear by Qur'an," *Weekly Trust*, 04-10/10/2003, 17.

[242] The grounds of conviction of Selah Dabo, Tukur Aliyu, the five rapists of Jigawa State, and Ade Debo were not reported.

[243] No sentence has been reported in the cases of Ibrahim Ayuba, Mohammed Ibrahim and Adamu Jugga.

[244] "Sharia: Man to Die for Raping 9-year Girl," *This Day*, 10/05/2002.

[245] "Sharia: Male convict to die by stoning," *Daily Champion*, 27/08/2002, 1-2.

appeal filed on his behalf by his family—after the thirty-day period for appeal had already elapsed—was admitted by the Jigawa Sharīʿa Court of Appeal. On appeal, Baranda withdrew his confession and was acquitted of the charge in August 2003 on the grounds of insanity and remanded in a psychiatric asylum.

As regards the punishment for defendants who were not and had not been married previously, only in two of the analysed cases, the rapist received a punishment which matched at least partly the punishment prescribed in the respective *sharīʿa* penal code. In July 2001, Abubakar Aliyu was brought before a *sharīʿa* court for committing "adultery" with a mentally deranged woman. He was sentenced to 100 strokes of the cane in addition to one year's imprisonment.[246] Aminu Ruwa, who confessed to raping a six-year-old girl, was sentenced to 100 strokes of the cane. He, in addition, was sentenced to paying the medical bill of his victim, estimated at 3,500 Naira (27 US$).[247] No prison term was mentioned.

Presumably, in the three remaining cases (the five Jigawa rapists, Hamisu Suleiman and Tukur Aliyu) the courts viewed the evidence as insufficient for pronouncing the *ḥadd* punishment. However, at least in the case of Hamisu Suleiman, the defendant is reported to have confessed to the charge, which is regarded sufficient evidence for conviction and the application of the *ḥadd* punishment. The judge stated that the court was lenient with Suleiman because he was a first offender and sentenced him to eighteen months in prison and a 15,000 Naira fine (110 US$).[248] The five Jigawa rapists received prison sentences of five months with an option of 5,500 Naira (42 US$) fine each.

The last case defies easy categorisation. Tukur Aliyu was sentenced to forty strokes of the cane and a fine of 10,000 Naira (71 US$). Described as a traditional Islamic teacher (*malam* in Hausa) in charge of teaching the Qurʾān to young children known as *almajirai*, Aliyu is said to have sexually abused a four-year-old girl who was under his supervision. He was caught when the little girl escaped from his house and was found by neighbours walking in the street with bloodstained clothes. The girl told them what had happened to her.[249] The circumstances of his arrest and the punishment he received present striking similarities with the case of Saminu Abbas of Kano State, who was charged before a *sharīʿa* court in May 2003 after raping a four-year-old girl. In this case, the girl returned

---

[246] "Man Sentenced for Committing Adultery with Lunatic," *This Day*, 14/07/2001. Although the report speaks of adultery, sexual intercourse with a woman of unsound mind is always considered rape.

[247] "Man gets 100 strokes for indecency," *The Guardian* (Nigeria), 20/11/2002, 16.

[248] "Rape suspect bags 18 months jail term," *Daily Trust*, 21/08/2003, 23.

[249] "Man, 45, gets 40 lashes for raping four-year-old girl," *Daily Independent*, 20/10/2003.

home crying. On indication by a group of children, who told her mother that Abbas had taken her daughter to his home, the mother examined the girl and found stains of blood on her underwear.[250] No sentence was reported in this case, but the press report mentions that Abbas was indicted on the basis of Section 187, Kano State Sharīʿa Penal Code. This section defines the offence of gross indecency, including acts such as "kissing in public, exposure of nakedness in public and other related acts of similar nature in order to corrupt public morals." It is made punishable with forty lashes, one year in prison and a fine of 10,000 Naira. The same offence is defined by the Zamfara code (Section 138). Thus, Tukur Aliyu may not have been convicted of rape but of gross indecency. Whereas the press reports describe the offences as rape or attempted rape, respectively, the grounds of conviction remain unclear. Possibly, in the absence of confessions or testimonies of four male eye-witnesses, the judges sought to punish the culprits by way of *taʿzīr*, and "gross indecency" was the *taʿzīr* offence provided for in the *sharīʿa* penal codes which they thought matched best the offence committed.[251]

In addition to these trials for rape or gross indecency, Yanusa Yargaba of Jigawa State was convicted of attempted rape of a blind woman in August 2001.[252] Yargaba allegedly entered a blind couple's home illegally at night and tried to rape the woman. His conviction was founded on a confession made in court and the statements of three witnesses. The judge sentenced him to hundred strokes of the cane. Although attempted rape is not defined in the *sharīʿa* penal codes,[253] and for the accusation of *zinā* penetration needs to take place, this sentence is remarkably close to the *ḥadd* punishment for *zinā*.

In conclusion, it seems that in cases of rape, *sharīʿa* judges tended to seek ways of avoiding the imposition of *ḥadd* punishments on the accused who were mainly brought before them by members of the public. In addition, while several defendants were ordered to pay fines, the only rapist ordered to pay *ṣadāq al-mithl* was Ado Baranda. The high proportion of underaged victims shows that forceful sexual intercourse which takes place within family compounds is either not considered an offence or dealt with between the affected parties. In addition, adult women are reluctant to report rape cases to the police for fear of being accused of *zinā*. As a result, most of the rape trials in *sharīʿa* courts treat cases of paedophilia.

[250] "Man in *Sharia* court for raping 4-year-old girl," *Daily Trust*, 26/05/2003, 23.
[251] The Zamfara code groups "gross indecency" under *ḥadd* offences. However, in the classical doctrine, it must be considered *taʿzīr*, as in Kano.
[252] "Man to Get 100 Lashes for Attempted Rape," *This Day*, 27/08/2001.
[253] There is only a provision for "attempts to commit an offence punishable by imprisonment," which cannot apply to attempted rape (Ostien 2007: 4:66).

*aims to deter people from homosexuality*

## Sodomy

A similar impression is gained from the three known cases of sodomy (see the appendix, p. 174). Penalising sodomy aims at deterring people from homosexuality. This assumption is substantiated by the fact that the *sharīa* penal codes also prohibit lesbianism (Imam 2004: 134fn5). In contrast, the 1959 Penal Code for the Northern Region made "carnal intercourse against the order of nature with any man, woman or animal," which included sodomy, punishable with imprisonment (Ostien and Umaru 2007: 49), but did not mention lesbianism explicitly. In practice, however, at least in two of the three sodomy cases the victims were little boys. Thus, these acts are better described as paedophilia than as homosexuality.

Jibrin Babaji was arrested by a *hisba* or *sharīa* enforcement group on indication of two citizens and handed over to police.[254] Attahiru Umar was reportedly apprehended by fellows of the *almajiri* he raped.[255] The convictions of Babaji and Umar were based on confession in court. Babaji is also reported to have answered in the affirmative when asked by the judge if he was a Muslim.[256] Umar reportedly confessed to the offence after having been identified by two witnesses.[257]

Attahiru Umar and Jibrin Babaji were sentenced to death by stoning. Similar to Ado Baranda, Jibrin Babaji was acquitted on appeal after he pleaded to being insane. The three boys, who allegedly accepted money from Babaji in return for allowing him to have sex with them, were given six strokes of the cane after the trial of first instance, but were later rehabilitated by the court that granted the appeal of Babaji. The judge who had sentenced them in the first instance was ordered to pay them compensation.[258] No information has come to light regarding a possible appeal against Umar's death sentence. Like the abovementioned rapist Selah Debo, it is not unlikely that Attahiru Umar has remained in jail awaiting the execution of the death sentence.[259] For being unmar-

---

[254] "*Sodomy: Sharia* court sentences man to death by stoning," *Daily Trust*, 25/09/2003.

[255] "Sharia Court Sentences Man to Death by Stoning," *This Day*, 14/09/2001. How Barkeji were brought to the court's attention was not reported.

[256] "*Sodomy: Sharia* court sentences man to death by stoning," *Daily Trust*, 25/09/2003.

[257] "Nigerian sentenced to stoning," BBC News, 14/09/2001. The grounds of Barkeji's conviction were not reported.

[258] "*Sodomy:* Judge to pay N3000 for wrongful conviction," *Daily Trust*, 23/03/2004, 5.

[259] Both cases were cited in the media as examples for stoning cases after the period for appeal had elapsed. Attahiru Umar's cases was last mentioned in "Niger sharia court sentences two to death by stoning," *The Guardian* (Nigeria), 29/08/2002, 1-2, that is almost a year after the judgment. The case of Selah Dabo was signalled in November 2004 by the Legal Aid Council, a federal agency which provides legal representation for indigent accuseds in serious cases, two months after the judgment ("Sharia: Legal Aid Council to appeal against 30 convictions," *Vanguard*, 17/11/2004).

impose hadd punishments

ried—"even though he had sexual knowledge of another man," as the judge pointed out—Abdullahi Barkeji received the *ḥadd* punishment for non-*muḥṣan* defendants: one hundred strokes of the cane and one year's imprisonment.[260]

These trials—few though they are—demonstrate that in cases of sodomy the courts were less reluctant to impose the *ḥadd* punishments for *zinā* than in rape cases. It appears that, in a region in which child marriage is common, sexual intercourse with immature girls is more acceptable to fellow men (and judges) than with little boys.

### Incest

The more prominent of the two reported incest cases involved Umaru and Altine Tori of Bauchi State. Fifteen-year-old Altine was forced by her stepfather Umaru Tori to have sexual intercourse with him on several occasions while they were alone on the family's farm land. The crime was reported to the police by an uncle of Altine's after noticing that she was pregnant. In court, Umaru Tori confessed to having raped his stepdaughter four times and was sentenced to death by stoning in December 2003. Later, he reportedly denied responsibility for Altine's pregnancy and filed an appeal, which was upheld, on 24 May 2005, by the state's *sharīʿa* court of appeal.[261] The appellate court ordered the case to be retried by the upper *sharīʿa* court.[262]

As for Altine, in the initial trial, the prosecuting police officer reportedly testified in court that at the time of the offence the girl called for help and tried to escape from her stepfather.[263] This statement might have been considered sufficient to cause *shubha* and prevent the *ḥadd* punishment for *zinā* from being applied to Altine. In spite of this, Altine, who only admitted two forceful sexual contacts, was apparently convicted of incest like her step-father on the basis of her pregnancy out of wedlock and sentenced to 100 strokes of the cane to be administered after the delivery of her baby.[264] The court seems to have taken the position that she had given herself voluntarily to her stepfather. In an appeal filed in her name, her defence counsel argued that, among other

[260] "Man Gets 100 Strokes, One-Year Jail for Sodomy," *This Day*, 28/02/2002, 5.
[261] "Shariah Court Entertains 11-Month-Old Appeal," *Weekly Trust*, 30/11/2004.
[262] Amnesty International Annual Report Nigeria 2006.
[263] "Incest: Sharia Court sentences man to death by stoning," *Daily Trust*, 06/01/2004, 1-2.
[264] "Sharia: Man to die by stoning for impregnating step-daughter in Bauchi," *The Guardian* (Nigeria), 06/01/2004. The Bauchi State Sharīʿa Penal Code makes incest punishable with one hundred lashes and imprisonment for a term up to seven years for unmarried defendants (Section 136(a)). In Altine's case there was no mention of a prison term.

grounds, there was no definitive proof of the offence as required by Islamic law.[265]

In the second known trial for incest, it appears that only the man was indicted. Umar Isa Zurena of Jigawa State was charged with incest in November 2003 after his niece, pressed by her family, disclosed that her pregnancy was caused by him. He was taken to court by the young woman's father. There, she is reported to have testified that her uncle raped her on two occasions, offering her money and threatening to beat her if she disclosed what had happened.[266] No judgment has been reported for this case.

These cases show that the offence of incest can be a means of prosecuting sexual abuse within the extended family, in particular those family members who are in charge of children outside the compounds and those who have access to the women's quarters. However, it is in the discretion of the court whether or not to consider the girl or woman affected a victim or an accessory in the offence.

### Consensual unlawful sexual intercourse (*zinā*)

In general, the described cases of rape, sodomy and incest convey the impression that *sharīʿa* court judges of lower instances have tended to avoid inflicting *ḥadd* punishments on male defendants to the greatest extent possible. Only for crimes which in the patriarchal societies of northern Nigeria may be considered repulsive for violating the feeling of manhood (sodomy) or the family honour (incest), this indulgence is absent. However, it is equally absent in trials of consensual unlawful sexual intercourse, in which the majority of the defendants are women.

Since the *sharīʿa* penal codes of the various states expressly define the offence of rape as intercourse against the will or without the consent of the woman, the offence of *zinā*, as defined in the codes, refers to consensual sexual intercourse between a legally responsible man and a legally responsible woman who are not married to one another. While this assumption seems to hold true in most cases, it is not always possible to assert that the women's consent was free from coercion. For instance, Bariya Ibrahim is reported to have named three middle-aged men as being the possible father of her pregnancy. She stated that all three had paid her to have sex with her, adding that it had been against her wishes.[267] Since she could not prove her allegations, she risked being

[265] "Shariah Court Entertains 11-Month-Old Appeal," *Weekly Trust*, 30/11/2004. The final hearing was slated for 7 December 2004. However, the outcome of the appeal could not be established. It is not clear whether Altine and Umaru Tori filed their appeals together.
[266] "Man, 20, in court for impregnating niece," *Weekly Trust*, 22/11/2003.
[267] "Nigerian girl gives birth and faces 180 lashes," AFP, 29/12/2000.

convicted, in addition to *zinā*, of *qadhf* or false accusation of *zinā*. In another case, involving Hafsatu Idris and Ahmadu Haruna, the female defendant claimed that she had been raped. Nevertheless, she was indicted for *zinā*, alongside the alleged rapist.[268] These examples show that women do have cause to be apprehensive about addressing the courts over sex-related offences, as failure to prove their allegations exposes them to the risk of being charged with consensual sexual intercourse.

Cases of consensual intercourse came to the attention of the courts principally in two ways. A number of unmarried women who were found pregnant or had a baby out of wedlock were reported to police or the *sharīʿa* courts by neighbours or *ḥisba* groups.[269] After it became known that she had a baby without being married, Amina Lawal was taken to the village head and later handed over to police (Ostien 2007: 5:52-3). Hafsatu Abubakar was reported to the police by a *sharīʿa* implementation committee for having a baby out of wedlock.[270] Bariya Ibrahim was first brought by her uncles to the village's district head, who summoned the three men named by the girl as possibly responsible for her pregnancy and questioned them extensively. At this stage, members of a *ḥisba* group heard about the case and reported it to the police (BAOBAB 2003: 10). It appears that in this case the intervention of the *ḥisba* group aborted the traditional conflict resolution mechanism. Another case which shows the effects of a thwarted mediation is the trial of Hafsatu Idris: her newly wedded husband divorced her after noticing that she was pregnant at the time of the wedding. She claimed having been raped by Ahmadu Haruna. The three families involved were seeking an out-of-court settlement of the affair, when Ahmadu Haruna dragged Hafsatu's uncle to court for denting his image in the town. The case was first taken to a lower *sharīʿa* court which ordered further police investigations. The second police report contained the charge of *zinā* and the case was transferred to an upper *sharīʿa* court where Hafsatu Idris and Ahmadu Haruna were jointly indicted.[271]

The second way in which courts became aware of cases of consensual unlawful intercourse is that, unaware of the changes in the legislation, the family of a woman sought civil redress in a *sharīʿa* court after the alleged father refused to accept the paternity of the child or did not fulfil his obligations incurred during traditional mediation. Ahmadu Ibrahim was dragged to court by the father of Fatima Usman, who demanded that Ahmadu live up to his promise made before the village council of

---

[268] "Rape victim's father accuses police of changing FIR," *Daily Trust*, 24/03/2004, 29.
[269] On the role of *ḥisba* groups, see, for example, Peters (2003: 29-30) and Last (2008: 50-5).
[270] "Mother of 2-week Baby on Capital Offence Charge," *This Day*, 11/01/2002.
[271] "Rape victim's father accuses police of changing FIR," *Daily Trust*, 24/03/2004, 29.

elders that he would sustain his illegitimate child (Ibrahim and Lyman 2004: 20). The family of Safiyya Hussaini went to a *sharīʿa* court to compel Yakubu Abubakar to accept responsibility for a pregnancy for which she said he was responsible.[272] Adama Yunusa dragged her fiancé to court to force him to assume his responsibilities as father of her unborn child. As a result, she was indicted for *zinā*.[273] The case of Attine Tanko and Lawal Sada came to the attention of the court after Attine confessed to her father that she was pregnant and that Lawal was the father of the child.[274] Also in this case, it appears likely that the father wanted to force Sada to assume his responsibilities.

Eighteen trials for the offence of *zinā* have been identified (see the appendix, p. 175f).[275] In all identified cases, women were indicted, while only twelve male defendants appeared in court. Four of the men were immediately discharged and acquitted due to lack of evidence against them.[276] Some of the eight women, who stood trial for *zinā* without a male counterpart, failed to prove their allegations of who was responsible for their pregnancy and were threatened, in addition to the punishment for *zinā*, with being convicted of *qadhf* or false accusation of *zinā*.[277]

Only in one case, the woman was acquitted and the man convicted: Yunusa Rafin Chiyawa was accused of illegal intercourse with the wife of one of his neighbours. The woman swore on the Qurʾān that she had been hypnotised by Chiyawa.[278] As a result, she was considered not to be criminally responsible at the time of the offence. Two other women, Maryam Abubakar and Hafsatu Abubakar, were acquitted in the trial of first instance, both after attributing their pregnancies to their former husbands. Both had been charged without a male counterpart.

Pregnancy of an unmarried or divorced woman is clearly the main indicator that has led to charges of *zinā*. At least fourteen of the nineteen female defendants were pregnant or had given birth out of wedlock at the time of trial. The only woman who was married at the time of trial was the co-defendant of Yunusa Rafin Chiyawa. In all fourteen cases of

---

[272] "The travails of convict Safiyatu," *The Comet*, 24/11/2001, 8-9.

[273] "Sharia: Woman Gets 100 Strokes over Pregnancy," *This Day*, 06/05/2002.

[274] "Second teen mum in Nigeria awaits flogging for pre-marital sex," AFP, 11/01/2001.

[275] In the previously published version of this article (Weimann 2009: 456), an unnecessary counting error occurred. There, nineteen trials for illicit consensual sexual intercourse were mentioned, whereas footnote 127 only lists eighteen. This error was a corollary of another error in a footnote (Weimann 2009: 458 fn 131), which mentions Hafsatu Idris twice, thus seemingly elevating the number of indicted women to nineteen. The first mention of Hafsatu Idris is correct.

[276] These men are Yakubu Abubakar (Safiyya Hussaini); Yahaya Mohammed (Amina Lawal); Umaru Shehu (Hafsatu Abubakar) and Dauda Sani (Hajara Ibrahim).

[277] These were Bariya Ibrahim Maguza, Hajo Poki, possibly Hajara Ibrahim.

[278] "Nigerian man faces death for adultery," BBC News, 27/06/2002.

unmarried (expecting) mothers indicted for *zinā*, the pregnancy was considered circumstantial evidence.[279] In the trial of first instance, many of the women were convicted on the basis of their confession.[280] It is reasonable to assume that these women were ignorant of the relevant provisions of Islamic law when they confessed in court. Faced with accusations of illicit pregnancy or childbirth, these women admitted sexual relations and pointed to the man responsible for it, probably motivated by the wish that the father assume responsibility for his child. The men, however, have no incentive to acknowledge the charges.[281] In none of the reported cases are eye-witnesses reported to have testified to the offence.

At least in twelve of the eighteen *zinā* trials with female defendants, the accused women were convicted of the charge in the first instance.[282] All women seem to have received the respective *ḥadd* punishment for *zinā*: five were sentenced to death by stoning; seven to 100 lashes. Some verdicts do not stop there: in addition to 100 lashes, Aisha Musa received one year's imprisonment (BAOBAB 2003: 12); and Adama Yunusa was banned from the area in which she lived.[283] Both additional punishments are traditionally reserved for men. In the trial of first instance, Hajara Ibrahim was even sentenced to death by stoning and 100 lashes.[284]

At the same time, only three men were convicted of the offence of *zinā* proper together with their female partners: Sani Mamman, the co-defendant of Zuweira Aliyu, and Lawal Sada, the co-defendant of Attine Tanko, were convicted and sentenced to 100 lashes and one year's imprisonment; only Fatima Usman and Ahmadu Ibrahim were jointly sentenced to death by stoning.

---

[279] Hajara Ibrahim, Attine Tanko, and Bariya Ibrahim were pregnant at the time of trial. Fatima Usman, Hawa'u Garba, Hafsatu Abubakar, Safiyya Hussaini, Daso Adamu, Hajo Poki, Maryam Abubakar Bodinga, and Aisha Musa were indicted after giving birth to a child out of wedlock. Amina Lawal and Hafsatu Idris were found pregnant, but gave birth before the start of their trials. Adama Yanusa sued her fiancé four months into her pregnancy. No pregnancy or illegitimate childbirth has been reported for Amina Abdullahi, Zuweira Aliyu, Zuwayra Shinkafi and the co-defendant of Yunusa Chiyawa.

[280] This has been reported for Safiyya Hussaini, Amina Lawal, Hajara Ibrahim, Bariya Ibrahim, Hafsatu Abubakar, Hawa'u Garba, and Adama Yunusa.

[281] An exception is Hussaini Mamman, who admitted in court that he had a child with Hawa'u Garba, saying he wanted to marry her, but her parents refused. "Nigerian couple arraigned in Islamic court on adultery charge," AFP, 18/06/2001.

[282] No sentences have been reported for the trials of Hawa'u Garba and Hussaini Mamman, and Hafsatu Idris and Ahmadu Haruna, respectively. It remains unclear on which provisions of the Zamfara State Sharīʿa Penal Code the sentences of Zuwayra Shinkafi (thirty lashes) and Sani Yahaya (eighty lashes and ten months' imprisonment) were based.

[283] "Sharia: Woman Gets 100 Strokes over Pregnancy," *This Day*, 06/05/2002.

[284] "Sharia court sentences woman to death by stoning," *Daily Trust*, 13/10/2004.

At least in eight of the sixteen *zinā* trials of first instance in which the defendants were found guilty, appeals were filed to a higher court.[285] Some women who had been sentenced on the basis of their confession now revoked.[286] Among the sentences appealed were the six stoning-to-death verdicts. Five of these death sentences were reversed and the defendants discharged and acquitted, although partly after protracted proceedings: in case of Amina Lawal's trial, e.g., one year and a half passed between the sentence of first instance and her acquittal in the second appeal. In the sixth trial, a final verdict has never been reached: Fatima Usman and Ahmadu Ibrahim were sentenced to death by stoning in Niger State in August 2002. They appealed to the state's *sharīʿa* court of appeal. Pending the outcome, they were admitted to bail. While the appeal was pending, the state's High Court called into question the jurisdiction of the *sharīʿa* court of appeal to decide the case. The appeal, therefore, has never been decided by the *sharīʿa* court of appeal but has also never been transferred to the High Court; the couple are still on bail, and they are unlikely ever to hear from the authorities about this matter again (Ostien and Dekker 2010: 604). In none of the cases in which a *ḥadd* sentence of first instance was overturned was it replaced by a *taʿzīr* punishment; the appellants were discharged and acquitted.

With regard to more recent stoning-to-death sentences, such as those against Hajara Ibrahim or Daso Adamu, the appeal was granted within less than three months after the verdict of first instance. Thus, it seems that after an initial period of uncertainty about how to deal with this kind of sentences, the acquittals of Safiyya Hussaini, Amina Lawal and others now serve as precedents for appellate courts to reject pregnancy as proof of *zinā* in *muḥṣan* women. Appeal judges accepted the argument of the delayed pregnancy. In many of the acquittals of female

[285] Safiyya Hussaini was acquitted in March 2002 by a *sharīʿa* court of appeal. Adama Yunusa's sentence of 100 lashes was upheld but the banishment revoked in May 2002 by a *sharīʿa* court of appeal. Maryam Abubakar Bodinga was acquitted in October 2002 by an upper *sharīʿa* court. Amina Lawal, after her sentence was upheld in a first appeal by an upper *sharīʿa* court in August 2002, was acquitted in September 2003 by a *sharīʿa* court of appeal. Yunusa Rafin Chiyawa was acquitted in November 2003 by an upper *sharīʿa* court. Hajara Ibrahim was acquitted in November 2004 by an upper *sharīʿa* court. Daso Adamu was acquitted in December 2004 by an upper *sharīʿa* court. The final outcome of the trial of Fatima Usman and Ahmadu Ibrahim has not been established (last reported hearing before a *sharīʿa* court of appeal in April 2004).

[286] The revocation of the confession is explicitly reported for Safiyya Hussaini and Amina Lawal. The confession of Hajara Ibrahim was annulled by the appeal judge on the grounds that it was not made four times. "Islamic court overturns stoning sentence," *Independent Online* (South Africa), 10/11/2004.

defendants or appellants, this argument was used as one of the main grounds on which the judges based their decision.[287]

Another development is of importance: the attitude of the higher courts to accusations of *zinā* brought before them by members of the public or *ḥisba* groups has been more cautious than that of the lower courts. In the case of Daso Adamu, the appeal judge stated that the first instance trial was improper because Daso Adamu "didn't present herself to court but was dragged and tried against her wish."[288] Similarly, the appeals court that annulled the stoning sentence against Safiyya Hussaini emphasised that the investigation of *zinā* cases on the basis of mere suspicion, such as an unmarried woman found pregnant, is unlawful (Peters 2006: 241). The court stated the following:

> We agree with the appellant's counsel that based on this verse [Qur'ān 49:12], it is *haram* to initiate an action against a person for *zina* based on other people's reports. Imam Shafi'i said that a leader does not even have the right to summon a person accused of *zina* for the purpose of investigating the accusation [...] It is not permissible for a leader to order somebody's arrest, in order to investigate him for allegedly committing *zina*, based simply on what other people report. The way the police went to Safiyatu's house just because they heard that she had committed *zina* is contrary to Islamic law.[289]

The appellate courts may have chosen to quash sentences such as death by stoning in order to prevent the cases from being appealed in a federal court, which might test the constitutionality of the *sharīʿa* penal codes (Peters 2006: 240-1). This analysis explains why in no case the *ḥadd* punishment was replaced by a *taʿzīr* punishment. But the annulment of the stoning sentences is also the result of the influence of informed Muslim defence teams at the appeal trials. In the climate of the heated debate about the introduction of the *sharīʿa* after 1999, Muslim critics of the way in which Islamic criminal law was introduced had a difficult standing in the public discourse.[290] Instead, the defence of people indicted before *sharīʿa* courts, in particular women accused of *zinā* on the strength of pregnancy out of wedlock, became an important arena for critics of the new legislation and its implementation. Muslim human rights activists,

---

[287] This applies at least to the cases of Daso Adamu, Amina Lawal, Maryam Abubakar, Hafsatu Abubakar and Safiyya Hussaini.

[288] "Sharia Court Nullifies Death Penalty On Woman," *Vanguard*, 11/12/2004.

[289] Quoted from the judgment of the Sokoto State Sharīʿa Court of Appeal of 25 March 2002, published in English translation in Ostien (2007: 5:48).

[290] One example is the public debate surrounding the so-called Miss World Riots in Nigeria 2002. See Chapter Five and Weimann (forthcoming).

lawyers and scholars formed defence teams to rectify the procedural and substantial shortcomings of the trials of first instance, thereby creating the precedents which by now have made it unlikely that more accusations which do not respect the procedural safeguards of Islamic criminal law will be allowed in court.[291] The international protests, by contrast, often enough had detrimental effects for the accused, as they contributed to further aggravating the antagonism within the Muslim community.[292]

## *Conclusion*

Initially a political project by some gubernatorial candidates, the "restoration" of Islamic criminal law in northern Nigeria was quickly appropriated by Muslim reformers because it overlapped with the centrality of legal positivism in their doctrine. Their aim was not to Islamise the state but to enforce a legalist interpretation of the *sharīʿa*. With regard to illicit sexual intercourse, the aim clearly was to discourage all forms of extramarital sexuality. The Hausa cultures' tolerance of certain forms of extramarital sexuality was deliberately ignored. The "modernist project" aimed at changing the behaviour of the Muslim population by way of creating deterring precedents in court. Procedural guarantees and individual circumstances seem to have been secondary. But the urgency with which the project was pushed forward may have backfired. The improper application of the law not only provoked international protests—which more often than not strengthen the radicals—but, more importantly, also offended the feelings of both Westernised and traditional Muslims.

At the higher levels of the judiciary, Islamic procedural guarantees regarding evidence have been emphasised, and practically all judgments by lower courts which did not respect these guarantees have been revoked. The long awaited acquittal of Amina Lawal in September 2003 was celebrated by Muslim organisations of all affiliations as a "victory of the *sharīʿa*." The two most important developments in the judicial practice with regard to the offence of illicit sexual intercourse certainly are that the courts accepted the doctrine of the delayed pregnancy and rejected accusations based on suspicion.

The doctrine of the delayed pregnancy provides an effective defence for divorced women charged before a *sharīʿa* court on the basis of a preg-

[291] That this cooperation was not without friction can be seen from the account of the lead defence lawyer of Amina Lawal, Aliyu Musa Yawuri (2007).

[292] In an open letter to its supporters, BAOBAB for Women's Human Rights, in May 2003, discussed the problematic effects of international protests on *sharīʿa* trials in Nigeria. The text of the letter is available at <http://www.counterpunch.org/iman05152003.html>.

nancy out of wedlock. Since among the Hausa only few divorced women in their reproductive age remain unmarried for more than five years, in most cases pregnancy will no longer be accepted as sufficient proof of *zinā*. Although the Hausa cultures know the concept of a "sleeping pregnancy" (*kwantacce*),[293] its use for legitimising children and, thereby, avoiding conviction of *zinā* in court is probably a recent phenomenon in the country. People not familiar with the concepts of Islamic criminal law must get the impression that they are denying the obvious.[294] Islamic legal concepts, especially the legal consequences of a confession, were rarely explained to the defendants. Due to the ignorance of this doctrine, many women confessed, not knowing that in doing so they created the evidence against them. As a consequence, the doctrine of the delayed pregnancy was used mainly on appeal.

The rejection of accusations based on suspicion prevents charges levelled by a party not directly affected by the case from being admitted in court. After an initial period, in which *ḥisba* groups dragged suspects to *sharīʿa* courts without respecting the Islamic rules of evidence, it seems now that the privacy of the family compound has been confirmed. This limits the possibilities of the *sharīʿa* implementation groups to survey life and potential conflicts arising from extramarital intercourse in the private space of the family compounds. Potentially immoral behaviour in this realm has effectively been withdrawn from the jurisdiction of the *sharīʿa* courts, while the consequence of such acts, i.e. pregnancy out of wedlock, is no longer accepted as proof of *zinā*.

These developments exclude actors that are not parties in the dispute from interfering and, thereby, create opportunities for informal mediation between the affected parties. They are an implicit recognition of the traditional conflict resolution mechanisms. The confirmation of these mechanisms, however, constitutes a major impediment for the attempt to change social behaviour through deterrence from court rulings. Thus, certain aspects of judicial practice in Islamic criminal law in northern Nigeria help to recreate local customs rather than to reform society.

Local customs which have been confirmed by judicial practice include those regarding the prevailing patriarchal gender relations. The different attitudes with which *sharīʿa* court judges particularly in the lower instances treated male and female defendants is a clear indication. Traditionally, for Hausa men, control of female sexuality is a constant

---

[293] On the meaning and the social function of *kwantacce*, see Bossaller (1994). For further reading on the issue of prolonged pregnancy refer to Bossaller (2004) and Nils Fischer's review of this book in *Die Welt des Islams*, 48:2 (2008).

[294] This may be one reason why the first appeal of Amina Lawal failed, and why in the trial of Hafsatu Abubakar the judge did not force the former husband to take responsibility for the child.

concern. Hausa folklore shows that men regard female sexuality as dangerous and disruptive, and women are viewed as inherently licentious and potentially troublesome (Wall 1998: 348). The judicial practice in *sharīʿa* courts, especially at the lower levels, has reaffirmed the control of men over women. In view of this, it is not astonishing that adult victims of rape are reluctant to seek redress in courts by themselves.

Due to the lenience with which the lower *sharīʿa* court judges have treated male sex offenders, the effects of the *sharīʿa* penal codes on male misbehaviour have remained minimal. The introduction of the offence of illicit intercourse has to all appearances not affected the high incidence of child rape in northern Nigeria. To the contrary, in Kano metropolis cases of rape of young girls, mainly between three and eleven years of age, have increased significantly in recent years. Here again, the victims are mainly girls hawking the products of their mothers.[295]

Whereas judicial practice confirms male dominance, the introduction of the offence of *zinā* limits the legal options of women. The risk of being charged with *zinā* when confessing publicly to extramarital sexual relations puts them in a disadvantageous position compared to their male counterparts. Unmarried mothers are unable to sue the fathers of illegitimate children in order to make them assume their responsibilities. They remain economically disadvantaged and are a burden for their kin, which further weakens their social position. As disputes involving extramarital sexual relations must be dealt with in secrecy, the courts are no longer the last resort for settling disputes for which the parties involved cannot find a solution.

Overall, however, judicial practice in cases of illicit sexual intercourse has helped to mitigate the effects of the introduction of the Islamic criminal legislation on the traditional Muslim societies in northern Nigeria. The reformers have reacted to these developments. Since late 2004 no new indictments for *zinā* based on pregnancy out of wedlock have been reported. Instead, the reformers seem to have concentrated on issues such as rape and homosexuality,[296] which are topics unanimously rejected by a majority of Nigerians, be they Muslim or not. The *sharīʿa* penal codes continue in place; the impact—positive or negative—which they could have had on Muslim societies in northern Nigeria has been limited to a minimum.

shari'a penal codes impact is minimal.

[295] "NIGERIA: Child rape in Kano on the increase," IRIN, 03/01/2008.

[296] Recent cases involving homosexuals and transvestites are referred to in Ostien (2007: 3:54).

# Chapter Three: Islamic Law and Muslim Governance in Northern Nigeria: crimes against life, limb and property in *sharīʿa* judicial practice[297]

Abstract: A decade ago, twelve northern Nigerian states introduced Islamic criminal legislation. Many governors of these states supported the move only with reluctance. They were caught between popular demands for the introduction of the *sharīʿa* and the exigencies of their office, established by the Nigerian Constitution. Their situation may be compared to that of the colonial period emirs whose legitimacy was closely linked to the implementation of Islamic criminal law, but who were forced to implement British orders containing its application. In this article, I analyse the judicial practice of modern *sharīʿa* courts with regard to crimes against life, limb and property, a major concern for northern Nigerian Muslims in the past and at present. I conclude that because both the emirs and the governors have been unable to find lasting solutions to the problem of reconciling the two legal systems, they have opted for delaying tactics.

The introduction of Islamic criminal law in twelve northern states of the Nigerian federation, starting in 1999, coincides with the country's return to democratic elections and civilian rule. This is a remarkable development, particularly in light of the fact that earlier projects to Islamise criminal law were undertaken mainly by totalitarian regimes in an effort to discipline the population.[298] In northern Nigeria, it seems to be the other way round: after the governor of Zamfara State enacted Islamic criminal legislation, the governors of eleven other states ceded to popular pressure and introduced Islamic criminal legislation. Shortly after the introduction of this legislation, *sharīʿa* courts in northern Nigeria passed sentences of amputation for theft (*sariqa*) and of death by stoning for illicit sexual intercourse (*zinā*). These sentences raised major con-

[297] Originally published in *Islamic Law and Society*, 17:3-4 (2010), and reprinted with permission from Brill Academic Publishers.
[298] Peters (1994: 270). In this article, Peters analyses the situation in countries in which Islamic criminal law was introduced by legislation. At the time, these were Libya (1972-1974), Pakistan (1979), Iran (1982) and Sudan (1983, 1991).

cerns relating to human rights as guaranteed by the Nigerian Constitution and international treaties. National and international media paid special attention to the stoning sentences. Indeed, a majority of the criminal trials before *sharīʿa* courts that were reported in the media were linked to sexual offences. In the day-to-day administration of justice before *sharīʿa* courts in northern Nigeria, however, these trials constitute only a small percentage of offences tried under Islamic criminal law.

Popular pressure on state governors was not merely the result of a wish to sanitise society and restore Muslim values, as the predominance of sex-related trials in the public discourse seems to suggest. Murray Last notes "a pervasive anxiety over insecurity felt on both a physical and a spiritual plane" among northern Nigerian Muslims (Last 2008: 41). This feeling of insecurity is probably at the root of popular support for the introduction of Islamic criminal law. On a spiritual level, it helps to explain the wish to eradicate immoral behaviour in a bid to bring society as a whole in line with the divine injunctions and, thereby, to avert God's punishment. The question of physical security has always been an issue of concern in what is now northern Nigeria. Today, the feeling of insecurity in northern Nigeria, as elsewhere, is nurtured by rapid demographic growth and the influx of strangers from beyond Hausaland or from the countryside into formerly closed communities (Last 2008: 43). Insecurity in Muslim northern Nigeria is largely perceived to be a consequence of external threats. Thus, it is not surprising that Muslims identify restoring security with isolating the Muslim territories from negative external influences by "closing the border" (Last 2008: 46). Creating a territory in which Islamic criminal law is applied may be understood as a surrogate for the political unity of a Muslim northern Nigeria which is unobtainable at present.

Islamic criminal law is widely held by Muslims in northern Nigeria (and elsewhere) to be a panacea for current problems, including the threat to security. Proponents of Islamisation have always pointed to the benefits of Islamic criminal law, including its deterrent effect, its simple and fast procedure and its perceived instrumentality in bringing about a real Islamic society:

> With disapproval, attention is drawn to the slowness of justice under Western law, where trials can drag on for many years. Such statements express a longing that exists with many groups in Muslim societies for a less complicated and orderly society, where good deeds are immediately rewarded and evil deeds punished right away. (Peters 1994: 269)

The deficiencies of the Nigerian judicial system are well known. It suffers from slow procedures and corruption. Linked to the popular demand for Islamisation was certainly the hope that judicial procedures would be simplified and, therefore, less prone to corruption and partiality, and that the performance of the justice system would be greatly enhanced.[299]

In Nigeria, the implementation of Islamic criminal law has taken place within a secular constitutional order of Western inspiration. The question of the constitutionality of Islamic criminal legislation in northern Nigeria has been widely discussed.[300] In this article, I focus especially on the political implications for the state governors, who need to reconcile public demands for the *sharīʿa* with the exigencies of their office. Their situation is comparable to that of the emirs of the colonial period, who also faced the challenge of implementing Islamic criminal law under the supervision of a non-Muslim political authority. Therefore, I describe the historical development of the application of Islamic criminal law in northern Nigeria with particular attention to the colonial era, before turning to the political context surrounding the recent introduction of Islamic criminal legislation. Since crimes against life, limb and property pose the greatest threat to the physical security of the population, I analyse a sample of trials before *sharīʿa* courts for theft, homicide and bodily harm.[301] In the conclusion, I discuss similarities and differences between the situation of the colonial emirs and the current governors and the solutions which they did or did not find to the problem of reconciling Islamic law and a secular political order.

## *Historical development of the application of Islamic criminal law*

At the beginning of the nineteenth century, a *jihād*, led by Usman ɗan Fodio, resulted in the establishment of the Sokoto Caliphate over much of what is nowadays northern Nigeria.[302]

The authority of the caliph and the local emirs was closely identified with the application of Islamic criminal law based on the Mālikī school of *fiqh* or Islamic law (Christelow 2002: 188). Apart from *alƙali* (Arabic *al-qāḍī*) courts, the caliph and the emirs had their own judicial councils, which handled most disputes over land and houses, matters relating to slavery, homicide, theft, public order, administration, and taxation

[299] See, e.g., Yadudu (2001).
[300] See, e.g., Peters (2003) and Human Rights Watch (2004).
[301] Although armed robbery (*ḥirāba*) also qualifies as a crime against limb, life and property, this offence has not been included in the analysis, since I have knowledge of only one case, which was very poorly documented (p. 34).
[302] For the history of the *jihād* and its leaders, see Hiskett (1973). For the history of the Sokoto Caliphate, see Last (1967).

(Christelow 1994: 13). With regard to the judicial authority of the ruler (*siyāsa*) as opposed to that of the *qāḍī*, Mālikī law follows the doctrine of *siyāsa sharʿiyya*, as developed by Ibn Taymiyya (d. 728/1328) and Ibn Qayyim al-Jawziyya (d. 751/1350). According to this doctrine, the ruler's judicial decisions must comply with the *sharīʿa*. However, to increase the efficiency of administration, the law of evidence was widened to allow circumstantial evidence, which is seldom accepted in classical *fiqh* (Johansen 2002). In what are known as "trials of suspicion" (*daʿāwī al-tuham*), Mālikī law allows state authorities to investigate suspects of doubtful reputation who are accused of theft, highway robbery, homicide or illicit sexual intercourse. The authorities may imprison or beat the suspects to obtain confessions (Ibn Farḥūn 1995: 2:129). This means that, in the exercise of their judicial powers, the councils of the caliph and the emirs were to follow the rules of the *sharīʿa*, using their discretionary powers only with regard to matters of evidence. In practice, as shown by Allan Christelow's analysis of early colonial records of the Kano judicial council, the council was prudent in the use of its discretionary powers in cases of theft and violence. Although cases were investigated—which seems to indicate that the council used the possibilities granted by the doctrine of *siyāsa sharʿiyya*—judicial discretion appeared not so much in the making of judgments as in the manipulation of the rules of testimony and oath (Christlow 1994: 11).

Western authors, including Joseph Schacht, have expressed the view that Islamic criminal law, as it relates to *ḥadd*, was hardly applied in practice. Rather, they contend, the ruler exercised his prerogative in administering justice based on *siyāsa* (Umar 2006: 198-9). Based on an analysis of Egyptian court records, Rudolph Peters comes to a different conclusion:

> This view is not correct, at least not for nineteenth century Egypt. Examination of Egyptian court records from this period shows rather that the provisions concerning the *ḥudūd* were often fully applied, but that convictions other than to flogging were rare, due to the difficulties [of fulfilling the Islamic standards of proof]. This does not mean that the culprits went scot-free, because they could always be punished on the strength of *taʿzīr*. (Peters 1994: 252)

After the British conquest in 1320-22/1903-04, the political structures in place in northern Nigeria were maintained under British overlordship. Submission to a non-Muslim political authority challenged the emirs' legitimacy, which was closely linked to application of Islamic law.[303] A

[303] The development of the legal system in Northern Nigeria under colonial rule is described by Ostien and Dekker (2010). Christelow (1994) analyses the judicial practice of

majority of emirs and Muslim judges confirmed or appointed by the British seem to have justified the decision of keeping their positions with the argument that, in the face of British military superiority, it was necessary to preserve the physical and spiritual survival of Muslims.

The British tried to provide the emirs with arguments justifying their acceptance of British interference with Islamic law. Whereas in India the British did not want to impose punishment on the strength of *siyāsa*, on the grounds that it was a form of arbitrary justice (Peters 2009), in Northern Nigeria they invoked this very doctrine. Joseph Schacht, for one, argued that the doctrine of *siyāsa* conferred all judicial powers on the ruler—in the Nigerian context the emirs or the British colonial power. Based on this power, the emirs, acting on behalf of the British authorities, should have been able to suspend the application of certain aspects of Islamic law. However, Schacht also observed that during the colonial period the emirs increasingly renounced the use of *siyāsa* and, "in the absence of any desire on the part of the British administration to interfere with the law applicable to the Muslim populations, pure Islamic law acquired an even higher degree of practical application than before" (Schacht 1964: 87). He explains this preference for strict *sharīʿa* as a response to the interference of British judges with the emirs' verdicts: adherence to the provisions of the *sharīʿa* was easier to defend vis-à-vis the British judges than the exercise of *siyāsa* (Abun-Nasr 1988: 46).

It is questionable whether the emirs accepted the justifications proffered by the British for their interference in the application of the law (Umar 2006: 198-202). As noted, the Mālikī doctrine of *siyāsa*, based on Ibn Taymiyya's and Ibn Qayyim al-Jawziyya's *siyāsa sharʿiyya*, cannot be invoked to justify a political decision—the more so if it was imposed by a non-Muslim overlord—to limit the applicability of Islamic law. Rather, the attitude of most emirs during the colonial period was one of passive resistance, probably inspired by the Islamic doctrine of *taqiyya* (dissimulation), which combines outward cooperation with inward rejection of colonial rule (Umar 2006: 155-6).

One way for the emirs and their legal advisers to justify their compliance with the new political and judicial order seems to have been the reference to the passage of time (*dahr*, *zamān*), the idea that, following the deaths of the Prophet and his Companions, an unstoppable process of moral and religious decline began (Umar 2006: 177). This concept implies that God, and not the temporal British military and political he-

the judicial council of Kano in the early colonial period. The conflict between Islamic and English law was studied extensively by J. N. D. Anderson (e.g. 1957). For a Muslim perspective on the transformation of Islamic law during the colonial period, see Yadudu (1991). The perception of colonialism by the Muslim elite and their responses to it are analysed in Umar (2006).

Colonial administration soon started to interfere with Islamic law.

gemony, will prevail. In line with this idea, the judicial council of Emir ʿAbbās of Kano classed judgments based on legislation introduced by the British in the judicial archives under the category of *ḥukm zamāninā* ("verdict of this era") to mark them as not based on the *sharīʿa* (Christelow 1994: 12).

Whereas initially substantive Islamic law was allowed to govern civil and criminal matters without hindrance (Yadudu 1991: 27-8), the colonial administration soon started interfering with the local judicial system in cases that were "repugnant to natural justice or morality, or inconsistent with any provisions of any Ordinance."[304] In effect, the British retained firm control over, and contained aspects of, Islamic law through the instruments of judicial review and transfer of cases (Umar 2006: 45). The colonial administration could transfer a case from native courts, i.e. the *alkali* courts and the judicial council, to English courts, which applied the Nigerian Criminal Code (Anderson 1957: 87). Certain categories of penal sentences, including capital sentences, had to be approved by the governor-general after review by the resident (Peters 2009). However, where a case was disposed of at first instance by a native court, it was only by the governor's exercise of the prerogative of mercy that discrepancies between the two systems of law could be rectified (Anderson 1957: 88).

The British introduced appellate instances in the Islamic judicial system. In particular, they conferred appellate jurisdiction on the emirs' judicial councils over decisions taken by *sharīʿa* courts. The British rationale was that emirs, as political figures, were more easily susceptible to political pressure and, therefore, through them the colonial authorities could retain control over the application of Islamic law, in particular in politically sensitive cases (Umar 2006: 189-90).[305]

The relation between Islamic and English law changed in 1947, after conflicts arose over homicide law. During his tenure, Governor-General Lugard (1914-19) fought to keep appeals of homicide judgments, which he considered politically sensitive, in the hands of his administration (Umar 2006: 16). Now, the British colonial judiciary apparently wanted to impose the rules of English law with regard to the awarding of punishment in homicide cases. It is plausible that this was partly motivated by the symbolic value of capital justice as a sign of sovereignty (Peters 2009). The West African Court of Appeal overturned the death sentence of Tsofo Gubba, who had been convicted of culpable homicide by the

[304] Native Court Ordinance, 1933, section 10, quoted in Anderson (1957: 88).

[305] The use of these appellate instances as a means to control and contain the application of Islamic law was the reason why as early as 1950 the traditional rulers of northern Nigeria identified the preservation of Muslim identity with the creation of Islamic appellate courts (Abun-Nasr 1988: 40).

emir of Gwandu's judicial council for having killed his wife's lover.[306] The court of appeal reversed the decision on the grounds that provocation is a mitigating circumstance, a concept not recognised under Islamic law. It concluded that native courts could not exercise their jurisdiction in a manner inconsistent with the provisions of the secular Nigerian Criminal Code. For acts which constituted an offence against the Criminal Code, native courts could not impose punishments in excess of the maximum punishment permitted by the Criminal Code. Thus, if a death sentence was passed in accordance with Islamic procedure, but the evidence was deemed insufficient under English law, it would be quashed. This decision undermined the emirs' legitimacy, since they now had to enforce rules that had no base in the *sharīʿa*. Negotiations between the traditional rulers and the colonial administration in this matter seem to have broken down: in an unusual step, the Sultan of Sokoto, Siddiq Abubakar III, voiced his criticism publicly in a speech before the House of Chiefs of the Northern Region (Boyd and Maishanu 1991: 28). Against this background, it is not surprising that after this reform the emirs told British officials that they would prefer the British to take over the jurisdiction of criminal law instead of constantly revising their decisions (Abun-Nasr 1988: 46).

With the independence of Nigeria on 1 October 1960, the legal order in what had now become the Northern Region changed radically.[307] The application of Islamic criminal law was abolished; henceforth, criminal matters were tried under the 1959 Penal Code, an essentially English code that contained a number of special provisions based on Islamic criminal law (Peters 2003: 12). The 1959 Penal Code has been inherited by the successor states of the Northern Region, which to date number nineteen.[308] After the adoption of the 1959 Penal Code, Islamic law continued to be applied in uncodified form only in civil cases.

As a result of the breakup of the regions and the reorganisation of the judicial system by the military government in 1967, the status of Islamic law within the Nigerian legal system increasingly acquired religious and political importance for Muslims in the north, and Islamic law gradually became the basic element of the political identity of Muslims in northern Nigeria (Abun-Nasr 1993b: 201-2). When some northern Nigerian states moved to re-introduce Islamic criminal law after 1999, the emirs, having lost their political and judicial powers, played no active role in

[306] On this case and its implications, see, e.g., Anderson (1957: 88-9); Umar (2006: 53-5) and Peters (2009).

[307] For the debate on the status of Islamic law in Nigeria after independence, see Abun-Nasr (1988, 1993b) and Ostien (2006).

[308] The laws of the original regions or states continued to apply in, and became the laws of, the new states carved out of them (Ostien 2006: 234).

the process. Nevertheless, they have gone along with it, and probably could not have done otherwise, if they were to retain spiritual authority over their constituencies (Blench et al. 2006: 73-4).

## *The re-introduction of Islamic criminal law*

Since Nigeria's return to civilian rule in 1999, political power in the states is held by elected state governments and the state Houses of Assembly. Their offices are established by the 1999 Constitution of the Federal Republic of Nigeria and their legitimacy is linked, on the national level, to the conformity of their policies with the provisions of this constitution. At the same time, notwithstanding frequent accusations of electoral fraud, the gubernatorial elections of 1999, 2003 and—to a lesser extent—2007 have shown that, under the new dispensation, electoral victory on the state level depends, at least to a certain extent, on winning popular support.[309]

As in all civilian political systems, the governors need to reconcile constitutional constraints and the demands of their particular mix of constituents. In Muslim-majority states of northern Nigeria, they—like the colonial period emirs—had to balance their subordination to a secular political system and their constituents' demands for an assertion of the Islamic character of their governance. Nevertheless, there are important differences between the colonial period emirs and the present-day governors. The roles have been reversed: while emirs had to integrate demands imposed on them by the colonial authorities into their traditional system of governance, present-day governors must manage their secular offices in a way that resembles an Islamic model to the greatest (constitutionally) possible extent.

Under the 1999 Constitution, the states do have considerable liberty in shaping the administration of justice in their territory. They are empowered to introduce legislation on criminal matters. The constitution

---

[309] According to the EU Election Observer Mission Nigeria 2003 (EU EOM), in many Nigerian states, the 19 April 2003 gubernatorial elections were "marred by serious irregularities and fraud – in a certain number of States, minimum standards for democratic elections were not met." Widespread election fraud was noted, among the *sharīʿa* states, in Kaduna and, to a lesser extent, in Katsina. In Gombe and Kebbi, the EU EOM was not present on election day. As a result of the elections, a number of unpopular governors lost their posts: in Borno State, Mala Kachalla was succeeded by Ali Modu Sheriff; in Gombe State, Abubakar Habu Hashidu was replaced by Mohammed Danjuma Goje; in Kano State, Ibrahim Shekarau defeated Rabiu Musa Kwankwaso. Shekarau won the election primarily for his stated commitment to the implementation of the *sharīʿa*. In the 2007 gubernatorial elections, governors elected to office in 1999 could not stand for elections again, as the constitution limits the mandate of the governors to a maximum of two four-year terms. The governor of Kano State, Ibrahim Shekarau, was re-elected. On the role of *sharīʿa* in the 2003 elections, see Kogelmann (2006).

explicitly establishes an Islamic judiciary. Section 275 provides that "any State that requires it" shall have a *sharīʿa* court of appeal. This court exercises appellate and supervisory jurisdiction in civil proceedings involving questions of Islamic personal law, in particular as regards marriage, inheritance and maintenance, "in addition to such other jurisdiction as may be conferred upon it by the law of the State" (Section 277 (1)). This highly contentious passage has been called the "delegation clause" by Philip Ostien because it plausibly may be read, and has been read, as delegating to the states the power to give their *sharīʿa* courts of appeal any jurisdiction they please, including Islamic criminal law.[310]

States which introduced Islamic criminal law replaced their area courts, which hitherto applied uncodified Islamic law in civil cases and the Penal Code in criminal cases, by *sharīʿa* courts, placed under the administrative responsibility of the *sharīʿa* court of appeal. These courts apply uncodified Islamic law in civil cases, but handle criminal cases in accordance with the newly introduced *sharīʿa* penal codes. This involved little change of personnel, most area court judges simply becoming *sharīʿa* court judges. In addition, the jurisdiction of the state *sharīʿa* courts of appeal, formerly restricted to matters of Islamic personal law, has been expanded to all civil and criminal matters, so that all appeals from inferior *sharīʿa* courts can be directed to them (Ostien 2006: 252).

However, the situation is not as clear as it may seem from Section 277 (1). In all other sections referring to the states' *sharīʿa* courts of appeal, the 1999 Constitution relentlessly uses the phrase "Islamic personal law." There is no doubt that the drafters of the constitution intended to limit *sharīʿa* court of appeal jurisdiction to questions of Islamic personal law. In particular, appeals from the *sharīʿa* courts of appeal of the states to the federal Court of Appeal are restricted to "civil proceedings before the Sharia Court of Appeal with respect to any question of Islamic personal law which the Sharia Court of Appeal is competent to decide" (Section 244 (1)) (Ostien and Dekker 2010: 581). However, it cannot be the intention that sentences by the state *sharīʿa* courts of appeal in criminal matters be left unappealable. Since the introduction of Islamic criminal law, the High Courts of Borno and Niger States have declared the expansion of state *sharīʿa* court of appeal jurisdiction beyond questions of Islamic personal law as unconstitutional. As a consequence, in these states, appeals from the *sharīʿa* courts in Islamic criminal law go to the high courts (ibid.). In other states, the *sharīʿa* courts of appeal have received and decided appeals involving Islamic criminal law from lower

[310] Ostien (2006: 248-52). He believes that the "delegation clause" is a drafting error which somehow slipped into the draft of the 1979 Constitution and has not been deleted in the 1999 Constitution.

*sharīʿa* courts. To present, the federal courts have not decided an appeal of a sentence in Islamic criminal law brought before them from one of the *sharīʿa* states. Thus, the question of the constitutionality of the Islamic criminal legislation has remained unanswered.

In criminal matters—unlike personal and civil matters—the *sharīʿa* courts cannot apply Islamic law in the traditional manner of a jurists' law due to the constitutional requirement that criminal offences and their punishments be specified in a written law enacted by the federal or state parliament (Section 36 (12), 1999 Constitution). As a consequence, the only practicable way for the governors to introduce Islamic criminal law was by way of state legislation. To be applicable within the legal framework set by the Nigerian Constitution, Islamic criminal law had to be codified.[311] Codification of Islamic law means that the state takes control and decides what God's law is or, at least, how and to what degree society should conform to God's will.[312] In the codification of Islamic law, choices have to be made between various, often conflicting opinions on a given issue as contained in the classical *fiqh* works. To make these choices, the cooperation of experts in Islamic law is essential. They are needed both for their expertise and in order to legitimise state-enacted *sharīʿa* codes. The necessary participation of these experts limits the freedom of the state in codifying Islamic law, while it enables them to exert pressure on the government by threatening to withdraw their support.

After his election in 1999 as governor of Zamfara State, Ahmad Sani, who holds the traditional title of the Yarima of Bakura, quickly started to act on his campaign promise to "restore" the full *sharīʿa*: on 8 October 1999, he assented to a law establishing *sharīʿa* courts for Zamfara State, subordinated to the state *sharīʿa* court of appeal, with the power to determine both civil and criminal proceedings "in Islamic law." The law also created a Council of ʿUlamāʾ for the State, with the power to "codify all the Islamic penal laws and their corresponding punishments, and the rules of criminal procedure and evidence as prescribed by the Qurʾan, Hadith and Sunna of the Prophet (SAW), *Ijmah*, *Qiyas* and other sources of Islamic Law."[313] A draft for a *sharīʿa* penal code was made by the Zamfara State Ministry of Justice in collaboration with the newly established

[311] In the early stages of *sharīʿa* implementation, in some states, such as Katsina and Kano, cases were tried according to uncodified *sharīʿa*. However, the sentence of Safiyya Hussaini, e.g., was quashed, among other reasons, on the ground that the *sharīʿa* penal code was not in place at the time of the offence. Therefore, it appears that a continued application of uncodified *sharīʿa* in criminal matters would have been contested on constitutional grounds. See Chapter One and Sada (2007: 23-4).

[312] On the effects of codification of Islamic law see Peters (2002a) and Layish (2004).

[313] Quoted in Sada (2007: 23).

Council of ʿUlama. It was revised by a group of seven lecturers in law from the Centre for Islamic Legal Studies (CILS) and the Faculty of Law at Ahmadu Bello University in Zaria (Kaduna State). Their final draft, which was prepared under time pressure, was enacted by the state House of Assembly and signed into law by Governor Sani on 21 Shawwāl 1420/27 January 2000. The code came into force on that day (Sada 2007: 24). Although the code is a codification of Islamic criminal law, it leaves room for the application of uncodified Islamic criminal law for offences not specified in the code.[314] This provision clearly contravenes the constitutional principle that criminal offences and their punishments be specified in a written law.

Following the lead of the Zamfara State government, governors in eleven other Muslim-majority northern states were forced to profess, at least verbally, their commitment to implementation of the *sharīʿa*, which in public discourse was often reduced to Islamic criminal law.[315] Few of the governors were enthusiastic about this measure. In Borno, Gombe and Yobe, where Islamic criminal law was introduced under pressure from the public, the law has largely remained a dead letter. The then governor of Katsina State, Umaru Yar'Adua, was accused of impeding the implementation of Islamic criminal law (Chapter One, p. 29). In Jigawa State, the "gradual approach" of the state government was met by accusations of lack of resolve (p. 37). In Kano State, the then governor, Rabiu Musa Kwankwaso, was reluctant to introduce a *sharīʿa* penal code. Muslim scholars tried to mobilise the public and, in February 2000, called on the governor, urging him to take action. The scholars already had prepared a *sharīʿa* penal code bill of their own, which they planned to submit to the state House of Assembly if the governor's response was not encouraging. The state government ceded to the pressure and introduced legislation establishing *sharīʿa* courts that were to apply Islamic criminal law as found in the classical sources. This law remained a dead letter. To put more pressure on the government, the *sharīʿa* penal code bill prepared by the scholars was introduced in the state House of As-

[314] Section 92 (General Offences) of the 2000 Zamfara State Sharīʿa Penal Code: "Any act or omission which is not specifically mentioned in this Sharia Penal Code but is otherwise declared to be an offence under the Qur'an, Sunnah, and *ijtihad* of the Malikî school of Islamic thought, shall be an offence under this code and such act or omission shall be punishable: (a) with imprisonment for a term which may extend to five years, or (b) with caning which may extend to 50 lashes, or (c) with a fine which may extend to ₦5,000.00, or with any two of the above punishments." This or a similar provision is also found in the *sharīʿa* penal codes of Bauchi, Gombe, Jigawa, Kebbi, Sokoto, and Yobe (Ostien 2007: 4:60).

[315] In addition to the introduction of Islamic criminal law, several states have introduced other measures, such as the segregation of men and women in public transport. See Ostien (2007, vol. 3).

sembly as a private bill. This, finally, prompted the governor to take proactive steps: two committees were set up, a Technical Committee headed by Prof. Auwalu Hamisu Yadudu, and a Sharia Implementation Advisory Committee (SIAC) under the chairmanship of Sheikh Isa Waziri. The Yadudu committee recommended that the private bill be withdrawn and a separate *sharīʿa* penal code be prepared and submitted as an executive bill to the House of Assembly. This code was drafted in Hausa by a subcommittee of the SIAC, headed by the lawyer Muzammil S. Hanga, and subsequently translated into English by the Kano State Ministry of Justice. However, Governor Kwankwaso, upon receipt of the draft, saw a need to set up another ten-member committee under the chairmanship of Dr. Ibrahim Na'iya Sada, the CILS director, which was given one week to review the draft, in a bid to have the legislation in place by 1 Ramaḍān 1421/26 November 2000, as promised by Governor Kwankwaso. The review committee observed that certain provisions tended to conflict with the Nigerian Constitution or existing federal laws. These were amended or deleted by the committee, including the provision which allows for the application of uncodified Islamic criminal law for offences not specified in the code. The resulting draft was introduced to the state House of Assembly and adopted, with modifications (Sada 2007: 25-30).

Soon after the introduction of Islamic criminal legislation, the governors embarked on reforming it. The twelve *sharīʿa*-implementing states commissioned and funded the CILS to draft a "harmonised *sharīʿa* penal code" that would be enacted by all twelve states to replace the diverse *sharīʿa* penal codes in place. This provided the chance not only to remove divergences between the different codes, but also to improve their often poor legislative quality (Ostien 2007: 4:20-1). At present, only Zamfara State appears to have adopted the "harmonised *sharīʿa* penal code"—in a photocopied version still bearing the header of the CILS—in November 2005 (Ostien 2007: 4:34).

The result of this legislative process was that Islamic criminal legislation in the different states differs in form and substance. Most codes are based on the Zamfara *sharīʿa* penal code. Kano State has produced its own code, while Niger State has amended the existing Penal Code to include provisions on Islamic criminal law. A similar situation applies to the *sharīʿa* criminal procedure codes: eight states introduced an independent *sharīʿa* criminal procedure code; Katsina and Yobe State still use the 1959 Criminal Procedure Code, while Kano and Borno State added to it a new chapter on trials by *sharīʿa* courts.

## *Provisions of the* sharīʿa *penal codes*

In general the individual *sharīʿa* penal codes provide for offences and punishments to be imposed and applicable to all Muslims and those non-Muslims who voluntarily consent to being tried by a *sharīʿa* court. This implies that non-Muslims who do not consent continue to be tried under the Penal Code (Ostien 2007: 4:45). The *sharīʿa* penal codes maintain most of the provisions of the 1959 Penal Code under the heading of *taʿzīr*, or discretionary punishments, to which are added chapters defining the *ḥadd* offences and the Islamic law of homicide and bodily harm (Peters 2006: 223). The *sharīʿa* penal codes were drafted in great haste, which "explains the poor legislative quality of the codes with lapses such as faulty, sometimes even incomprehensible wording, incorrect cross references, omissions and contradictions."[316] In the following sections, I discuss the provisions of the *sharīʿa* penal codes with regard to theft, homicide and wounding and contrast them with the classical doctrine of Mālikī *fiqh*.

### *Sharīʿa* penal codes on homicide and bodily harm

The provisions of the *sharīʿa* penal codes in northern Nigeria[317] concerning the Islamic law of homicide follow the classical Mālikī model, albeit with modifications.[318] In the classical doctrine, the prosecution, the continuation of the trial and the execution of the sentence are conditional upon the will of the victim or, in cases of homicide, the victim's next of kin (*awliyāʾ al-dam*, sing. *walī al-dam*). In Mālikī law, these are the closest adult male agnates. Under the *sharīʿa* penal codes, it is the state prosecutor who brings the accused to trial, not the victim's next of kin.

In the classical doctrine, the legal effects of homicide or bodily harm depend very much upon the perpetrator's intent. The basic distinction is between intentional (*ʿamd*) and accidental (*khaṭaʾ*) homicide or wounding. Intent is established by examining the weapon or means employed in the offence. If this is such that it would normally produce death or the injury suffered by the victim, the act is assumed to have been intentional. If death or injury were caused by an instrument or an act that normally would not have this effect, classical Mālikī law tries to establish whether or not the intention to kill or wound exists by looking at other factors, such as anger or hatred on the part of the perpetrator. If

[316] Peters (2003: 14). See also Sada (2007: 25).

[317] For the *sharīʿa* penal codes, I rely on Philip Ostien's edition of the harmonised *sharīʿa* penal code and harmonised *sharīʿa* criminal procedure code produced by the CILS, which shows variations between the harmonised versions and the codes in place as well as the old Penal Code (Ostien 2007: 4:36-139 and 4:221-317).

[318] For a summary of the classical doctrine, see Peters (2005: 12-19 and 38-53).

the killing or wounding was intentional, the victim or the next of kin, respectively, can demand retaliation (*qiṣāṣ*). In the classical doctrine, *qiṣāṣ* is performed by the victim or the next of kin in a manner similar to that which the perpetrator used to wound or kill his victim.

In the *sharīʿa* penal codes, the basic principle of retaliation (*qiṣāṣ*) is respected. This means that if the victim's next of kin demand it, intentional homicide is punished with death "in the like manner he [the perpetrator] caused the death of his victim" (Ostien 2007: 4:292). However, whereas the classical doctrine allows retaliation for wilful wounding or homicide to take place only if there is equivalence in value between the attacker and the victim, i.e. if the attacker's *diya* (see below) is not higher than the victim's (except in the case of a woman killed by a man), the codes are silent about this requirement (Peters 2003: 172).

Many *sharīʿa* penal codes include in the definition of intentional homicide deaths resulting from causes "not intrinsically likely or probable to cause death," with some codes specifying that this refers to the object used, e.g. a light stick or a whip. The Kaduna code states that causing death with one of the aforementioned objects "in a state of anger" constitutes intentional homicide (Ostien 2007: 4:84-5). This definition of intentional homicide is close to the classical doctrine. All instances in which the Penal Code accepts the plea of provocation in cases of homicide and hurt have been omitted in the *sharīʿa* penal codes (ibid.: 4:11-2).

If the victim or the next of kin remit retaliation, they are entitled to receive financial compensation (*diya*) which accrues to the victim's estate, or they can pardon the perpetrator. Also according to the *sharīʿa* penal codes, in most cases of wilful homicide and grievous hurt, the plaintiff has the option of remitting the *qiṣāṣ* punishment and accepting monetary compensation (*diya*).[319]

According to Rudolph Peters, the classical doctrine treats *diya* as a remedy for a civil tort (Peters 2005: 7). Payment of *diya* does not imply fault, as evidenced by the fact that as a rule it is not paid by the perpetrator but by his solidarity group (*ʿāqila*). A liability for paying *diya* is also created in cases in which killing or wounding is accidental (*khaṭaʾ*). Negligence on the part of the defendant is not required. The *sharīʿa* penal codes define unintentional, i.e. accidental, homicide as causing another person's death by mistake or accident. Most codes state that it is "punished" with the payment of *diya* (Ostien 2007: 4:85). The description of *diya* as punishment is contrary not only to the classical doctrine but also to the provision of the *sharīʿa* penal codes that there is no criminal re-

[319] See Ostien (2007: 4:85) for homicide and (2007: 4:90) for hurt.

sponsibility unless for acts committed intentionally or negligently (Peters 2003: 27-8).

In classical Mālikī law, the full amount of *diya* is defined as 100 camels, 1,000 dinars or 12,000 dirhams. This full amount of *diya* is payable in the case of homicide of a free Muslim man. The bloodprice for women, non-Muslims and slaves is calculated as a fraction of the full *diya*. In cases of wounding, the financial compensation for the loss of members or faculties or for certain wounds is also calculated as a fraction of the full *diya*. Most of the *sharīʿa* penal codes, while specifying the fractions of *diya* to be paid for particular wounds or damages (Ostien 2007: 4:137-9), fail to define the equivalent of the *diya* in modern currency and simply cite the classical definition (ibid.: 4:54; Peters 2003: 27-8). Only Niger State, in its 2000 amendment to the Penal Code, defines the full amount of *diya* as 4 million Naira (35,000 US$) (Ostien 2007: 4:141; Peters 2003: 27). As in the classical doctrine, *diya* is paid to the victim or the *awliyāʾ al-dam*, respectively, by the *ʿāqila*, which most codes define as the agnatic relatives of the killer.[320] The *sharīʿa* criminal procedure codes of Kano and Bauchi State go a step further and stipulate that *diya* is to be paid by "close relations of the convict." In cases in which these relatives are not available or are not financially capable of making such payment, the convict is ordered to pay the full amount. If neither the convict nor his relatives are capable of paying, the state government assumes responsibility for effecting the payment of *diya* (Ostien 2007: 4: 323).

All *sharīʿa* penal codes except that of Bauchi State distinguish between "hurt" and "grievous hurt" (Ostien 2007: 4:89-90).[321] Instances of grievous hurt are specified in a list that enumerates permanent partial disablements, such as emasculation, permanent deprivation of a sense or the power of speech, deprivation of any member or joint or disfiguration of the head or face (Ostien 2007: 4:89). In cases of grievous hurt, the victim can demand retaliation "in the like manner the offender inflicted such injury on the victim" (ibid.: 4:293). Other cases of hurt are punished with a maximum of six months' imprisonment or twenty lashes and payment of damages.

In the classical doctrine, in addition to retaliation or financial compensation, the state authorities or the court may inflict punishment on the strength of *taʿzīr* or discretionary punishment. In Mālikī law the *taʿzīr* penalty is fixed: a person who commits wilful homicide but who, for procedural reasons, cannot be sentenced to retaliation, must be sen-

---

[320] There are no specific provisions on who receives the *diya* in the rules on homicide and hurt, but the terms *diya* and *ʿāqila* are defined accordingly (Ostien 2007: 4:53 (*ʿāqila*) and 4:54 (*diya*)).

[321] A similar distinction is found in the 1991 Sudanese Penal Code, S. 138 Grievous Hurt (*jirāḥ*) and S. 142 Hurt (*adhan*). I thank Olaf Köndgen for this information.

tenced to one year's imprisonment and 100 lashes. While most *sharīʿa* penal codes follow classical Mālikī *fiqh* in this respect, the Kano and Katsina codes provide for up to ten years' imprisonment (Ostien 2007: 4:85; Peters 2003: 27).

Under Islamic law, an accusation of homicide or bodily harm is proven either by confession of the accused or concurring testimonies of two male adult Muslim witnesses of good reputation in the presence of a judge. In principle, oaths do not count as evidence in the law of *qiṣāṣ*, but there is one exception: the *qasāma* procedure.[322] It is a means to compensate for insufficient evidence in homicide cases in which the body is found bearing marks of violence. The victim's *awliyāʾ al-dam* must prove that there is strong suspicion (*lawth*) as to the identity of the murderer. Based on this, the court can decide to allow the *qasāma* procedure to take place. In Mālikī law, the next of kin swear fifty oaths in order to substantiate their claim. The *qasāma* procedure establishes liability for the *diya*, and may result in a death sentence for the defendant, if the plaintiff swears that the killing was intentional. The validity of the *qasāma* procedure has been contested by some Muslim jurists, but it has been used in northern Nigeria both in the past and, as we will see, in recent times.

### *Sharīʿa* penal codes on theft

Under classical Islamic law unlawfully seizing property (*ghaṣb*) is essentially a tort with civil remedies: return of the stolen object or damages.[323] In addition, the thief may be sentenced to a discretionary punishment (*taʿzīr*). Under special circumstances, however, he may be sentenced to the *ḥadd* punishment for theft (*sariqa*), which—for first offenders—is amputation of the right hand.[324] The jurists define the *ḥadd* crime of theft narrowly: theft is the surreptitious seizure of (movable) property with a certain minimum value (*niṣāb*) from a place which is locked or under guard (*ḥirz*). Classical Mālikī doctrine defines the *niṣāb* as three silver dirhams or one-quarter of a gold dinar. A further requirement for the fixed punishment to apply is that the thief must not have the goods legally at his disposal or be a co-owner. For example, a shop assistant who takes away goods or money from the shop he attends to, or a person who steals state property, cannot be punished with amputation.

In the *sharīʿa* penal codes, *sariqa* or theft is punishable by amputation of the right hand from the wrist for first offenders. The modern defini-

---

[322] On the origins and the doctrine of the *qasāma* procedure in Islamic law, see Peters (2002b).

[323] For the classical doctrine on theft, see Peters (2005: 55-7).

[324] This *ḥadd* penalty is based on Qurʾān 5:38: "As for the thief, both male and female, cut off their hands. It is the reward of their own deeds, and exemplary punishment from God." See Peters (2005: 56).

tion of *sariqa* respects many of the classical restrictions for the application of the *ḥadd* punishment (Ostien 2007: 4:73). These include that the value of the stolen goods must exceed a minimum value (*niṣāb*). However, the codes fail to define the exact monetary value of the *niṣāb*. The stolen property must have been kept in a safe place or *ḥirz*, defined as any location or place "customarily understood to represent safe keeping or custody or protection" (Ostien 2007: 4:52). Presumed or real co-ownership of, or entitlement to, the stolen goods is accepted as a defence that precludes the imposition of the *ḥadd* punishment (ibid.: 4:74).

Uniquely, the Kano code treats as *sariqa* embezzlement of public funds or of funds of a bank or company by officials and employees and makes it punishable with amputation and "not less than five years' imprisonment." Section 134B reads—in its original English wording:

> Whoever is a public servant or a staff of a private sector including bank or company connives with somebody or some other people or himself and stole public funds or property under his care or somebody under his jurisdiction, he shall be punished with amputation of his right hand wrist and sentence of imprisonment of not less than five years and stolen wealth shall be confiscated. If the money or properties stolen are mixed with another different wealth it will all be confiscated until all monies and other properties belonging to the public are recovered. If the confiscated amount and stolen properties are not up to the amount, the whole wealth shall be confiscated and he would be left with some amount to sustain himself.[325]

This provision in the Kano code has its own history. It was first included in the draft produced by the Hanga subcommittee. The review committee, headed by Ibrahim N. Sada, after discussion, decided to re-designate it as an offence attracting *ta'zīr* punishment. However, the Kano State House of Assembly, in the bill it finally enacted, based on the advice of prominent Kano-based Muslim scholars, restored it to the original draft position (Sada 2007: 30-1).

From the perspective of Islamic law, there is some support from less authoritative Mālikī jurists, who regard amputation as a lawful punishment for these offences, albeit not as a *ḥadd* punishment but by way of *ta'zīr* (Peters 2005: 172). There seems to be an element of populism in the decision to assimilate embezzlement of public funds to the *ḥadd* crime of theft. The possibility to call a corrupt politician a thief may appeal to the

[325] Ostien (2007: 4:74). The other *sharī'a* penal codes, with the exception of Katsina, define similar offences under the heading "Criminal Breach of Trust" (Kaduna under *ta'zīr*) and make them punishable with between five (Kebbi) and fifteen (Zamfara) years' imprisonment, fine and a maximum of sixty lashes (ibid.: 4:79).

population of a country ranked among the most corrupt in the world. However, to the present time, there is no evidence that this section has been applied in practice.

In the classical doctrine, unlike homicide or bodily harm, the prosecution of theft is not a private matter. Once the case has been reported to the government and the victim has demanded the application of the *ḥadd* punishment, he cannot pardon the defendant. The return of the stolen goods by the thief before the judgment, however, prevents amputation. If the stolen object still exists, it must be given back to its rightful owner. If it has been destroyed, according to Mālikī jurists, the victim may demand damages in addition to the penalty if the thief is rich, but otherwise only the penalty (Ibn Farḥūn 1995: 2:193).

The classical rules of evidence with regard to *ḥadd* offences, including *sariqa*, are formalistic (Peters 2005: 12-4). In principle, convictions may be based either on confession of the defendant or the testimony of two male, or one male and two female, adult Muslim witnesses of good reputation who give concurring testimonies in the presence of the *qāḍī* with regard to what they have seen themselves. Only confessions made in court are valid. In a court presided over by a *qāḍī*, statements obtained under coercion and torture are not accepted. With regard to *ḥadd* punishments, such as theft, the assertion of having confessed under torture is tantamount to withdrawal of confession.

If the evidence is insufficient for the *ḥadd* punishments, under classical doctrine, the judge is relatively free to impose a discretionary punishment if he is convinced that the accused is guilty. According to most *sharīʿa* penal codes, with the exception of those in Katsina and Kano, if the requirements of *ḥirz* and *niṣāb* are not met, the court can sentence the accused for committing the offence of "theft not punishable with *ḥadd*." The maximum punishment in those cases is one year in prison and fifty lashes (Ostien 2007: 4:74-5).

## Role of the governors in implementing Islamic criminal law

The governors had only limited influence on the formulation of the new legislation. The codification of Islamic criminal law was mainly the work of a younger generation of university-trained lawyers or scholars of Islamic law. The driving force in the process is said to have been "mainly young and educated Muslims associated with Muslim activism and supported by Islamic scholars, particularly graduates of Arab universities" (Sanusi 2007: 177). Participation in the "*sharīʿa* project" was seen as an opportunity for social mobility and personal advancement (ibid.: 184). The need to introduce Islamic criminal law by way of state legislation has created an opportunity for some to distinguish themselves and to acquire social recognition. Possibly, economic reward was also a motivation: numerous commissions needed to be staffed and positions filled. The introduction of the *sharīʿa* brought about an institutionalisation of the religious sphere, the effects of which will become apparent only in the long term.

The ideas and measures promoted by the pro-*sharīʿa* lobbies did not necessarily match the intentions of the governors, who must take into consideration the wider interests of their states within the Nigerian federation and internationally. Moreover, the political office holders also had personal interests to consider: implementing harsh sentences in a bid to please their mostly Muslim constituencies would have ruined the governors' hopes of continuing their career on a national level.[326] Thus, they may have felt the need to control the application of the *sharīʿa*, in particular Islamic criminal law, and if necessary contain certain aspects thereof.

At the same time, the governors have reasons to be apprehensive of appeals of cases involving Islamic criminal law reaching the level of the federal courts. In view of several potential conflicts between the Nigerian Constitution and the Islamic criminal legislation, the federal courts are likely to rule that the *sharīʿa* penal codes in place in northern Nigeria are unconstitutional. The annulment of Islamic criminal law by the federal level would severely damage the governors' credentials as Muslim leaders. The governors could not be expected to actively seek clarification of the constitutional issues on the federal level.

The ability of governors to control the application of Islamic criminal law is restricted by the limitations of the powers conferred to them by the Nigerian Constitution. Their lack of judicial powers means that the administration of justice has become the exclusive remit of the state judiciary, which—at least theoretically—is independent of the state government. In addition, the governors have only limited control over law enforcement in their respective states,[327] and do not have the authority to establish their own law enforcement agencies. The only official law enforcement authority, even in states that have introduced Islamic criminal law, is the secular nation-wide Nigeria Police Force (NPF). NPF officers are not stationed in their home areas, which compromises their immediate effectiveness in the community (Last 2008: 55). It may also

[326] Many governors of *sharīʿa* states showed interest in being nominated as candidates for the office of the President of Nigeria in the 2007 elections. One of them, former governor of Katsina State Umaru Yar'Adua was eventually elected. See Ostien (2007: 4:203) and Chapter One.

[327] According to Section 215 (4) of the 1999 Constitution, the state governor has the right to issue directives to the commissioner of police, but the commissioner has the right to refer the matter to the federal government.

affect their commitment to the implementation of Islamic criminal law. In several states, *sharīʿa* enforcement, or *ḥisba*, groups were established, partly with statutory backing of the state government.[328] In other states, such as Kano and Katsina, independent *ḥisba* groups emerged in opposition to what was perceived as a lack of resolve on the part of the state government in implementing *sharīʿa* (Chapter One, p. 39).[329] In response, the Katsina State government issued a directive to the *sharīʿa* courts not to accept any more cases brought before them by independent, i.e. not state-controlled, *ḥisba* groups.[330] In the past, there have been clashes between the NPF and *ḥisba* groups. This notwithstanding, Murray Last (2008: 51) concludes that, due to the limitations of their mandate, the *ḥisba* are acting as concerned citizens, not as a police force. Even in the field of law enforcement, state governors are torn between constitutional restrictions on their powers and pressure exerted by non-state agents.

Nevertheless, the state governments retain a certain influence on the judiciary. Whereas they have limited powers to interfere with the progress of trials in *sharīʿa* courts, they do have means to control and contain the application of Islamic criminal law in other ways. For example, they can decide to assign specific cases to specific courts. Besides the newly established *sharīʿa* courts applying the *sharīʿa* penal codes and the *sharīʿa* criminal procedure codes, magistrate and high courts in the "*sharīʿa* states" continue to apply the old Penal Code and the Criminal Procedure Code. Homicide, wounding and theft are offences under both types of law and, therefore, can be tried by either the magistrate courts or the *sharīʿa* courts. Cases in which all parties are Muslims normally should be brought before *sharīʿa* courts. Ultimately, it is in the discretion of the state attorneys-general to decide which type of court should hear a case. Only the more serious cases, however, reach their offices. Those that do are almost all assigned to the magistrate or the high courts.[331] Transferring cases to non-Muslim courts, it will be recalled, was an important instrument with which the colonial administrators contained the application of Islamic law. Apparently, present-day governors use this method to avoid verdicts that might bring them into conflict with the constitution and the federal government. Some governors have lost this option. In Zamfara State, in October 2002, a separate law was passed

---

[328] See Chapter One for Zamfara (p. 26), for Jigawa (p. 36), for Bauchi (p. 45).

[329] In response, Kano State enacted a law establishing a state-controlled *ḥisba* board. For a comparison of the independent and the state-controlled *ḥisba* groups, see Gwarzo (2003: 305-8).

[330] "Sharia implementation in Katsina, the journey so far," *Weekly Trust*, 26/07-01/08/2003, 8.

[331] Philip Ostien, personal communication, June 2009.

removing the criminal jurisdiction of magistrate courts to try off committed by Muslims. As a result of this law, all cases involving M lims have been transferred from the magistrate courts to the *shar* courts in Zamfara State (Human Rights Watch 2004: 21).

As in the colonial period, if a case has been decided by a *sharīʿa* court, the governors can avoid a potential conflict of laws only by invoking their constitutional prerogative of mercy. Section 212 of the 1999 Constitution allows state governors, among other options, to grant a pardon to the defendant, to substitute a less severe form of punishment for any punishment imposed or to remit the whole or any part of any punishment. According to the *sharīʿa* criminal procedure codes, severe punishments, such as death penalties, amputation for theft or retaliation, cannot be executed without prior confirmation of the state governor. Some *sharīʿa* criminal procedure codes apparently attempt to exempt *ḥadd* and *qiṣāṣ* punishments from the requirement for the governor's approval, but these provisions will surely be held ineffective if ever challenged in higher courts.[332]

## Judicial practice

In general, it appears that the largely oral character of early colonial judicial procedure, identified by Allan Christelow (2006: 301), has been maintained. Confession, witness testimony and oaths seem to be the main means to produce evidence during trial.[333] In this respect, the local tradition lives on.

Legal pluralism accords the governor the possibility to influence the administration of justice by assigning particular cases to particular courts. The same applies to other parties involved. Plaintiffs and defendants have tried to use the possibilities opened by the competition of legal systems to their personal advantage.

Apparently arbitrary decisions have been made as to which courts should handle which cases (Human Rights Watch 2004: 19-21). There are allegations that police and judicial officials were bribed or otherwise pressured to take cases before *sharīʿa* courts instead of magistrate courts. For example, in 2001 Altine Mohammed was initially taken to a magistrate court in Kebbi State. However, at the request of the grand *qāḍī*, who owned the items he was accused of stealing, the case was transferred to the upper *sharīʿa* court in Birnin Kebbi, where Mohammed was sentenced to amputation (ibid.: 20). There also have been reports of de-

---

332 For a discussion of the sections in the *sharīʿa* criminal procedure codes with regard to the consent of the governor, see Ostien (2007: 4:201-3).

333 See, e.g., the lively description of proceedings in a northern Nigerian *sharīʿa* court by Wiedemann (2006).

e police to take them to the magistrate court rather [334]

ceiving compensation has also been a motivation ... be transferred from a magistrate court to a *sharīʿa* ... Jamilu Nasiru and Yawale Muhammadu, accused of hav- ...y removed the eyes of seven-year-old Umar Mamman, were ... a magistrate court in Sokoto, where they were convicted of con- ...racy and causing grievous hurt and sentenced, on 4 June 2007, to five years' imprisonment. Not satisfied with this, Umar Mamman raised the case to a lower *sharīʿa* court in Wamakko asking for *diya*.[335]

Even non-Muslims have opted for a trial before a *sharīʿa* court. In July 2001, two Christians, Emmanuel Oye and Femi Lasisi, insisted that they be tried before a *sharīʿa* court in Sokoto State. They had been charged with "idleness" and "belonging to a group of thieves." Possibly, they reckoned that the punishment awaiting them under Islamic criminal law would be less severe than under the secular Penal Code.

The unsatisfactory quality of many sentences passed by *sharīʿa* courts has frequently been criticised. Two major factors have led to perfunctory verdicts. One is the badly drafted and often incomplete legislation, in particular the absence, in some states, of *sharīʿa* criminal procedure codes. The second factor is insufficient knowledge of Islamic criminal law on the part of the judges. Most *sharīʿa* judges previously exercised their profession as *alkalai* in the former area courts, where they administered uncodified *sharīʿa* in civil matters and applied the Penal Code in criminal matters. Preparation or training for implementing the new codes was lacking.

The following analysis of judicial practice in northern Nigerian *sharīʿa* courts after the introduction of Islamic criminal law is based on two samples of trials, first for homicide and bodily harm and second for theft. This choice reflects the importance of crimes against life, limb and property for the physical security of the population and, therefore, for governance. By contrast, national and international public opinion largely concentrated on trials of sexual offences, in particular illicit sexual intercourse (*zinā*).[336]

## Judicial practice in cases of homicide and bodily harm

Only a small number of trials for intentional homicide and bodily harm have come to my notice, despite the fact that such trials should attract the attention of the local media, since they address the issue of personal

---

334 Philip Ostien, personal communication, June 2009.

335 "Nigeria: Group Seeks Justice for Boy, 7," *This Day*, 16/05/2008.

336 For an analysis of judicial practice in *zinā* cases, see Chapter Two.

safety and physical integrity. With regard to homicide, I am aware of only one trial.[337]

In the pre-colonial era, in most homicide cases, the result was payment of compensation to the victim's family by the killer, who was lashed and imprisoned for one year (Christelow 2002: 193). By contrast, the murder case of Sani Yakubu Rodi of Katsina State ended in a capital punishment. Rodi was convicted of intentional homicide and, upon the request of the victims' *awliyāʾ al-dam*, on 5 November 2001 he was sentenced to death. The death sentence was carried out on 3 January 2002 after the then governor of Katsina State, Umaru Yar'Adua, had confirmed the verdict (Human Rights Watch 2004: 32).

Rodi was accused of a brutal murder. On 8 June 2001, the wife of the Katsina State Director of Security and their two children, aged four years and three months, respectively, were stabbed to death at their residence. Reportedly, Rodi was caught on the premises on the same day, wearing blood-stained clothes and having in his possession a double-edged knife.[338] Rodi is reported to have repeatedly denied the charge.[339] However, neither he nor his family appealed the verdict. Rodi's family accepted the sentence, as they were convinced that he was guilty.[340]

The indictment was based on the circumstances of Rodi's arrest. Considering that these constituted *lawth*, the court allowed the *qasāma* procedure to take place. The husband of the murdered woman and his younger brother, acting as the victims' *awliyāʾ al-dam*, each swore twenty-five times on the Qurʾān.[341] This is in line with Mālikī criminal procedure, which stipulates that in cases of intentional homicide, if there are two or more *awliyāʾ al-dam*, the fifty oaths are shared equally among them (Ibn Farḥūn 1995: 1:274). Initially, the court ruled that Rodi

[337] However, Human Rights Watch (2004: 21) speaks of a number of murder cases involving Muslim defendants which have been brought before *sharīʿa* courts.

[338] "*Sharia* court sentences man to death by knifing," *The Guardian* (Nigeria), 15/11/2001, print edition.

[339] Human Rights Watch (2004: 32) reports that Rodi pleaded guilty in one of the hearings. However, a confession would be sufficient evidence for conviction and, thus, the *qasāma* procedure would have been unnecessary. Possibly, Rodi confessed after the procedure had taken place and it had become clear that the evidence was sufficient for him to be convicted.

[340] "Family will not appeal death sentence against Nigerian man," AFP, 22/11/2001. The family of the defendant is not a party to the case. However, in some trials of illicit sexual intercourse (*zinā*), stoning-to-death sentences were appealed by family members, pleading insanity of the defendant. For an example, see Chapter Two (p. 68).

[341] "*Sharia* court sentences man to death by knifing," *The Guardian* (Nigeria), 15/11/2001, print edition.

was to be executed by stabbing with the same knife with which he murdered his victims.[342]

The mode of execution subsequently was changed to hanging by the state government. According to some reports, this was done with a view to avert riots.[343] Another reason may have been that the execution of the sentence might have been contested on constitutional grounds. Stabbing to death may have qualified as a form of cruel, degrading or inhuman punishment, which is prohibited by the 1999 Constitution (Section 34). From a historic perspective, the change of execution method reproduces the colonial rule, introduced by the British through a legislative enactment stipulating that death penalties under Islamic law must be carried out by hanging (Anderson 1957: 87n3). The leader of the 'Yan Izala movement[344] in Katsina State, Sheikh Habibu Kaura, who witnessed the execution of Rodi, protested against the decision not to allow retaliation.[345]

The state government, on its part, attempted to find justification in Islamic legal doctrine. In a press interview, Aminu Ibrahim, Katsina State Grand Qāḍī and chairman of the state's *sharīʿa* commission, explained that, in the absence of eyewitnesses to the crime and due to Rodi's refusal to confess, the indictment was based on circumstantial evidence: the knife found in his hands, and the blood found on him and the knife. This is why the *qasāma* procedure was invoked to complement the evidence. According to Ibrahim, by passing the sentence in its initial form, the court forgot to take this fact into account.[346] The grand *qāḍī*'s argument for changing the mode of execution, explicitly mentioned in the verdict, appears to be that the *qasāma* procedure may lead to a death sentence, but not to retaliation. There seems to be support for this interpretation in classical Mālikī rules of procedure. In his *Tabṣirat al-ḥukkām*, Ibn Farḥūn (d. 799/1396) states that in cases of intentional homicide, the *qasāma* oaths must be sworn by those who normally would be entitled to *qiṣāṣ*, i.e. the closest male agnates. However, he is vague about the effects of the *qasāma* procedure: the *awliyāʾ al-dam* are entitled to the murderer's life (*yastaḥiqqūna al-dam*); if they wish, they kill him (or have him killed) or they pardon him. He does not use the word *qiṣāṣ*

342 "*Sharia* court sentences man to death by knifing," *The Guardian* (Nigeria), 15/11/2001, print edition.

343 E.g. "Nigeria's first Sharia execution," BBC News, 04/01/2002.

344 *Jamāʿat izālat al-bidʿa wa iqāmat al-sunna* (Society for the removal of innovation and reinstatement of tradition) or 'Yan Izala is a Muslim reform movement which is equally opposed to the *ṣūfī* brotherhoods and Western influence. See Loimeier (1997) and Kane (2003).

345 "Sharia: Katsina executes murder convict," *Vanguard*, 04/01/2002.

346 "Controversy over Sani Rodi's hanging," *New Nigerian Newspaper*, 16/01/2002, 14.

in this context (Ibn Farḥūn 1995: 1:273-4). Thus, even if the state government prevented the retaliation sentence for political motives, it sought justification for this containment of Islamic criminal law in Islamic legal doctrine.

In pre-colonial and colonial times, the judicial councils used the *qasāma* procedure as an instrument to establish liability in murder cases. It was one of the instances in which the judicial council was able to use its discretion, as illustrated by the following examples from Kano emirate. In a time of famine, a man was caught stealing food from a granary. He was followed, beaten and castrated, sustaining injuries so severe that he died after nineteen days. The perpetrators were not found, so the council invoked the *qasāma* procedure against the owner of the granary, even though there was no evidence that he took part in beating the food thief. This was no doubt a popular measure in a time of drought (Christelow 2006: 316-7). By contrast, the council did not invoke the *qasāma* procedure against a member of the traditional aristocracy accused of killing his wife (Christelow 1994: 167). In the case of Sani Rodi, it may be significant that the next of kin who demanded retaliation was a high-ranking state government official in charge of security matters. This leaves room for speculation regarding the extent to which the *qasāma* procedure retains a subjective element and, thereby, exposes the court to political pressure. The court's decision whether or not to invoke the *qasāma* procedure may well have been influenced by the social prestige of the complainant.

The trial of Sani Rodi shares a number of features with the judicial practice of the emirs' judicial councils in the colonial period, i.e. the use of discretion in the application of Islamic rules of evidence based on political expediency and the containment of certain aspects of Islamic criminal law in order to avoid conflict with a supreme non-Islamic political authority.

In three of the seven trials for grievous hurt punishable by retaliation of which I am aware, the conviction of the defendant was based on a confession. In January 2003, Adamu Musa Hussaini Maidoya of Bauchi State was convicted of cutting his wife's right leg with a cutlass in a rage of jealousy, on the strength of his confession. The sentence was upheld by the state's *sharīʿa* court of appeal in August 2006, more than three years after the trial of first instance, on the grounds that Maidoya had not withdrawn his confession.[347] In early 2008, the sentence was yet to be executed, pending the signature of the governor of Bauchi State.[348] In March 2004, Sabo Sarki of Bauchi State was convicted, on the strength of

[347] "Sharia Court of Appeal affirms first amputation in Bauchi," *Daily Trust*, 21/08/2006.
[348] "Six sharia convicts await stoning death in Nigeria," Reuters, 15/02/2008

his confession, of having forcefully removed the eyes of a fourteen-year-old boy in order to sell them to a man who intended to use them in a ritual. Sarki reportedly was arrested together with two accomplices,[349] but for reasons that are unclear these were not convicted. Possibly they did not confess and, therefore, the evidence against them was insufficient. In Zamfara State, Dantanim Tsafe pleaded guilty in court, in February 2000, of knocking out his wife's teeth. By contrast, Ahmadu Tijjani of Katsina State was convicted, in May 2001, of partially blinding the plaintiff in a quarrel based on the testimonies of seven eyewitnesses to the fight.[350] In marked difference to judicial practice in pre-colonial and colonial times, I am not aware of any trial for homicide or bodily harm in which the defendant was sentenced to a *taʿzīr* punishment on the grounds that the available evidence was insufficient for retaliation.

It appears that the courts encourage plaintiffs to forego retaliation and accept *diya*. In the trial of Ado Bako of Kano State, who was convicted, in September 2001, of causing permanent damage to one of the plaintiff's eyes, the question of retaliation does not seem to have played any role, the defendant being sentenced to paying *diya*. If he was unable to pay, he would have to spend six years in prison.[351] Sabo Sarki was sentenced to pay *diya*. However, the plaintiff insisted on retaliation. The court asked Islamic scholars and Sarki's family for assistance to persuade the boy to accept compensation.[352] Other plaintiffs, as in the cases of Ahmed Tijjani[353] and Adamu Maidoya,[354] insisted on retaliation. Nevertheless, the state governors are reluctant to assent to demands of *qiṣāṣ*. I am not aware of any retaliation sentence for grievous injury that has been executed to date in northern Nigeria.

If *diya* is to be paid, it must be calculated in modern local currency. To illustrate the difficulty of finding a modern equivalent of the full amount of *diya*, I compare trials in which the plaintiffs sought justice after having been blinded totally or in only one eye. According to the *sharīʿa* penal codes, depriving a person of his sight warrants the full amount of *diya*. If one organ out of a pair is damaged, the financial compensation is half of the full amount of *diya* (Ostien 2007: 4:138). In May 2001, half the amount of *diya* to be paid by Ahmad Tijjani was calculated to be 1.5 million Naira (13,400 US$).[355] In September 2001, half the

349 "Shariah court convicts man over ritual," *Daily Trust*, 30/03/2004, 5.
350 "In Katsina, it's an eye for an eye," *The Guardian* (Nigeria), 26/05/2001, 1-2.
351 "Kano Govt Compensates Man for Losing Eye," *Leadership*, 11/04/2008.
352 "Boy turns down N6m compensation for eyes," *Daily Trust*, 13/05/2004.
353 "In Katsina, it's an eye for an eye," *The Guardian* (Nigeria), 26/05/2001, 1-2.
354 "The Justice She Wants," *Newswatch*, 18/11/2002, 48-49.
355 "In Katsina, it's an eye for an eye," *The Guardian* (Nigeria), 26/05/2001, 1-2; and "Nigerian court orders 'eye-for-an-eye' ... literally," AFP, 06/06/2001.

amount of *diya* was set at 2,070,000 Naira (18,500 US$) in the case of Ado Bako.[356] In March 2004, in the case of Sabo Sarki, the full amount of *diya* was said to be equivalent to 5.5 million Naira (37,000 US$).[357] In 2007, the Wamakko *sharīʿa* court in Sokoto State, to which Umar Mamman had turned asking for *diya* from Isa Bello, Jamilu Nasiru and Yawale Muhammadu for blinding him, set the full amount of *diya* at 11,160,000 Naira (75,000 US$).[358] This series shows that the full amount of *diya*, which serves as a basis for calculating the lesser amounts, has varied between 3 million and over 11 million Naira, or approx. 26,700 US$ and 75,000 US$. It may be argued that fixing an equivalent of the *diya* in local currency subjects the actual amount of compensation to the perils of inflation. From this perspective, the calculation of *diya* for each individual case on the basis of the classical definition makes sense. But failure to define a modern equivalent of the *diya* creates legal uncertainty, as illustrated by the considerable difference between the two first cases, which were decided within a period of a few months.

The fact that the *sharīʿa* penal codes regard *diya* as a punishment, not as compensation for a civil liability, may have contributed to considerable confusion. In February 2000, a *sharīʿa* court in Zamfara State ordered Dantanim Tsafe to pay 157,933.70 Naira (1,500 US$) for knocking out his wife's front teeth in a quarrel. Tsafe's wife is reported to have pleaded for the "fine" to be set aside, as her husband was unable to pay. The judge reduced the "fine" to 50,000 Naira (470 US$), adding that, if he failed to pay, Tsafe would have to "submit his teeth for forceful removal."[359] The confusion over the nature of *diya* may be at the root of the wife's plea to set aside the compensation to which she was entitled.

In Bauchi and Kano, in accordance with their *sharīʿa* criminal procedure codes, the state governments pay compensation when the defendants, and presumably their *ʿāqila*, are unable to pay the *diya*. In the trial of Sabo Sarki, the court ruled that if the defendant was unable to pay the *diya*, the Bauchi State government must pay compensation to the plaintiff.[360] Since Ado Bako was unable to pay the *diya* after his sentencing in September 2001, the Kano State government paid, in April 2008, i.e. possibly after the end of his six years' prison term, 500,000 Naira (4000 US$) as compensation to the victim.[361]

---

356 "Kano Govt Compensates Man for Losing Eye," *Leadership*, 11/04/2008.

357 "Shariah court convicts man over ritual," *Daily Trust*, 30/03/2004, 5.

358 "Group Seeks Justice for Boy, 7," *This Day*, 16/05/2008.

359 "Zamfara amputation: Raising the stakes of Sharia implementation," *The Guardian* (Nigeria), 29/02/2000, 8. See also "*Sharia*: Farmer fined N158,000 for beating wife," *The Comet*, 15/02/2000, print edition.

360 "Shariah court convicts man over ritual," *Daily Trust*, 30/03/2004, 5.

361 "Kano Govt Compensates Man for Losing Eye," *Leadership*, 11/04/2008.

In one trial for injury not punishable with retaliation in April 2002, Luba Mainasara of Zamfara State was convicted on the strength of her confession of beating her fellow wife with a pestle and was sentenced to 20 lashes and a fine of 3,000 Naira (22 US$). In addition, she had to pay 50,000 Naira (370 US$) as compensation to her fellow wife.[362]

## Judicial practice in theft cases

The trials for theft reported in the media or by non-governmental organisations (NGOs) are only a part of the total number.[363] Already in September 2004, Human Rights Watch reported:

> According to the information available to Human Rights Watch, there have been more than sixty amputation cases since 2000. However, as with other types of sentences passed by Shariʿa courts, accurate statistics are unavailable, and cases are often unreported, so the real figure might be higher. It has also been difficult to confirm the details and progress of each case. There is no central record of cases and no concerted attempt to record and maintain an overview of cases, either within state governments' ministries of justice or even among nongovernmental organizations. (Human Rights Watch 2004: 36)

The present study is based on a sample of fifty-one trials for theft initiated before *sharīʿa* courts in northern Nigeria between February 2000 and December 2003.[364] This set of trials involves 64 defendants, at least 52 of whom were sentenced to amputation of the right hand. The cases recorded, however, are not evenly distributed over the aforementioned period as a considerable part of the data originates from surveys carried out in specific areas over limited periods of time. In December 2003, Human Rights Watch (2004: 40) interviewed twenty-six prisoners in Zamfara, Kano and Kebbi States who had been sentenced to amputation between 2001 and 2003 but whose sentences had not yet been carried out. Twelve of these trials were reported exclusively by Human Rights Watch, whereas seven were also reported by the media. Another report mentioning individual cases was published by the Nigerian non-

---

362 "Sharia Court Orders Housewife to Pay Mate N50,000," *Daily Trust*, 03/04/2002, print edition.

363 For occasional press reporting on numbers of cases in individual states, see Chapter One.

364 The exact number of trials remains unclear since, as in the case of the "Zaria 6," media sources sometimes mention several people sentenced to amputation without specifying the circumstances in which they were tried. The appendix lists 44 cases of theft. The number of 51 is achieved by treating the "Zaria 6" as six and the trials of Haruna Musa, Aminu Ahmed and Ali Liman as three separate cases.

governmental organisation BAOBAB for Women's Human Rights (2003). It mentions the names of ten defendants supported by the group in eight trials taking place in Sokoto State in 2002. Two of the cases mentioned were also reported in the media. Naturally, these two sources take the perspective of the accused and focus on the alleged violations of their rights by police and the courts, e.g., confessions extracted under police torture. In addition to these sources, I have identified seventeen cases of theft reported only in the media. These are more or less evenly distributed over the period from 2000 to 2003. The relatively small overlap between the NGO reports and the available media reporting may be indicative of the scale of trials for theft. The small number of cases mentioned by more than one source suggests that an even greater number remains unreported.[365] The sentences of amputation of hands for theft in northern Nigeria probably number several hundred (Ostien and Dekker 2010: 592).

The identified trials took place in the states of Sokoto (13), Zamfara (12), Kano (8), Kebbi (6), Kaduna (6), Katsina (4), Jigawa (1), and Bauchi (1). The first decision of the respective trials, or the first known hearing, was reported in 2000 (4), 2001 (14), 2002 (20), and 2003 (13).

In pre-colonial times, the infliction of mutilating punishments seems to have been extremely rare (Umar 2006: 45). A great many, perhaps most, theft cases were probably resolved by returning the lost property or would not have met the minimum value required for amputation (Christelow 2002: 190). Presumably, thieves were also punished on the strength of *taʿzīr*. Now, the *ḥadd* punishment has become the rule. As mentioned, I am aware of fifty-two amputation sentences for theft. Three of these were carried out. In Zamfara State, the right hand of Buba Bello Jangebe, who was sentenced in February 2000, was amputated on 20 March 2000 and that of Lawali "Inchi Tara" Isah, sentenced in December 2000, on 3 May 2001. In Sokoto State, Umaru Aliyu was sentenced in April 2001 and his right hand amputated on 5 July 2001. No execution of an amputation sentence has been reported after that date.

The items stolen include livestock, bicycles, motorbikes and car spare parts, textiles and clothing, food staples, but also cash, electric appliances and electronic equipment. The value of the items ranges from 400 Naira (3 US$) for a shirt to 50,000 Naira (385 US$) for eighteen sheep. The highest value was reported in connection with Aminu Bello: he was convicted, in December 2001, of stealing property worth 65,000 Naira

---

[365] According to media reports, the people awaiting amputation in Bauchi state rose from twelve in June 2003 to twenty-eight in November 2004. For the same period, I have identified only one individual case in the state (Chapter One, p. 48).

(580 US$) from a Christian woman who appeared as the plaintiff in a Sokoto State *sharīʿa* court.[366]

Of the fifty-two people sentenced to amputation, at least twenty-one were convicted on the basis of a confession in court. Some defendants reportedly were advised to do so by the police or the prosecution under the promise that they would receive a more lenient sentence if they did.[367] Seven defendants are said to have admitted the allegations against them in court after being tortured in police custody.[368] In addition to these, at least six others were sentenced to amputation, although they told the judge that they had confessed to police under torture.[369] Some amputation sentences relied, to some extent, on partial admissions by the defendant. For instance, Abubakar Mohammed admitted taking the television but not the video recorder he was accused of stealing (Human Rights Watch 2004: 48). Fifteen-year-old Abubakar Aliyu was reportedly convicted of theft after he admitted having opened the door of the apartment from which he was accused of stealing money.[370] Sirajo Idris, accused of stealing a television set and a suitcase, admitted entering the house which he said was his uncle's (BAOBAB 2003: 19).

Under strict Islamic law, confession under torture is not accepted in the *qāḍī*'s court.[371] Also in practice, judicial systems based on Islamic law have been shown not to be more likely to tolerate torture than secular ones: Islamic law neither encourages nor prevents investigative torture in practice (Reza 2007). An explanation must be sought elsewhere: the frequent disregard for Islamic rules of evidence in northern Nigerian *sharīʿa* courts is probably due to a combination of a lack of knowledge of the Islamic rules of procedure on the part of the judges and activities of pressure groups which attend the court hearings "to see whether Sharia

---

[366] "Another thief sentenced to hand amputation in Nigeria," AFP, 27/12/2001.

[367] Allassan Ibrahim and Hamza Abdullahi (Kano State, June 2003; HRW 2004: 52); Danladi Dahiru (Kano, August 2001; ibid.: 54); Abubakar Abdullahi (Zamfara, February 2002; ibid.: 56); and Haruna Bayero (Kano, April 2002; ibid.: 53).

[368] Yahaya Kakale (Kebbi, December 2001); Aminu Bello; Mohammed Bala and Abubakar Mohammed (Kano, January 2002; ibid.: 55-6); Sirajo Mohammed (Zamfara, April 2003; ibid.: 47-8); Bawa Magaji and Altine Hassan (Sokoto, 2002; BAOBAB 2003: 18-9).

[369] Abubakar Lawali and Lawali Na Umma (Zamfara, May 2003; HRW 2004: 46-7), Altine Mohammed (Kebbi, July 2001; ibid.: 46), Abubakar Yusuf (Zamfara, April 2003; ibid.: 51), Abubakar Hamid (Kebbi, October 2002; ibid.: 45-6), Umaru Guda (Sokoto, 2002; BAOBAB 2003: 19).

[370] "Sharia court orders amputation of 15-year-old boy," *The Guardian* (Nigeria), 15/07/2001, last page.

[371] In the classical theory, the *qāḍī* does not have the right to investigate. He acts as an arbitrator between the litigants and makes his decision on the basis of their testimonies and oaths (Johansen 2002: 177).

law would be enforced."[372] Moreover, in Nigeria the acceptance in court of confessions extracted under torture is not limited to *sharīʿa* courts. The NPF is notorious for routinely torturing suspects to extract confessions. According to Amnesty International and the Nigerian non-governmental organisation Legal Defence and Assistance Project (LEDAP) (2008: 3 and 10), more than half of all prisoners awaiting the execution of a death sentence in Nigeria's prisons were sentenced to death on the basis of a confession. Thus, the figures mentioned above seem to mirror the national situation.

Some amputation sentences for theft were based on witness statements. In 2002, a certain Malam Aliyu of Sokoto State was convicted of theft on the strength of the testimony of two witnesses who alleged that he had stolen the items presented as exhibits and kept them in the place in which they were found (BAOBAB 2003: 20). Also in Sokoto State, in July 2001, thirteen witnesses are said to have testified against Lawali Garba.[373]

As mentioned earlier, in addition to sufficient evidence, the imposition of the *ḥadd* punishment of amputation is conditional on the fulfilment of a number of factors. For one, the value of the stolen item must exceed the minimum stipulated value (*niṣāb*). In the absence of a modern monetary equivalent, the *niṣāb* has been set at different values by different judges. Referring to the case of Umaru Aliyu who, in April 2001, was convicted of stealing one sheep worth 3,000 Naira, an upper *sharīʿa* court judge in Sokoto, Bawa Sahabi Tambuwal, fixed the *niṣāb* at 869 Naira (8 US$). The judge had invited two Islamic scholars to explain to the people sitting in the court room the Naira equivalent of *rubʿ dīnār* (one-quarter of a dinar).[374] Since the value of the sheep was higher than this, the punishment was amputation. In line with this definition, the same judge did not sentence Mohammed Ali to amputation in December 2001 because the value of the kitchen goods he was convicted of stealing was "less than $8."[375] However, in the same state of Sokoto, also in April 2001, a lower *sharīʿa* court judge, Umaru Sifawa, set the *niṣāb* at 15,000 Naira (130 US$) and, consequently, did not sentence Lawali Bello and Sani Mohammed to amputation for stealing two goats valued at 2,600 Naira (23 US$).[376] According to Tambuwal's definition of the *niṣāb*, they might have been sentenced to amputation. In September 2000, Kabiru Salisu was

[372] Yawuri (2007: 133-4). He refers to the 19 August 2002 hearing in which Amina Lawal's stoning sentence was confirmed.

[373] "Sharia Claims Another Victim in Sokoto," *This Day*, 13/07/2001.

[374] Peters (2003: 22) and "Sharia: Man to Lose Hand for Stealing Sheep," *This Day*, 14/04/2001, 3.

[375] "Nigerian 'Christian' in Sharia court," BBC News, 11/12/2001.

[376] "Two Kids Share 40 Lashes for Goat Theft," *This Day*, 25/04/2001.

sentenced in Zamfara State to imprisonment and lashing, instead of amputation. The shirt that he was convicted of stealing was valued at 400 Naira (3 US$).[377] Musa Shuaibu's amputation sentence, which was handed down in August 2002, was quashed, in September 2002, on appeal before the Zamfara State Sharīʿa Court of Appeal on the grounds that the court of first instance failed to establish the monetary value of the alleged stolen goods which, in the view of the appellate court, did not exceed the *niṣāb*.[378] Another condition for the imposition of the *ḥadd* punishment is that the property was stolen from a safe place (*ḥirz*). Abdul Jolly Hassan of Bauchi State was not sentenced to amputation in June 2002 because the goats he stole were not properly caged.[379]

Some defendants were sentenced to amputation despite their claim that the stolen goods were compensation for unpaid debts. Human Rights Watch (2004: 41) reports that two co-defendants said they had stolen two pieces of clothing and seeds from their employer—totalling 5,000 Naira (35 US$)—because he had not paid them for their work.[380] In another case, also reported by Human Rights Watch (2004: 51), Abubakar Yusuf was sentenced to amputation of the right hand in April 2003 in Zamfara State, reportedly after taking a video camera, a photo camera and a generator from a friend who owed him money. To be in conformity with the letter of the codes, the value of the stolen goods minus the owed amount would have to exceed the *niṣāb* (Ostien 2007: 4:74).

Some of the defendants sentenced to amputation said they would not appeal the sentence. Among them were Buba Bello Jangebe, Lawali "Inchi Tara" Isah and Umaru Aliyu, whose hands were subsequently amputated. Their decision may have been influenced by promises of rehabilitation. After his amputation, Buba Bello Jangebe was given the post of a janitor in a secondary school owned by the Zamfara State government.[381] Umaru Aliyu was granted 50,000 Naira by the Sokoto State government.[382]

At least twenty-five of the fifty-two known amputation sentences were appealed. This high percentage is probably not representative but a result of the fact that the NGOs give support to the defendants on whom they report. It must be assumed that the majority of cases remain unreported and unappealed. Some appeals were granted on the grounds that the defendants were minors. In 2001 the amputation sentence of Abubakar Aliyu of Kebbi State, aged between 14 and 17, was converted

---

[377] "Two men flogged publicly in Nigeria for drinking, stealing," AFP, 25/09/2000.
[378] "Safiyat becomes honorary citizen of Rome," *The Guardian* (Nigeria), 06/09/2002, 56.
[379] "Man Escapes Amputation over Theft of 18 Sheep," *This Day*, 24/06/2002.
[380] The state in which this trial took place is not mentioned.
[381] "Zamfara amputes bicycle thief," *Punch*, 05/05/2001, 1-3.
[382] "Amputee Gets N50,000 Govt Gift," *This Day*, 31/07/2001.

into flogging and one year in a children's remand home (Human Rights Watch 2004: 57). In Sokoto State, Lawal Garba and Bashir Alkali, two teenage boys who were accused of theft and sentenced to amputation, were acquitted on appeal in March 2002 (BAOBAB 2003: 17). As mentioned above, Musa Shuaibu was acquitted on appeal on the grounds that the value of the stolen items did not exceed the *niṣāb*. In other cases, the appellate courts ordered retrials. In December 2002, the Kano State Sharīʿa Court of Appeal ordered the case of Mohammed Bala, but not that of his accomplice Abubakar Mohammed, to be retried by the court of first instance. Mohammed Bala was released on bail pending the decision (Human Rights Watch 2004: 55). In April 2004, an upper *sharīʿa* court in Kano State granted the appeal of Haruna Bayero and quashed the amputation sentence on the grounds that the court had not explained the effect of the confession to the defendant. The court ordered a retrial (ibid.: 56). In at least one case, the appeal was not granted. In 2002, the Kebbi State Sharīʿa Court of Appeal did not accept the withdrawal of Yahaya Kakale's confession and upheld the amputation sentence of the trial of first instance. According to Nigeria's National Human Rights Commission, a further appeal has been filed on his behalf to the Federal Court of Appeal in Kaduna. This would be the first case of Islamic criminal law to reach the federal courts (ibid.: 44). However, there are reasons to believe that this is not in the interest of state governors.

Those whose amputation sentences have not been appealed and who have not been released on bail remain remanded in prison pending confirmation of their sentence by the state governor. After the three initial amputations, however, the governors have not assented to any of the numerous amputation sentences that were subsequently pronounced. As a result, the convicts have remained in prison, frequently for several years. The reluctance of the state governments to confirm the judgments is due to their difficult position between the conflicting political imperatives of demonstrating their personal commitment to *sharīʿa* implementation and avoiding the implementation of harsh punishments, forbidden by the Nigerian Constitution. Already in 2003, Governor Ahmad Sani of Zamfara State acknowledged that he felt that the present situation was not "conducive for amputations" but denied that the convicts should be released, as "it will create chaos" (Human Rights Watch 2004: 39). At the same time, however, the governors feel pressure from different quarters. In Bauchi State, for one, against the background of twenty-eight people in the state's prisons in 2004 awaiting the amputation of a hand for theft, legal rights groups urged the state governor to set aside their sentences, while Muslim groups appealed to him to implement them (Chapter One, p. 49).

While a satisfactory solution on the political level is not in sight, pragmatic solutions are sought in individual cases. Haruna Musa, Aminu Ahmed, and Ali Liman, sentenced to amputation in Kano State in January and February 2002, were released on bail by an upper *sharīʿa* court in May and June 2003 (Human Rights Watch 2004: 40). In May 2005, the amputation sentences of six men, the "Zaria 6," who were convicted of theft by an upper *sharīʿa* court in Zaria (Kaduna State) between August and September 2003, were set aside on appeal on the grounds that the two years that they had already spent in prison were sufficient punishment (Chapter One, p. 44). In 2005 twenty-one persons sentenced to amputation of the right hand for theft were set free by the governor of Sokoto State, using his constitutional prerogative of mercy (Ostien and Dekker 2010: 604). This latter case may indicate a change in attitude of a state governor.

## *Conclusion*

After the return to civilian rule in 1999 under what has become known as the Fourth Republic, the governors of the northern states, newly elected in accordance with the 1999 Constitution of the Federal Republic of Nigeria, were exposed to immense popular pressure. They had to prove that they were representatives of the local population and not subject to external control, as had been the case under military rule, when the governors were appointed by the central government. They also had to address the security concerns of the population.

In the prevailing opinion of northern Nigerian Muslims, both issues had, over the years, become linked to the implementation of Islamic criminal law. Governors who did win the elections with the promise of implementing the *sharīʿa* were forced to introduce Islamic criminal law. Governors who pleaded for a "gradual introduction" of the *sharīʿa* feared popular anger and, possibly, defeat in the next elections. At the same time, the governors had to try to maintain their position within the secular political system of the Nigerian state. Implementing harsh sentences in a bid to please their mostly Muslim constituencies would have ruined the governors' hopes of continuing their career on a national level.

This situation is comparable to that of the emirs of the colonial period, who traditionally built their legitimacy on the application, in their judicial councils, of Islamic law, including criminal offences like homicide, wounding and theft, but were forced by the British to contain its application and even implement rules that had no base in the *sharīʿa*. Whereas the emirs sought to maintain an existing system seen as the safeguard of Islam and Muslim culture, the governors face popular expectations that the introduction of Islamic criminal law will bring rapid relief for the rampant feeling of physical and spiritual insecurity in northern Nigeria. They have been under immense pressure not only to promulgate Islamic criminal law by way of state legislation but also to enforce it.

The governors have only limited control of the legislative procedures in their states. In addition, the codification of Islamic criminal law requires the involvement of experts in Islamic law. Thus, there is room for intervention by other groups, such as Islamic scholars, Muslim legal experts, Islamic activists, and even state Houses of Assembly—which in northern Nigeria are not known for their opposition to the state government. Not a few saw in the project a means to enhance their position in society; for some this may have been a correct perception.

The result of populist politics and Muslim activism was a steadily increasing number of sentences that had to be approved by the governors but were politically inopportune and detrimental to the governors' position within the secular federal system. The ways in which the state governments can control, and if necessary contain, the administration of Islamic criminal law in northern Nigeria resemble to a large extent the methods used by the British colonial authorities prior to 1947: they can transfer cases to non-Islamic courts or exercise their prerogative of mercy. At least in the early years of *sharīʿa* implementation, however, using this prerogative would not have been a politically viable option for governors who wished to retain public support. Even today, Islamic criminal law must be maintained for political reasons. This is apparent in the fact that, like colonial officers, such as Lord Lugard, today's governors try to prevent the issue of Islamic criminal law from reaching the federal courts for fear of creating a precedent which, like that of Tsofo Gubba, might lead to an annulment of Islamic criminal legislation altogether.[383] Such an outcome would expose the governors to the accusation of representing an un-Islamic political system.

How can this dilemma be solved? Sentences to death by stoning for illicit sexual intercourse were appealed and ultimately quashed on the basis of procedural flaws in the first instance trials (Chapter Two). In spite of the apparent shortcomings of many of the trials described above, this seems to be more difficult in cases of bodily harm and theft,

[383] In his discussion of the reasons for the *sharīʿa* court of appeal's quashing of Safiyyatu Hussaini's stoning sentence, Peters (2006: 240-1) suggests that the court may have chosen to quash the sentence in order to prevent it from being appealed in a federal court, which might test the constitutionality of the *sharīʿa* penal codes. Ostien and Dekker (2010: 604-6) suggest that it is likely that Islamic criminal law will be challenged in the federal courts by non-Muslims because for certain offences the Penal Code prescribes harsher punishments than the *sharīʿa* penal codes.

possibly because in northern Nigeria the threat to physical security is felt more intensely than that to spiritual security. The only politically viable option for the governors has been to delay approval, and therefore execution, of the unwanted sentences.

The comparison between the emirs and the governors shows that neither group has been able to find a lasting solution to reconcile the application of Islamic criminal law with the exigencies of a non-Muslim political system. The emirs sought refuge in the idea that one day the non-Muslim occupation would end and Islam would prevail. Similarly, the governors apparently have no choice but to delay and wait for the situation to evolve in a way that will open the possibility of finding an accommodation in the future.

# Chapter Four: An Alternative Vision of *Sharīʿa* Application in Northern Nigeria: Ibrahim Salih's *Ḥadd offences in the sharīʿa*[384]

Abstract: After Islamic criminal law was introduced in north ern Nigeria in 1999/2000, sentences of amputation and stoning to death were handed down by *sharīʿa* courts. Within a short period of time, however, spectacular judgments became rare. Given the importance of religion in northern Nigerian politics, this development must have been supported by influential Muslim scholars. This article analyses an alternative vision of *sharīʿa* implementation proposed by influential Tijāniyya *ṣūfī* shaykh Ibrahim Salih. He calls for a thorough Islamisation of northern Nigerian society, relegating the enforcement of Islamic criminal law to the almost utopian state of an ideal Muslim community. In this way he not only seeks to accommodate the application of Islamic law with the realities of the multireligious Nigerian state but also tries to conserve the unity of Muslims in the face of a perceived threat for Nigeria's Muslims of being dominated by non-Muslims in the country.

At the beginning of the twenty-first century of the Christian era, Islamic criminal law was re-introduced into parts of northern Nigeria. This development coincided with the country's return, after long years of military rule, to a civilian system of governance. Soon after the introduction of the new legislation the media began to report amputations of hands and the imposition of sentences of stoning to death. In the Western world, in particular under the impression of the attacks of 11 September 2001 in the United States, the Islamisation of criminal law in northern Nigeria was mainly perceived in the context of heightened fears of an alleged worldwide attempt by radical Islamists to overthrow democratically elected governments and establish totalitarian Islamist regimes. A pivotal African nation was seen at risk of "sliding into lawlessness and terror, like Afghanistan under the Taliban" (Marshall 2002).

[384] Originally published in *Journal for Religion in Africa*, 40:2 (2010), 192-221, and reprinted with permission from Brill Academic Publishers.

In practice, however, the execution of harsh punishments such as amputation or stoning to death, was soon hampered by mounting opposition. The right hands of three convicted thieves were amputated between March 2000 and July 2001. No amputations have been reported after that date. Hundreds of amputation sentences for theft remain in place, but have not been executed because the governors of the states in which these verdicts have been handed down refuse to approve them (Dekker and Ostien 2009: 252-253; Chapter Three). The most prominent stoning sentences were those of two unmarried mothers who were convicted of illicit sexual intercourse on the basis of pregnancy or childbirth out of wedlock (Chapter Two). Safiyya Hussaini of Sokoto State, who was sentenced to death by stoning in October 2001, was discharged and acquitted for lack of evidence on 25 March 2002 (Peters 2006). Around that time Amina Lawal of Katsina State was sentenced to death by stoning for the same offence. Her sentence was confirmed on 19 August 2002 before being quashed in a second appeal on 25 September 2003.[385] The last stoning sentences against unmarried mothers were reported in 2004; they were quashed in a matter of weeks. No stoning sentence has been carried out in Nigeria to date. All death sentences imposed on unmarried mothers on the basis of pregnancy or childbirth out of wedlock have been revoked. Today, while the question of the constitutionality of the *sharīʿa* penal codes remains, Islamic criminal law continues to be administered in *sharīʿa* courts in northern Nigeria but spectacular cases like those mentioned have become rare. This is a remarkable development that needs explanation.

Northern Nigerian Muslim politicians need to ensure that their policies receive the support of religious leaders who legitimise their rule in the eyes of their Muslim constituencies. The governors' unwillingness to implement sentences of amputation and stoning is certainly due to the implications that the execution of such sentences would have for their personal political careers in the Nigerian federal system (Ostien 2007: 4:203; Chapter Three). Notwithstanding, their attitude must still be backed by influential Muslim currents, led by Muslim scholars whose mastery of the Arabic language and Islamic sciences allows them to legitimise certain interpretations of the religion. An important development, such as the observed change in the implementation of Islamic criminal law in northern Nigeria, must have been accompanied or preceded by a scholarly discourse.

While the dogmatic discussions surrounding the confrontations of *ṣūfī* brotherhoods (*ṭarīqa*s) and Muslim reform movements in northern

[385] The proceedings and judgments of the two trials have been published in English translation in Ostien (2007, vol. 5).

Nigeria until the mid-1990s have been amply documented,[386] little has been published to date about scholarly perceptions of the introduction of Islamic criminal law after 1999.[387] This chapter analyses an alternative vision of the application of Islamic criminal law in northern Nigeria proposed by the influential Maiduguri-based Tijāniyya shaykh Ibrahim Salih. The analysis is based on a scholarly work in Arabic and focuses on the theological arguments provided. It is difficult to assess the impact of Ibrahim Salih's views in this matter on the Muslim community in Nigeria with any degree of exactitude. However, it is argued that the widespread acceptance of his or similar ideas have probably been at the root of the observed change in the application of Islamic criminal law.

## *Ibrahim Salih in the northern Nigerian religious context*

Ibrāhīm bin Muḥammad al-Ṣāliḥ al-Ḥusaynī,[388] known as Shaykh Sharif Ibrahim Salih, was born in 1939 in Dikwa (Borno State) into a family of Shuwa Arabs, the only population of Arabic native speakers in Nigeria. His linguistic and geographic origins allow him to present himself as an independent Muslim authority in Nigeria. In the nineteenth century AD, the region now covered by Borno State was the core of the Muslim empire of Bornu, the only northern Nigerian Muslim polity to withstand the expansion of the Sokoto Caliphate despite several attempts by Sokoto to conquer it. Its *de facto* ruler and later Shehu of Bornu Muḥammad al-Amīn al-Kanemi defied Sokoto not only militarily but also on a dogmatic level in a famous correspondence with the leader of the Sokoto *jihād* Usman ɗan Fodio and his companions, in which al-Kanemi questioned the legitimacy of Sokoto's fight against Muslims (Hiskett 1973: 109-110; Brenner 1973: 40-42). This debate reinforced Sokoto's already existing intransigence toward dissenting voices. The view prevailing in Sokoto was that Muslims who refused to accept its authority were not only enemies but non-Muslims (Last 1967: 58 fn). Until today, many Muslim Hausa, the predominant ethno-linguistic group in northern Nigeria that culturally dominated the Sokoto Caliphate, tend to glorify the legacy of the Sokoto *jihād* and claim a position of leadership in

---

[386] E.g., Loimeier (1997); Seesemann (2000); and Kane (2003).

[387] Umar (2001: 140) believes that Muslim scholars of all currents were caught off guard by the project of Western-educated Muslim politicians to implement "full *shari'a.*" Loimeier (2007) discusses the attitudes and reactions of the different Muslim currents in Nigeria to the implementation of Islamic criminal law. O'Brien (2007) describes the relations and cooperation between different Muslim factions in Kano in implementing the *sharī'a.*

[388] For his complete *nisba*, see Hunwick (1995: 407). Biographical and bibliographical information on Ibrahim Salih is provided in Hunwick (1995: 407-415); Loimeier (1997: 271-273); Seesemann (2000: 138-140); and Kane (2003: 167-172).

Nigerian Islam on this basis, while non-Hausa, including non-Hausa Muslims, view it with more reservations.

Ibrahim Salih comes from a family with a long tradition of ṣūfism. His family claims descent from the Prophet. His father and grandfather were affiliated with the Tijāniyya,[389] while earlier generations were linked to the Qādiriyya (Loimeier 1997: 271). Whereas under the Sokoto Caliphate the Qādiriyya was the dominant *ṣūfī* brotherhood, affiliation with the Tijāniyya was viewed as a symbol of resistance. British colonial authorities were quick to view it with suspicion as well (Umar 2006: 35-40). It would be wrong, however, to consider the Tijāniyya, or any other *ṣūfī* brotherhood for that matter, to be an organised movement of political opposition. *Ṣūfī* brotherhoods are not monolithic blocks but rather split in a multitude of different networks that co-exist and compete with each other, each grouped around a number of spiritually, politically, and economically influential religious scholars (Loimeier 1997: 15).

The quest for establishing himself as an independent authority within the Tijāniyya characterises Ibrahim Salih's biography. As did other ambitious shaykhs, he tried to free himself from local sources of authority and build an independent position (Loimeier 1997: 272-273). While he considers himself to be a disciple of Aḥmad Abū al-Fatḥ (d. 1424/2003), a renowned shaykh of the Tijāniyya in Maiduguri (Seesemann 2009: 311), he sought and obtained other *silsila*s, or continuous chains of spiritual descent, that connect him with the order's founder Aḥmad al-Tijāni through Tijāniyya centres in Nigeria (Kano), Egypt (Cairo), Senegal (Kaolack) and Morocco.

In the 1960s and 1970s Ibrahim Salih concentrated on establishing his trade in books and his publishing house in Maiduguri. He developed trading contacts in Egypt, the Sudan, and the Central African Republic (Loimeier 1997: 272-273), which allowed him to be economically independent from donations of his supporters. During the same period Ibrahim Salih founded several *Islāmiyya* schools whose curricula combine Islamic and "Western" subjects, and contributed to the establishment of higher Islamic education institutions in his home state of Borno (Seesemann 2000: 139). Finally, in the 1980s, he began a prolific literary production that earned him a reputation for his scholarship.[390]

Ibrahim Salih should be counted among the most influential living Tijāniyya shaykhs, not only in Nigeria but in the greater part of Africa and beyond. He regularly leads Nigerian delegations to Tijāniyya conven-

---

[389] On the emergence, the doctrines, and the development of the Tijaniyya until the first half of the twentieth century AD, see Abun-Nasr (1965).

[390] Hunwick (1995: 408-415) reproduces a list, partly provided by Ibrahim Salih himself, of ninety-five works. Loimeier (1997: 273) refers to an interview with the Islamic periodical *The Pen* in 1989 in which Ibrahim Salih claimed to have written 132 "books."

tions in Morocco. To the east, his influence reaches far beyond Nigeria into Chad, the Central African Republic, and the Sudan, with particularly strong support in Darfur. By the early 1990s he began to make frequent appearances at international gatherings of Muslims, including the Muslim World League and the Organisation of the Islamic Conference (Seesemann 2009: 312). In Nigeria Ibrahim Salih has not avoided contact with the state. General Ibrahim Babangida, Nigerian military head of state from 1985 to 1993, regarded him as his personal *malam*, that is, a religious teacher and spiritual guide (Loimeier 2007: 49). During this period he regularly performed the Ramadan *tafsīr* in the Abuja National Mosque (Seesemann 2009: 312). His close links to the northern Nigerian political elite enhance his independent position.

In the 1990s Ibrahim Salih was appointed chairman of the *fatwā* committee of the Nigerian Supreme Council for Islamic Affairs (NSCIA). The NSCIA was founded in 1973 by a number of regional Muslim organisations with the aim of achieving a national consensus in matters pertaining to the development of Islam in Nigeria (Loimeier and Reichmuth 1993: 61). Its president is the Sultan of Sokoto, its vice president the Shehu of Bornu, and its secretary-general a Yoruba Muslim. Due to his chairmanship of the NSCIA's *fatwā* committee, Ibrahim Salih is frequently introduced as the Muftī of Nigeria by Muslim news providers such as IslamOnline.net, and by Arabic media. However, in contrast to the situation in some countries in the Middle East, the NSCIA is not backed by the Nigerian state but derives its authority solely from its ability to speak in the name of its distinguished leadership.

Another title used by Ibrahim Salih abroad is that of the chairman of the Assembly of Muslims in Nigeria (AMIN), a Muslim organisation with headquarters in the Nigerian capital Abuja.[391] AMIN's objective is to provide "the much-desired collective leadership for the *Ummah* by our *Ulama*."[392] AMIN's Arabic name is *al-Majlis al-Islāmī al-Nayjīrī*, which—possibly not without intention—is easily confused with the Arabic name of the NSCIA (*al-Majlis al-aʿlā lil-shuʾūn al-Islāmiyya bi-Nayjīriyā*). In addition, Ibrahim Salih is among the few Nigerian Muslim scholars with an extended presence on the Internet. The site *al-Siyāda* [Leadership] is available, albeit not without interruptions, in Arabic at <http://www.alsiyada.org> and English at <http://www.alsiyada.net>. While the Arabic version provides access to the text of a number of Ibrahim Salih's writings, the English version seems to double as official site

[391] For example, he used this title to register on the Internet site of the Muslim World League (<http://www.themwl.org/Bodies/Members/default.aspx?d=1&mid=1099&l=AR>).

[392] AMIN "Brochure of Information," leaflet dated November 2002. Copy in the possession of the author.

of AMIN, including public statements signed by Ibrahim Salih in his capacity as AMIN chairman.[393]

On the dogmatic level Ibrahim Salih views himself as having been assigned the historic task of reconciling the *ṣūfī*s with their opponents (Seesemann 2000: 159). The beginning of the antagonism between mystic brotherhoods and the legalist reform movement dates back to the early years of the Federal Republic of Nigeria. After independence in 1960 the premier of the Northern Region, Ahmadu Bello, pursued a policy of political and religious unity in order to ensure the North's domination in the Nigerian federation. Following his assassination in 1966 and the loss of the north's political unity—in 1967 the three Nigerian regions were replaced by smaller states—the superficial unity in the religious sphere in the north that had been maintained with great difficulty by Bello rapidly disintegrated. The Grand Qāḍī of the Northern Region, Abubakar Gumi, began to attack the *ṣūfī* brotherhoods as carriers of un-Islamic innovations (*bidaʿ*, sing. *bidʿa*) in Islam. On the basis of their ideological affinity to the Saudi Arabian reform movement, Gumi and his followers have been labelled as Wahhābīs by their *ṣūfī* opponents (Seesemann 2000: 145).[394] Beginning in 1977, Gumi made a series of public pronouncements of *takfīr*, thereby declaring as unbelievers those who adhered to *ṣūfī* beliefs, particularly the followers of the Tijāniyya (Brigaglia 2005: 430). In 1978 Gumi's supporters established an organisation of their own that was given the Arabic name *Jamāʿat izālat al-bidʿa wa-iqāmat al-sunna* [Society for the removal of innovation and the instatement of tradition] and became known in Hausa as 'Yan Izala, in an effort to transfer the struggle against the *ṭarīqa*s to the grassroots level. The 'Yan Izala advocate an Islamic positivist legalism. They emphasise direct access to the sources and have led the way in expanding Muslim women's access to Arabic and Islamic learning (Umar 2001: 132).

The ferocious attacks of the 'Yan Izala, based on the religious arguments of Abubakar Gumi, put the *ṣūfī* brotherhoods, especially the Tijāniyya, under great pressure. Numerous members of the *ṭarīqa*s left their religious leaders and joined either the 'Yan Izala or the growing movement of non-affiliated Muslims. The 'Yan Izala were particularly successful with their criticism of certain costly social customs, such as marriage and naming ceremonies, or donations to the shaykhs of the *ṭarīqa*s (Loimeier 1997: 328). Under the pressure of Gumi's attacks the

---

[393] In these statements Ibrahim Salih also describes himself as "chairman, Fatwa Committees of both *Jama'atu Nasril Islam* [JNI] and Supreme Council for Islamic Affairs of Nigeria [NSCIA]."

[394] Gumi's ideological background was provided mainly by the standard sources of contemporary *salafī* thought, with some additional, sparse references to Wahhābī theologians (Brigaglia 2005: 429).

*ṭarīqas* stopped their internal quarrels and formed a common front against Gumi and his supporters. They also responded to the new ways introduced by the 'Yan Izala by modernising their own approaches to, for example, education and the use of mass media.

Several attempts to solve the conflict between the *ṣūfī* brotherhoods and the reform movement by negotiations failed. For a long period, the conflict largely paralysed the activities of the two Muslim umbrella organisations, the NSCIA and *Jamāʿat Naṣr al-Islām* (JNI)[395] (Loimeier 1997: 291-292). During the 1980s, however, the conflict between the *ṣūfī* brotherhoods and the 'Yan Izala slowly receded into the background. Eventually a formal reconciliation between the *ṣūfī* brotherhoods and the reform movement took place in January 1988 (Loimeier 1997: 308). This superficial reunion was brought about not through a settlement of the contentious dogmatic issues, but by the increasing perception of a Muslim-Christian antagonism resulting—among other factors—from the growth of Christian Pentecostal and Charismatic movements and their missionary activities in northern Nigeria and a series of outbursts of ethno-religious violence.[396] The fragmentation of the Muslim camp was seen as the main factor responsible for the perceived preponderance of the non-Muslims in the country. Since 1988, the relationship between the *ṣūfī* brotherhoods and the reform movement has mainly been one of mutual tolerance.

A factor that has contributed to overcoming the antagonism between the *ṣūfī* brotherhoods and the reform movement is that the dividing line between the two camps has been blurred over recent decades. All major Muslim movements have suffered from internal fragmentation—even the 'Yan Izala split into twe competing factions in 1991 (Kane 2003: 217-226)—while at the same time certain factions seem to have converged with those of other movements. In particular, the modernisation processes within the *ṭarīqas* have brought them closer to the reform movement of the 'Yan Izala (Umar 2001). In addition, the number of Western-educated Muslims who are not affiliated with one of the existing religious movements and who reject the religious conflict on account of its political implications has grown considerably. These non-affiliated Muslims are a heterogeneous group. They comprise conservative bureaucrats and judges, but also young and radical Muslim intellectuals, mainly centred in the high schools and universities of northern Nigeria, and finally dissidents from the conflicting parties of the *ṣūfī* brotherhoods

---

[395] Like the NSCIA, JNI is presided over by the Sultan of Sokoto. Ahmadu Bello promoted its foundation as early as 1962 in a bid to gain the support of the Sufi brotherhoods for his policies (Loimeier and Reichmuth 1993: 47).

[396] Kane (2003: 179-206) provides an overview of the issues and crises that characterised Muslim-Christian relations in Nigeria in the 1980s and the early 1990s.

and the ‘Yan Izala. The energetic appearance of this new class of Muslim actors has also led to a revitalisation of JNI and the NSCIA, which are under pressure to act accordingly (Loimeier 1997: 310-312).

Notwithstanding these developments and the reconciliation efforts, the conflict between reformists and traditionalists has continued on a lower level. Disputes about issues apparently unrelated to religion are used as alternative battlegrounds.[397] In the light of the lingering conflict, advocating Muslim unity and seeking a compromise between the competing interpretations of the religion has become a major preoccupation. As the chairman of the NSCIA's *fatwā* committee, Ibrahim Salih occupies an important position that allows him to act as a mediator between rivalling Muslim factions. Ibrahim Salih believes that in order to achieve a reconciliation between traditionalism and mysticism, it is necessary to address exaggerations (*mubālaghāt*) in the teachings of the *ṣūfīs* in an effort to bring them into line with the original teachings of Islam (Seesemann 2000: 158-159). This attitude was reflected in his approach to the conflict between the *ṭarīqas* and Abubakar Gumi's reform movement.

Abubakar Gumi's criticism of the Tijāniyya, as expressed in his major programmatic work *al-ʿAqīda al-ṣaḥīḥa bi-muwāfaqat al-sharīʿa* [The correct creed according to the *sharīʿa*],[398] which was published in Arabic in 1972, concentrated on the central work of Aḥmad al-Tijāni, *Jawāhir al-maʿānī wa-bulūgh al-amānī fī fayḍ Sīdī Aḥmad al-Tijānī* [The Jewels of the meaning and the fulfilment of the wishes in the grace of Sidi Aḥmad al-Tijāni]. Gumi criticised this work for claiming that, besides the revelation meant for all Muslims, the Prophet also transmitted "special instructions" exclusively to "specially chosen persons," including after his death. Traditional *ṣūfī* leaders, like Nasiru Kabara for the Qādiriyya and Muhammad Sani Kafanga for the Tijāniyya, who were unwilling to give up or even revise the positions of the Tijāniyya as they were laid down in *Jawāhir al-maʿānī* (Loimeier 1997: 270), argued that the writings of the *ṣūfīs* were written in a special language that could only be understood by people having special knowledge. The joint counterpropaganda efforts of the *ṣūfī* brotherhoods allowed Dahiru Bauchi to establish himself as the spokesman for the brotherhoods, and in particular the Tijāniyya (Loimeier 1993: 153).

In contrast, in his defence of the Tijāniyya, which was published in 1982 in Egypt under the title *al-Takfīr akhṭar bidʿa tuhaddid al-salām wal-waḥda bayna al-Muslimīn fī Nayjīriyā* [Declaring others unbelievers is the most dangerous innovation threatening peace and unity among Muslims

[397] Cf., for example, Loimeier (2000b).
[398] For a summary of *al-ʿAqida al-sahiha*, see Loimeier (1997: 186-196).

in Nigeria],[399] Ibrahim Salih argued that none of the several existing versions of *Jawāhir al-maʿānī* was authentic. He even affirmed that some of the passages of the book's version currently in circulation were not in conformity with the *sharīʿa* (Loimeier 1997: 275, Seesemann 2000: 148). This approach has brought severe criticism from the traditional Tijāniyya shaykhs.[400] By questioning the authenticity of *Jawāhir al-maʿānī*, Ibrahim Salih certainly attempted to develop a new strategy in the religious discussion with the 'Yan Izala. At the same time, Ibrahim Salih's approach can be understood as the manifestation of a power struggle within the Tijāniyya. In particular, the competition between Dahiru Bauchi and Ibrahim Salih threatened to split the *ṭarīqa*. Ibrahim Salih never accepted Bauchi's claim to leadership, and his own popularity and political backing allowed him to side against Bauchi on several occasions (Loimeier 1993: 156, 1997: 266).

In a bid to save the unity of the *ṭarīqa*, the strategy adopted by the traditionalists within the Tijāniyya in Nigeria was to ignore the existence of *al-Takfīr* (Seesemann 1998: 66-67, 2000: 145-146). This seemed to work, until eventually a reaction to Ibrahim Salih's theses came from abroad. In 1985 a Tijāniyya shaykh of Darfur, Ibrāhīm b. Sīdī Muḥammad b. Muḥammad Salmā (1368/1948-1949 to 1420/1999), published a polemical reply, *al-Summ al-zuʿāf al-muḍamman fī kitāb al-takfīr li-ifsād al-ṭarīqa wal-itlāf* [The deadly poison secreted in the book *al-Takfīr* to corrupt and destroy the brotherhood], in which he accused Ibrahim Salih of being a "Wahhābi" trying to destroy the Tijāniyya.[401] Ibrahim Sidi authored at least seven works in which he attacked Ibrahim Salih and *al-Takfīr*, frequently employing offensive language and mentioning his adversary by name (Seesemann 2009: 325-326).

Ibrahim Salih responded to this attack by writing *al-Mughīr ʿalā ahl al-ahwāʾ wa akādhīb al-munkir ʿalā kitāb al-Takfīr* [The attacker of the heretics and the lies of the one who rejects the book *al-Takfīr*], printed in 1986 in Lebanon (Seesemann 1998). In this 584-page book he defended his earlier line of argument, expanded his ideas, and gave an exhausting presentation of the development and the teachings of the Tijāniyya (Loimeier 1997: 273). But he also defamed Ibrahim Sidi as an "insolent liar" (Seesemann 2000: 150). The exchange of polemics illustrates that despite his modernising efforts, Ibrahim Salih still depends on his legitimacy as

---

[399] This work was a response to the 1978 publication of a simplified and polemical Hausa version of Gumi's *al-ʿAqida al-sahiha* under the title *Musulunci da abin da ke rushe shi* [Islam and the things that lead to its destruction] (Hunwick 1995: 554).

[400] The polemical exchanges between members of the Tijaniyya on the issue of Ibrahim Salih's *al-Takfir* have been analysed in Seesemann (1998).

[401] Seesemann (1998: 49-57) has summarised and analysed the contents of *al-Summ al-zuʿaf*. See also Seesemann (2000: 146).

a Tijāniyya shaykh as an indispensable basis for his immense influence and his claim to religious leadership.

It is beyond doubt that Ibrahim Salih has succeeded in presenting himself as a modern Muslim scholar, whose writings address themes that relate to Islam's position in the contemporary world (Seesemann 2009: 323). His reputation has earned him an increasing following among younger Tijāniyya members with Western education, and acceptance as a religious leader even outside the Tijāniyya. Apart from his rapprochement with the reform movement, his popularity among Muslim intellectuals can be explained by the fact that, like them, he emphasises the importance of the Arabic language and stresses his ties with Borno. For these reasons many Muslims consider him as standing above the parties, in spite of his known affiliation with the Tijāniyya (Loimeier 1997: 276).

## *Attitudes toward Islamic criminal law*

Since the 1967 breakup of the Northern Region, which until then could be regarded as the political base for Islam in the Nigerian federation, Muslim religious and political leaders in northern Nigeria have at every opportunity stressed the importance of acknowledging the *sharīʿa* at all levels of the judiciary and in all spheres of law, and embodying the *sharīʿa* in the constitution of Nigeria (Loimeier 1997: 9). In the face of the loss of political unity, Muslims in northern Nigeria increasingly identified with the question of the status of Islamic law within the federation. The controversy over the creation of a federal *sharīʿa* court of appeal dominated the deliberations of the constituent assemblies of 1977-78 and 1988 (Abun-Nasr 1988, Ostien 2006).

In addition, the restrictions on Islamic criminal law became a major issue in the north. After independence the application of uncodified Islamic law in northern Nigeria was restricted to personal and civil matters tried before native courts, which in 1967 became area courts. In criminal matters, (secular) magistrate and native/area courts applied the 1959 Penal Code for the Northern Region, which after 1967 continued in force as the law of the newly created states. The Penal Code was a compromise negotiated by the British colonial authorities in an effort to reconcile the demands of the Muslim majority and the fears of the non-Muslim minorities in the then Northern Region of being subjugated to Islamic law. The British authorities took care that northern Nigerian Muslim scholars were consulted at every stage of the discussions leading to the adoption of the Penal and Criminal Procedure Codes for the Northern Region (Ostien 2007: 1:5). Although the Penal Code was initially received with an acquiescent or even hopeful attitude by northern Nigerian Muslims, over time the judicial situation in northern Nigeria came to be regarded by Muslim intellectuals and scholars as a consequence of the colonial power's subjugation of Islamic law.[402] Thus the introduction of Islamic criminal law after 1999 was understood by many Muslims as a step in the process of decolonisation (Last 2000).

Nevertheless, when the opportunity to Islamise criminal law came, it seemed to have taken many by surprise. Neither the followers of the *ṣūfī* brotherhoods nor the 'Yan Izala seem to have believed that implementing "full *sharīʿa*" was possible in the multireligious society of the secular Nigerian state. Given the enormous popular support, however, many were quick to identify with the initiative (Umar 2001: 145). Popular support for an immediate implementation of the *sharīʿa* was not only the result of political considerations but was rooted in a profound anxiety in northern Nigeria over the approaching end of time and therefore the felt urgency to obtain God's favour soon (Last 2008).

The most outspoken supporters of restoring the *sharīʿa*, including Islamic criminal law, were not Muslim scholars but prominent members of the northern political and economic establishment (Loimeier 2007: 66). This was the same social group that produced the initial patrons of the 'Yan Izala in the 1970s: their financial support merited them social and religious prestige that in turn enhanced their position in society (Kane 2003: 230). Similar aims can be assumed about the patrons of *sharīʿa* implementation. The patrons were seconded by young and educated Muslims and university graduates in Islamic studies who participated in the "*sharīʿa* project" because they saw it as an opportunity for social mobility and personal advancement (Sanusi 2007: 177). Again, this was the same group that, in the early days of the reform movement, constituted the majority of 'Yan Izala preachers who used their religious studies to achieve a position in society and a livelihood (Kane 2003: 228-229). The "*sharīʿa* project" was thus driven not by the religious establishment but by social groups motivated by the chance to advance their personal position.

The introduction of Islamic criminal law began as a campaign promise by Ahmad Sani when he ran for the office of governor in Zamfara State in the 9 January 1999 elections, the first such elections after fifteen years of military rule. Sani promised to introduce "religious reforms that will make us get Allah's favour."[403] After his election these reforms quickly came to be called "*sharīʿa* implementation" (Ostien 2007: 1:viii). Part of the reforms was the introduction of Islamic criminal law. In October 1999 Zamfara State replaced its area courts with *sharīʿa* courts that had the power to determine both civil and criminal proceedings "in Is-

[402] See, e.g., Yadudu (1991).

[403] *Tell*, 15 November 1999, 19. Quoted in Ostien (2007: 1:vii).

lamic law." The Zamfara State Sharīʿa Penal Code came into force, after revision by the Centre for Islamic Legal Studies (CILS) at Ahmadu Bello University in Zaria, on 27 January 2000 (Sada 2007: 23-24). Other northern Nigerian state governments came under enormous popular pressure to follow Zamfara's example. By late 2001 eleven other states had established *sharīʿa* courts competent to try criminal offences, and most had introduced Islamic criminal legislation (Chapter One).[404]

The authors and reviewers of the draft Zamfara State Sharīʿa Penal Code were aware of the limits to introducing Islamic criminal law in the contemporary Nigerian context. They tried to ensure that at least substantial conformity with the provisions of the Nigerian Constitution of 1999 was achieved (Sada 2007: 24).[405] Compromises thus had to be found. One of the CILS lecturers who participated in the review of the draft, Ibrahim Ahmed Aliyu, later remarked in an interview with a northern Nigerian newspaper[406] that the type of Islamic law implemented was not the real or ideal one; rather, it was the one available at the moment. He explained that the *sharīʿa* was normally not a codified law, but it had to be codified in order for it to be accepted under the prevailing circumstances—in reference to the constitutional requirement that criminal offences and their punishments be specified in a written law enacted by the federal parliament or a state parliament (Section 36 (12), 1999 Nigerian Constitution). He added that some of the substantive rules of the *sharīʿa* had been omitted, such as the *ḥadd* offence of apostasy, which would have contradicted the constitutionally guaranteed freedom of worship and the freedom for anyone, including a Muslim, to change his religion (Section 38 (1)).

The way in which Islamic criminal law was introduced and implemented was not applauded by all Muslim leaders. However, few spoke out against it publicly. Many preferred to conserve an attitude of observant neutrality. The Sultan of Sokoto, Muhammad Maccido, remained conspicuously silent when the *sharīʿa* penal codes were introduced, limiting himself to emphasising the importance of Muslims' enlightenment before the implementation of the *sharīʿa* (Loimeier 2007: 66). He also refrained from attending the ceremony that officially announced the commencement of *sharīʿa* implementation in the Zamfara State capital of Gusau in November 1999 (Last 2000: 142).

---

[404] In Kaduna the *sharīʿa* penal code was promulgated in June 2002, in Borno only in March 2003.

[405] The question of the constitutionality of the *sharīʿa* penal codes is discussed in Peters (2003: 31-36), Human Rights Watch (2004: 96-99), Ostien (2006), and Dekker and Ostien (2009).

[406] "Don exposes defects in Shari'ah code," *Weekend Triumph*, 20/04/2002.

One prominent Muslim critic was Ibrahim al-Zakzaki, leader of the Islamic Movement, a movement inspired by the Iranian revolution that is also known as Muslim Brothers or 'Yan Brotha (O'Brien 2007: 52-53). Due to its revolutionary orientation and massive support received from Iran, al-Zakzaki and his movement have been labelled as *shīʿīs* by their adversaries and the media. With regard to the introduction of Islamic criminal law, al-Zakzaki held that the *sharīʿa* could only be implemented in an appropriate way by a just Islamic state in an Islamic society, otherwise it would become a mere instrument of oppression of the masses (O'Brien 2007: 53-54). Like al-Zakzaki, Dahiru Bauchi argued that inasmuch as it was politically motivated and not introduced in a proper Islamic way, the introduction of the *sharīʿa* was illegal (Loimeier 2007: 65). Sanusi Lamido Sanusi, a member of the Fulani aristocracy of Kano and prominent banker, was one Muslim intellectual who was among the most outspoken critics of the way in which Islamic criminal law was administered.[407] His economic independence allowed him to criticise political and religious leaders without fear of reprisal. In contrast, many leading Muslim scholars feared that open criticism of the implementation of Islamic criminal law would endanger the accommodation between the *ṣūfī* brotherhoods and the reform movement. The situation thus had to be remedied in more subtle ways. It is in this context that Ibrahim Salih's contribution, including the production of *al-Ḥudūd fī al-sharīʿa*, must be understood.

## *Ibrahim Salih's* Ḥadd offences in the sharīʿa

Ibrahim Salih's *al-Ḥudūd fī al-sharīʿa* [*Ḥadd* offences in the *sharīʿa*], whose completion date is given as 10 Muḥarram 1421 / 15 April 2000, is an example of a scholarly work that formulates not only a religious but also a political vision.[408] On the face of it, *al-Ḥudūd fī al-sharīʿa* is a source book on the *ḥadd* offences. On a more profound level, however, the work presents an alternative concept of achieving compliance with the rules of Islamic criminal law, clearly opposed to the way in which Zamfara and other states tried to achieve it after 1999.

Ibrahim Salih begins his book with a discussion of the nature of the *sharīʿa* and a historical overview of its development. According to him, Islam was established in Nigeria via Bornu in the sixth decade of the first

---

[407] A selection of his articles is available at <http://www.gamji.com/sanusi/sanusi.htm>. See also Sanusi (2007). In April 2009 he was appointed governor of Nigeria's Central Bank and embarked on an unprecedented campaign of fighting corruption and mismanagement in the Nigerian banking system.

[408] I have used the text of the book available online at <http://www.alsiyada.org/hudud.htm> (accessed 27 August 2007). This page reproduces the table of contents of the print version, according to which the original is 108 pages long.

century AH (670 to 680 AD), when the Companion of the Prophet ʿUqba bin Nāfiʿ and his followers set foot on it. The peoples of the region recognised the divine origin, the comprehensiveness, and the justice of the *sharīʿa*. Ibrahim Salih compares the pre-Islamic societies of Nigeria, which he says were built on partisanship (*ʿaṣabiyya*) based on class (*jins*) or tribal affiliation, to the Indian caste system and to the pre-Islamic Arab tribes. In the subsequent discussion of the characteristics of the *sharīʿa*, Ibrahim Salih emphasises that God has made the *sharīʿa* easy to observe. Rules that people may find hard to follow because they are linked to habits are to be implemented gradually (*tadarruj fī al-aḥkām*), such as the prohibition of drinking alcohol, fighting *jihād*, or fasting during the month of Ramaḍān. These rules were revealed in Mecca but only enforced in Medina after the *hijra*. Thus the people were already committed to the *sharīʿa* before punishments began to be enforced on those who contravened its prescriptions and violated the social order that it established.

Ibrahim Salih rejects positive law on the grounds that it does not improve the people's situation with regard to social justice or the elimination of crime, be it in Nigeria, Africa, or the countries of the "civilised world." He mentions examples of injustice and unequal treatment including racial discrimination in the United States of America, and religious discrimination in the United Kingdom with regard to "coloured" people and in France on the grounds that the latter country banned the head scarf and deported North-Africans and Africans. Another example of religious discrimination cited by Ibrahim Salih is the pressure exerted on Muslims with regard to "the so-called Islamic terrorism."

Ibrahim Salih then turns to Nigeria. In an implicit reference to the Penal Code, he states that Muslims in Nigeria relinquished the *sharīʿa* entirely on their own accord, only because the colonial power requested it. As a result, in Nigeria and in most Muslim countries, the *sharīʿa* is not applied at present because of ignorance of its rules and ways of application since "very unfortunately, most of those working in the field of *sharīʿa* courts do not comply with the most basic characteristics of a Muslim judge (*qāḍī*)." Because of high levels of corruption, people began to avoid the *sharīʿa* courts and preferred to go to the civil (read magistrate) courts, which were less vulnerable to corruption but too bureaucratic to provide justice.

The solution to this problem lies in spreading Islamic knowledge, raising the level of Islamic consciousness, and educating Muslims about their religion and making them understand that each person can apply the *sharīʿa* to him/herself. Many areas of the *sharīʿa*, such as religious doctrine (*ʿaqīda*), religious practice (*ʿibāda*), relations between humans (*muʿāmalāt*), and the prohibition of homicide and bodily harm (*jināyāt*), can be observed successfully by any individual if he or she is committed, devout and feels God's presence (*al-ḥuḍūr maʿa Allāh*). As for the *ḥadd* offences and other criminal offences, which in a society committed to Islam should occur very rarely, they have to be punished by the public authority (*sulṭa*). However, the sole existence of *sharīʿa* courts is not sufficient: "With regard to having courts for the sole purpose of priding oneself on the highest levels without the rules (*nuṣūṣ*) of the *sharīʿa* being applied in them, this is a matter of little use, and I do not think that Muslims demand it." After this introduction, Ibrahim Salih discusses the *ḥadd* offences and their punishments, quoting extensively from the sources. He points out that *ḥadd* offences infringe on the right of God (*ḥaqq Allāh*) and will be punished in the next world. In addition to this, the punishment in this world serves as a deterrent with the aim of purifying society. In fact, all rights concerning the public sphere (*al-ḥuqūq al-ʿāmma*) are rights of God because God aims at the creation of a society in which every individual observes his duties and enjoys his rights. The author discusses the *ḥadd* offences in the following order: apostasy (*ridda*), illicit sexual intercourse (*zinā*), false accusation of illicit sexual intercourse (*qadhf*), theft (*sariqa*), armed robbery (*ḥirāba*), and consumption of alcohol (*shurb al-khamr*). This is followed by a section on the punishment for wilful or accidental killing.

Ibrahim Salih uses his discussion of the different offences to mention a number of points relevant to the Nigerian situation. For example, when discussing apostasy he insists that it is to be punished by the state, not in self-justice. *Ridda* can only be proven in court through detailed witness statements. Simply declaring that someone is an unbeliever (*takfīr*) cannot be the basis of an apostasy sentence. Another issue that he discusses in this context is the attitude that Muslims should adopt toward a government that fails to implement the *ḥadd* punishments, a description that, according to Ibrahim Salih, applies to most rulers and *imāms* in this age. He affirms that in such a case Muslims have the duty to implement the *ḥadd* punishments, on the condition that they have an *imām*, that is a supreme Islamic leader, or an individual who can represent the entire society. Violence is only permitted if the people have no peaceful means to change the situation, such as elections. Muslims need to choose a government that acts in accordance with the *sharīʿa*, enforces the *ḥadd* punishments, and protects the order of the Muslim community (*jamāʿa*). These two points seem to be a rejection of the aggressive position of Abubakar Gumi and the 'Yan Izala toward the *ṣūfī* brotherhoods on the one hand, and the revolutionary ideology of the Islamic Movement on the other. But in a subsequent passage, Ibrahim Salih equally criticises the Western concept of freedom of confession, which he claims has replaced religion under the system of "positive law": "The Declaration of Human Rights, for which the states of Europe call under the leadership of America, is tantamount to a veiled war against the revealed religions. Islam is the main target of this unjust war."

When detailing the conditions for the application of the *ḥadd* punishment of amputation for theft, Ibrahim Salih insists that once the accusation of theft has been brought before a judge, no intercession (*shafāʿa*) on behalf of the defendant is accepted. He explains that this will ensure that powerful people are treated in the same way as weak ones. However, he points out that the *ḥadd* punishment for theft does not apply to cases of embezzlement of public funds. Nevertheless, embezzlers need to be punished and brought to account, so that theirs will be a lesson for others. Although the punishment of amputation does not apply, this does not mean "that the impostor (*khāʾin*) will be forgiven and will not be demanded to return the public money that he has misappropriated." All necessary disciplinary measures (*ijrāʾāt al-taʾdīb*) have to be taken against him.

Also in the section on theft, Ibrahim Salih discusses the question of whether the *ḥadd* punishments are to be enforced in *dār al-ḥarb* (lit. "territory of war") or areas under non-Muslim rule in which the *sharīʿa* is not applied. His understanding is that the *ḥadd* offences must be prosecuted by a person of Islamic political or spiritual authority (*man lahū al-wilāya*). Due to the absence of such an authority in *dār al-ḥarb*, someone who commits a *ḥadd* offence there is not liable to punishment, even if he returns to *dār al-Islām* or an area under Muslim rule. On the other hand, a person who commits a *ḥadd* offence in *dār al-Islām* and then flees to *dār al-ḥarb* will be prosecuted.

After the discussion of the different offences, Ibrahim Salih turns to the question of the application (*taṭbīq*) of the law. He cautions that the application of the *sharīʿa* is not restricted to criminal law. Every aspect of life should be in compliance with the law; in a society of faith, utterances, deeds, or situations that are at variance with the religion and the *sharīʿa* are rarely committed by believers. Therefore application of the *sharīʿa* means the Islamisation of "everything in life." He cautions that it is not permissible to adhere to some rules and omit others. Only in cases of incapacity or necessity, can some rules be omitted, but the only persons competent to determine this are Muslim jurists (*fuqahāʾ*) who exercise Islamic jurisprudence in matters of law (*fiqh al-aḥkām*) and political issues (*siyāsa sharʿiyya*).[409]

---

[409] For a discussion of the doctrine of *siyasa sharʿiyya* in Mālikī law and its application in northern Nigeria, see Chapter Three.

Ibrahim Salih proposes a reform of the Nigerian judicial system, in particular an extension of the jurisdiction of the *sharīʿa* courts. He claims that the Penal Code, by which, according to him, the colonial power replaced the *sharīʿa* before leaving the country, does not encompass all the obligations that the *sharīʿa* demands from the Muslim. In addition, for some offences it requires punishments different from those of the *sharīʿa*. Therefore the jurisdiction of the *sharīʿa* courts in Nigeria needs to be extended in a way so as to cover all aspects of life as ordained by God. While not explicitly referring to the application of uncodified Islamic criminal law, he demands that the higher *sharīʿa* courts be given the power to judge all matters.[410] Lower *sharīʿa* courts must be independent from the magistrate courts and be supervised by the Grand Qāḍī (*qāḍī al quḍāt*). *Sharīʿa* court judges are to be selected by a committee of Islamic legal scholars (*ʿulamāʾ al-qānūn wal-sharīʿa*) and religious authorities (*ʿulamāʾ al-dīn*). Finally, Ibrahim Salih repeats the longstanding demands of northern Nigerian Muslims: the Nigerian constitution must be amended to allow all instances of *sharīʿa* courts to try all matters of law, and a federal supreme *sharīʿa* court must be created.

Apart from the reform of the judicial system, the application of the *sharīʿa* must be implemented in several stages. The first stage is the application at the family level. In particular, un-Islamic innovations (*bidaʿ*) with regard to marriage, divorce, and expenditures must be brought into line with the *sharīʿa*. Certain social customs come next, such as those pertaining to funerals. The third stage is combating idleness and begging. Fourth, the markets need to be brought into conformity with the rules of the *sharīʿa*. *Ḥisba* officials, chosen from among highly qualified and noble scholars, are to ensure compliance with the norms regarding weights and measures, the items sold, their quality and the prevention of fraud on the part of the merchants. This applies to both Muslim and non-Muslim traders. Fifth, *sharīʿa* norms need to be applied to the slaughter of animals. Sixth, corruption and the misuse of authority must be eradicated from all government agencies. Legislation must be put in place to deter those who act fraudulently regarding these *sharīʿa* rules. Seventh, the *sharīʿa* must be applied in the transport sector. *Ḥisba* boards must ensure that no forbidden goods are transported and that the be-

410 Before the introduction of Islamic criminal legislation, the *sharīʿa* courts of appeal of the states could hear appeals only in cases of Islamic personal law, in particular those regarding marriage, inheritance, and maintenance. Other cases judged first by area (now *sharīʿa*) courts, including criminal cases but also civil matters other than those pertaining to Islamic personal law, were appealed to the state's high court. Thus the application of uncodified Islamic law was restricted not only through the Penal Code but equally by the area courts' subordination in these civil cases to the secular branch of the judiciary. Cf. Ostien (2006).

longings of the people are not destroyed as a result of negligence or lack of compliance with traffic rules. Eighth, the *sharīʿa* must be applied in Muslim cities and quarters by means of Islamic legislation banning prostitution as well as consumption, production, and import of alcohol. Ninth, deterring punishments must be defined for deception, trickery, magic, and other acts that are incompatible with Islam, morals, and the foundations of a civilisation based on religious knowledge (*usus ḥaḍāriyya ʿilmiyya*). Only then can the tenth stage be implemented, which consists of establishing a commission of Islamic scholars and legal experts with a view to reviewing all existing laws in the country that are applicable to Muslims, including the Penal Code, to introduce the necessary modifications, to formulate rules in accordance with the Mālikī school of law and to identify unnecessary or unacceptable rules that are at variance with the *sharīʿa*. This will increase the acceptance of these laws "that were forced upon the Muslims of the north for the first time at independence without asking the scholars for their opinion," a statement that discredits the consultations of northern Nigerian scholars by the British authorities in the preparation of the Penal Code.

In the following sections Ibrahim Salih extensively discusses the office of the judge (*qāḍī*), which he describes as a burden, not a position for which people should apply. He details the competency, possible reasons for wrong judgments (*naqḍ al-qaḍāʾ*), qualities, and manners of the judge. In the conclusion Ibrahim Salih emphasises that enforcement of the *ḥadd* offences is the duty of the public authorities. In all Muslim countries there is an urgent need for the application of the *sharīʿa* "within a wise framework consistent with the wisdom of the Great Legislator in gradual application and carefulness."

There are two types of Muslims in this era. One type is Muslims whose commitment to Islam is formalistic (*shaklī*) and "with whom the enthusiasm for this religion can reach the level of calling for *jihād*." This applies to most of the Islamists, who believe that Islam is nothing but the commitment to the rules of the *sharīʿa* enforced by an authority that has been established in the name of Islam. Their religiosity is based on Islamist political thought (*al-fikr al-Islāmī al-siyāsī*). Its adherents call for the application of the *sharīʿa* without addressing the educational and dogmatic side. These attempts sometimes end in failure because they try to bring the people to the truth in one shove without gradual application of the rules. The second type of Muslims are those who believe that the application of the *sharīʿa* is conditional on receiving education on the religion of Islam. This type of Islam will eradicate all contradictions, customs, and traditions incompatible with the will of God and the society. Education will create a society in which those that violate God's regime and the society's regime will be few in number.

In Ibrahim Salih's view, Nigeria today is at a turning point. With the country's transition from a military regime to a Western-style democracy, "the Muslims in Nigeria felt for the first time that they were losing the battle and that the carpet was pulled away from under their feet by the non-Muslims." Although they form the majority of the population, Muslims have been marginalised in the army and the federal institutions. Moral decay, heretic tendencies, and unrealistic ideas have caused stagnation among the Muslims, who now seek relief through anything, be it true or false, as long as it is presented as Islamic.

However, even if among the increasing number of people active in the propagation of Islam (*daʿwa*) there were some who acted wrongly, the movement has contributed to the fact that many Nigerian Muslims are joining the global Islamic awakening (*al-ṣaḥwa al-Islāmiyya al-ʿālamiyya*). One of the positive results of this awakening was the call for the application of the *sharīʿa*. A negative consequence, however, was that it led to internal conflict and fragmentation of Muslims. This was caused by "uneducated sermons" (*al-waʿẓ ghayr al-muhadhdhab*), whose authors did not respect the ways in which *daʿwa* should be practiced, as mentioned in Qurʾān 16:125: "Call unto the way of thy Lord with wisdom and fair exhortation (*mawʿiẓa ḥasana*), and reason with them in the better way (*aḥsan*)."[411]

The heightened Islamic awareness has given "the brothers politicians" no choice, if they were to maintain the loyalty of their religiously motivated voters, than to comply with the demands "to fill the void in their hearts and to open the hope for them to return the lost glory, [the loss of] which was caused by the West's pressures continuously aiming at giving preponderance to the non-Muslims in the country." Most of the Muslim activists were influenced, in one way or the other, by Islam as understood by the "brothers Islamists" (*al-ikhwa al-Islāmiyyūn*), whose aim traditionally has been the establishment of an Islamic political system and the commitment to Islam in appearance and conduct. In this situation their attention was only directed to the application of the rules of the *sharīʿa*, believing that the Muslims' lost glory could be restored at the necessary pace by immediate adoption of a plan for applying the rules of the *sharīʿa*, at least in states with a Muslim majority population.

Ibrahim Salih points out that the announcement by some states of the application of the *sharīʿa* was natural and commendable. The noise made by the Christian citizens was astonishing, particularly in the light

[411] Ibrahim Salih interprets *aḥsan* as a comparative in the sense of "reason with them in a better way than they reason with you." Cf. Paret (2001: 295). This criticism is probably not only directed to the 'Yan Izala for their polemics against the brotherhoods but also to Ibrahim Salih's adversaries within the Tijaniyya, such as Ibrahim Sidi.

of assurances that the rules of the *sharīʿa* would not be applied to non-Muslims, except in cases related to the prevention of spreading corruption on earth (*manʿ intishār al-fasād fil-arḍ*), which in Ibrahim Salih's view comprises the offences of armed robbery and theft.[412] He adds that Christian-owned print media continued to publicise opinions that were detrimental to relations with Muslims and ridiculed Islam and the *sharīʿa*. For Ibrahim Salih, this triggered the riots in Kaduna and the Igbo-dominated states of south-eastern Nigeria.[413]

At the end of his "study," Ibrahim Salih makes a number of proposals with a view, as he puts it, to facilitating the task of the *ʿulamāʾ* to ensure an adequate and comprehensive application of the *sharīʿa* in all Muslim states of the country. There should be a serious effort to unite all Muslim scholars from the north and the south of Nigeria to set up a single plan for preaching, religious sensitising and orientation to be executed in a fixed period of time. In order to formulate this plan scholars must survey all sectors of the population, in particular young people of all schools of thought and intellectual orientation, intellectuals (*muthaqqafūn*), businessmen, and certain politicians. After these meetings the plan should be extended to cover all Muslims in all parts of Nigeria "until every Muslim feels part of the Muslim community (*jamāʿa*)." Muslims must be trained psychologically for taking responsibility. All remnants of past mutual low opinions and hatred must be eliminated. Priority must be given to economic development in order to combat unemployment and idleness. The aversion toward marriage and having children must be examined because it is an issue that conflicts with the general interest of Muslims. Related to this is the issue of standardising the amount of dowry to be paid (*tanẓīm al-muhūr*). All un-Islamic customs (*al-ʿādāt al-mubtadiʿa*) must be condemned. Non-Muslims should be invited to join Islam, and the people responsible for teaching them must be specified. The policies of past Nigerian governments that did not respect

---

[412] Under the *shariʿa* penal codes in place in northern Nigeria, non-Muslims cannot be tried by *shariʿa* courts unless they consent to it in writing. Ibrahim Salih seems to deliberately overlook this legal provision, which is due to the multireligious character of Nigeria. Whereas the promise to apply the punishments for armed robbery and theft to non-Muslims would certainly appeal to a Muslim audience, it is inconceivable that Ibrahim Salih is unaware of the impracticability of such a position. It may be a subtle way of suggesting that the *shariʿa* penal codes are incomplete.

[413] In several states the announcement or the fear that Islamic criminal law would be implemented triggered violent clashes between Muslims and non-Muslims, which became known as "*shariʿa* riots." With at least 2,000 people killed in clashes in February and May 2000, Kaduna State was particularly hard hit (Human Rights Watch 2003: 4), but violence also erupted in Bauchi, Plateau, and Gombe (Chapter One). Islamic criminal law was not introduced in Plateau State. These clashes provoked anti-Muslim riots in some southern home states of Christian victims, the majority of whom were Igbos.

the rights of the Muslims must be reviewed. Muslims must establish media equal to or surpassing the media owned by non-Muslims. Muslim members of the federal government are to be counselled on areas of interest and priorities from an Islamic perspective without asking them to do things they cannot or should not do. Finally, every state needs to apply the *sharīʿa* in a way that is in agreement with its particular circumstances, the state of the country, and the situation of the Muslims locally and internationally. Only this last point needs the intervention of the public authorities, for example with regard to the enforcement of the *ḥadd* punishments. All the other issues can be implemented instantaneously.

One of the final sentences of the book again stresses the issue of unity: "Our means to achieve these goals is to work for mutual acquaintance of Muslims in the north and Muslims in the south, just like the politicians did in the different parties. They are united through worldly interest, so we should be united through religious interest."

In *al-Ḥudūd fī al-sharīʿa*, Ibrahim Salih provides the religious foundations for Islamic criminal law in the manner of a source book. The publication of the book a few months after Zamfara State began implementing Islamic criminal law indicates that it is a direct response to the introduction of Islamic criminal legislation in northern Nigeria. The emphasis put on the office of the judge can be seen as a reaction to inappropriate sentences in criminal matters issued by *sharīʿa* courts immediately after the introduction of *sharīʿa* penal codes. In addition to the discussion of the substance of the law, Ibrahim Salih presents an alternative approach for the application of the *sharīʿa*. In his understanding, the application (*taṭbīq*) of the *sharīʿa* refers first and foremost to the compliance of the individual believer with the norms set out by the Islamic religion on the basis of personal conviction, not so much to the enforcement of a set of legal rules by the courts and the public authorities. Compliance with the law is achieved through religious education; the enforcement of Islamic criminal law is the last step of a comprehensive campaign for an Islamisation of the society. Consequently, he condemns the overhasty enforcement of the *ḥadd* offences but welcomes the states' announcement of the application of the *sharīʿa*. In this regard, Ibrahim Salih's position resembles that of the Egyptian Muslim Brothers in the 1940s,[414] who believed that Islamic law can be applied to the full extent only in a "truly Muslim society." The Muslim Brothers strongly criticised the implementation of the punishment of amputation of the hand in Saudi Arabia "while the rulers swim in the gold stolen from the state treasury and the wealth of the people" (Mitchell 1969: 240-241). In Nige-

[414] I thank Rudolph Peters for this remark.

ria, the faction that, with regard to the implementation of the *sharīʿa*, is closest to the intellectual heritage of the Muslim Brothers is Ibrahim al-Zakzaki's Islamic Movement, as expressed in his open criticism of the implementation of Islamic criminal law.

Despite this intellectual proximity to the Muslim Brothers with regard to the enforcement of Islamic criminal law, Ibrahim Salih explicitly blames "Islamists" and "Islamist political thought" for being behind the demands for the immediate implementation of Islamic criminal law. This apparent contradiction must be seen as an attempt by the author to safeguard the fragile unity between the main Muslim rival factions in Nigeria, the *ṣūfīs* and the reformists. As a representative of a *ṣūfī* order, putting the responsibility for the inadequate implementation of Islamic criminal law on radical members of the reform movement would have inevitably revived the old antagonism. In general, Ibrahim Salih is careful to not accuse Muslim scholars or activists of acting with evil or selfish intentions. He rejects as premature and precipitate the approach of forcing *sharīʿa*-compliant behaviour on the population through implementation of the *ḥadd* punishments. But instead of accusing the protagonists of the *sharīʿa* project of acting in a way that is incompatible with Islam, he prefers to put the blame for the inadequate enforcement of the *ḥadd* punishments on Muslim politicians, who used the topic of the *sharīʿa* for their personal advancement.

Another concession to the reform movement may be Ibrahim Salih's affirmation of the idea of a global conspiracy of the West against Islam and the Muslims. It serves to emphasise the need for unity: non-Muslims in Nigeria are the main adversaries of the Muslims, and Muslims in Nigeria must be united against the alleged attempts by non-Muslims to dominate the state. Ibrahim Salih thus tries to strike a difficult balance between criticising different groups and currents in Nigerian Islam and advocating the unity of Muslims in Nigeria. He criticises the hostile attitude of the 'Yan Izala and the revolutionary project of the Islamic Movement, but he also includes central topics of the criticism levelled against the traditional *ṣūfī* brotherhoods, including un-Islamic marriage customs and expenditures. At times his efforts for Muslim unity seem to put the consistency of his arguments at risk. For instance, he states that certain Muslim activists have acted wrongly and that diverging opinions have led to a fragmentation of Muslims, but in general he evaluates the heightened awareness created for Islamic issues as positive. What he criticises is the lack of manners in the confrontation.

Probably not unconnected to his criticism of the style in which dogmatic confrontations have been carried out in the past, Ibrahim Salih rejects by implicit means the claim of Hausa scholars in the tradition of the Sokoto Caliphate to leadership in Nigerian Islam. He affirms that

Islam was brought to Nigeria by ʿUqba bin Nāfiʿ through his home region of Borno. Historical sources indicate that ʿUqba bin Nāfiʿ conquered the oasis of Kawar, halfway between Fezzan and Lake Chad, in 46/666-7 (Vikør 1999: 148-153). However, there are no historical records to indicate that he subsequently continued to Borno. Therefore, rather than a historical comment, the reference to the Companion of the Prophet is intended to give particular authority to the author himself and relativises the Sokoto *jihād* and its intellectual legacy. In this way Ibrahim Salih portrays himself as an "honest broker" among Nigeria's Muslims. His repeated references to Muslims from the north and the south of the country need to be understood within this context.

In addition to the advocation of Muslim unity, Ibrahim Salih also presents a political vision. He recognises the political reality: Nigeria will not be an Islamic state. His ideas about *dār al-ḥarb* and *dār al-Islām* seem to point to a concept of legal systems running in parallel in separate legal jurisdictions. The territorial jurisdiction of Islamic law proposed by Ibrahim Salih justifies the application of Islamic criminal law in certain states of the country that have an Islamic government. With regard to the legal system, Ibrahim Salih rejects positive laws and the procedure followed by magistrate courts on the grounds that the judicial system inherited from British colonialism does not deliver justice. Nevertheless, he does not advocate a return to the application of uncodified Islamic law but suggests a revision of the existing legislation, including the Penal Code, to bring it in line with Islam. Instead of an Islamic state, Ibrahim Salih advocates a concerted effort by Muslims to elect governments that apply the *sharīʿa* and to influence the federal policies in their interest using all legal means.

## Changing attitudes

Ibrahim Salih's strategy of blaming the politicians for what went wrong in the implementation of Islamic criminal law is also quite apparent in subsequent statements. In an interview with IslamOnline.net on 29 September 2003,[415] Ibrahim Salih stated that the criticism of the way in which the *sharīʿa* was implemented was due to "the hastiness of some in implementing it without thinking." Once again emphasising a gradual approach in the implementation of the *sharīʿa*, he affirmed that Nigeria was determined to implement the *sharīʿa* in spite of external and internal pressures. The contentious issue was the implementation of Islamic criminal law (*ʿuqūbāt*). This, however, was but one part (*rukn*) of the *sharīʿa*. Even Muslims differed on the implementation of the *ḥadd* penal-

---

[415] "Muftī Nayjīriyā: nuʾayyid al-taṭbīq al-mutaʾannī lil-sharīʿa" [Muftī of Nigeria: We support a thoughtful application of the *sharīʿa*], IslamOnline.net, 01/10/2003.

ties, such as stoning to death and amputation of the hand. Again, he blamed the rush in implementing these penalties on the politicians:

> Some of the brothers among the state governors who implemented the *sharīʿa* wanted to mix a good and pious deed with an evil one: the implementation of the *sharīʿa* is a pious deed; the evil one is their wish to achieve a reputation by creating noise around them, so they did not look at the issue from all its angles.[416]

This interview took place at a time when first steps to remedy the situation had already been taken. Shortly after introducing separated *sharīʿa* penal codes, the twelve *sharīʿa*-implementing states commissioned and funded the CILS to draft a Harmonised Sharīʿa Penal Code. The plan was to produce a draft code that would be enacted by all twelve states to replace the diverging legislation in place. This also provided the chance to improve the often poor legislative quality of the codes (Ostien 2007: 4:20-21).[417] In the interview with IslamOnline.net, Ibrahim Salih stated—probably in reference to the Harmonised Sharīʿa Penal Code—that a great number of scholars and intellectuals from the different Nigerian states came together to correct the errors in the application of the *sharīʿa*. A committee was formed to select the *sharīʿa* rules to be applied (*intiqāʾ al-aḥkām*) and to formulate them in the style of a legal code (*ṣiyāgha qānūniyya*) that was consistent with the modern spirit (*rūḥ al-ʿaṣr*). A "white paper" (*kitāb abyaḍ*), designed to be an alternative for the Penal Code, was finalised in August 2002, and printed and distributed in all states that wished to have it, including states that had no Muslim majority.

Notwithstanding this effort, it appears that at present only Zamfara State has adopted the Harmonised Sharīʿa Penal Code—in a photocopied version still bearing the header of the CILS—in November 2005 (Ostien 2007: 4:34). By the time of the publication of the Harmonised Sharīʿa Penal Code in August 2002, the euphoria about the implementation of Islamic criminal law seemed to have already subsided. Disillusionment was widespread as a result of the new legislation's incapacity to end non-Islamic activities (consumption of alcohol, prostitution) and its alleged political instrumentalisation (Human Rights Watch 2004: 90). Nevertheless, a majority of people still believed that a better application of Islamic law—emphasising education, social protection, and maintenance of order—could radically improve the living conditions of Muslims in the north (O'Brien 2007: 57). Public opinion polls show that support for the

---

[416] Ibid.

[417] For an annotated version of the Harmonised Sharīʿa Penal Code, see Ostien (2007: 4:33-139).

*sharīʿa* in general actually increased between 2001 and 2007 in the states implementing it, particularly strongly in the lower- and middle-level economic segments of the population (Kirwin 2009: 144-146). This may be indicative of changing attitudes toward the *sharīʿa*: previously the prevailing opinion all but identified it with the implementation of Islamic criminal law, whereas now a majority of the Muslim population seem to understand it as a broader Islamisation of society with a focus on alleviating physical and spiritual penury. If this interpretation of the situation is correct, it amounts to the population's rejection of the politicisation of religion.

A number of governors who followed Zamfara's example in introducing Islamic criminal law only reluctantly under strong popular pressure appear to be ready to accept the blame of acting prematurely. Despite the adoption of Islamic criminal legislation in their states, they relied on the idea of a gradual implementation of the *sharīʿa*, as promoted by Ibrahim Salih, to counter accusations that they were not sincere about the implementation of the *sharīʿa*.[418] Even governors who owed their election to the promise to implement the *ḥadd* penalties and initially defied non-Muslim protests by assenting to amputation sentences soon grew reluctant to continue in this way. This indicates that they had come under pressure not only from Christian and secular quarters, but also from the Muslim side.

The gubernatorial elections of April 2003 provided the first opportunity to see whether the governors had been able to retain popular support within their state with their respective stances on the *sharīʿa*.[419] Only in Kano State was the electoral campaign clearly centred on the issue of the *sharīʿa*. The gubernatorial candidate and eventual winner of the elections, Ibrahim Shekarau, promised to implement the *sharīʿa* in a way that seemed to be close to that promoted by Ibrahim Salih. His campaign promise to extend the application of the *sharīʿa* in the state was translated into a societal reorientation programme termed "A Daidata Sahu" (Hausa for "close the ranks [in prayer]"). The focus of this programme was not placed on the prosecution of *ḥadd* offences but on social change through education, social protection measures, and moral "purification" (O'Brien 2007: 64-65). Remarkably, in Kano the implementation of the *sharīʿa* has not been dominated by the 'Yan Izala or the *ṣūfī* brotherhoods. In fact, important positions in the *sharīʿa* and *ḥisba* commissions and the state judiciary have been occupied by representatives of each camp (O'Brien 2007: 68). Thus it seems that the flawed implementation of Islamic criminal law, which was unacceptable to many

[418] For examples, see Chapter One: Jigawa (p. 37), Kano (p. 39), and Borno (p. 42).
[419] On the role of *sharīʿa* in the 2003 elections, see Kogelmann (2006).

Muslims in northern Nigeria, has stimulated a response toward greater cooperation and pragmatism in a broadly defined project to Islamise northern Nigerian society from below through Islamic education and the creation of Muslim awareness among the population.

## Conclusion

The analysis of Ibrahim Salih's *al-Ḥudūd fī al-sharīʿa* and subsequent developments shows that the remarkable change in judicial practice in Islamic criminal law in northern Nigeria within a few years following its introduction in 1999 paralleled the emergence of a scholarly Muslim discourse that replaced the emphasis on implementing the *ḥadd* punishments with a call for Muslim unity and increased cooperation, with a view to strengthening the Muslim community in Nigeria in their perceived confrontation with non-Muslims. Outside observers of the implementation of Islamic criminal law in northern Nigeria often had the impression of a near-homogeneous Muslim front advocating the implementation of Islamic criminal law on a national level. This view overlooks the fact that verbal support for the implementation of the *sharīʿa* was an almost desperate attempt to save the appearance of unity in the Nigerian Muslim community, which continues to experience internal divisions and even conflict. By endangering Muslim unity, Islamic criminal law challenged the mutual tolerance between the reform movement and the *ṣūfī* brotherhoods, and thus the authority of those who stood for this agreement.

The religious establishment had to react to a development that they had not predicted but that rapidly gained unexpected popular support. Among Muslims in northern Nigeria, the opinion prevailed that under the new civil dispensation the non-Muslims were attempting to dominate the country. The "restoration of the *sharīʿa*" quickly became a popular mark of Muslim identity; anyone openly criticising it risked being accused of harming the interests of the Muslims. In addition, the social mobility created by the introduction of the *sharīʿa* challenged the influence of established Muslim scholars in society and politics; they feared losing control over part of their constituencies. Ibrahim Salih's alternative vision for the implementation of the *sharīʿa* was also an attempt to reclaim leadership in northern Nigerian Islam.

The work can be read as a position paper by Ibrahim Salih. The ideas expressed in it have almost certainly served as a guideline in oral statements during sermons and seminars given by him or his adepts. Ibrahim Salih attempts to present a sustainable vision of the application of Islamic criminal law in northern Nigeria, adapted to the Nigerian realities. Such a vision must reconcile the fact that Nigeria is a multireligious state with an essentially secular constitutional order on the one hand, and the demand of implementing a religious law on the other. In addition, it had to be based on a concept of Islam broad enough to accommodate both the mysticism of the *ṣūfī* brotherhoods and the legal positivism of the reform movement. The answer found by Ibrahim Salih was to postpone the state's enforcement of the *ḥadd* penalties to a utopian time when society would be fully Islamised. In this way, Islamic criminal law remains the symbol of an ideal Muslim community in which Islamic law is almost completely respected, rather than a practical possibility.

An additional strategy to preserve Muslim unity was to put the blame for the flawed implementation of Islamic criminal law almost exclusively on politicians rather than Muslim scholars and activists. This avoided accusing any Muslim faction of wrongdoing, which in turn would have invariably led to a counterattack and further fragmentation. The criticism of politicians in *al-Ḥudūd fī al-sharīʿa* is probably a response to the ideas and emotions of a considerable portion of Nigerian Muslims, which generally remain unexpressed. One element of these popular sentiments is the feeling that politicians are intrinsically liars and that the political processes are flawed to an extent that so-called democracy only leads to more disorder, falsehood, and corruption. In such a situation, the *sharīʿa* in the hands of the religious scholars acts as a corrective of the politicians' abuses of their authority.

Many Muslims in northern Nigeria now seem to agree that instead of the enforcement of Islamic criminal law, priority should be given to a comprehensive Islamisation of society, starting at the grassroots level with concrete measures, such as the segregation of men and women in public places and transport, combating prostitution and the consumption of alcohol, but also improving the population's health and living conditions and access to education. Cooperation between rival Muslim factions may be easier on this level than on the highly politicised level of enforcing Islamic criminal law on all Muslims. This agreement is based on the assessment that the Muslim population of Nigeria must counter non-Muslim attempts to control them and deprive them of their rights. The change in attitude toward the implementation of Islamic criminal law is not a concession to non-Muslim protests or an effort to appease tensions in Muslim-Christian relations. Its aim is to conserve Muslim unity in a bid to avoid succumbing to the enemy due to internal fragmentation.

# Chapter Five: The *Fatwā* and the Beast: Islamic authority and Muslim unity in northern Nigeria in light of the 2002 Miss World Crisis

Abstract: In 2002, the Miss World beauty contest was scheduled to take place in Nigeria. After riots broke out in the Muslim north of the country, the contest was relocated to London. Shortly afterwards, a northern Muslim politician made a public statement that was interpreted as a "fatwa" on a young Christian journalist for alleged slander of the Prophet. These events and the discussions that followed revealed not only the state of Muslim-Christian relations in the country but also the struggle for leadership and religious authority among Nigeria's Muslims. The present article analyses the 2002 Miss World crisis in light of the development of Islamic authority in Nigeria. Decades of intra-Muslim conflict have left Muslim religious authority highly fragmented. It is argued that a new strategy of building authority has developed, which advocates Muslim unity in the face of an alleged Christian threat. This strategy makes it difficult for its representatives to contain radical currents within their own camp.

Nigeria's return to a civilian government in 1999 was immediately followed by the introduction of Islamic criminal law in some northern states of the federation. Locally and internationally, the Islamisation of criminal law was perceived as a political project promoted by a few populist state governors who exploited wide-spread popular discontent over deteriorating living conditions and anti-Western sentiments. The support which these governors received from the population forced governors of other states to follow the example, with limited possibilities to contain the effects. By late 2001, twelve northern Nigerian states had introduced Islamic criminal law.

While the implementation of the *sharīʿa* was supported by radical groups composed mainly of young Muslim activists, established *ʿulamāʾ* seem to have been more sceptical. Their response, however, was not outspoken criticism of the politicians' populist approach but rather silent advocacy aiming at a reform of the reform with political and judicial authorities. Such efforts have mitigated the possible effects of the implementation of Islamic criminal law with regard to certain offences like, for example, illicit sexual intercourse (*zinā*) (Chapter Two).

The question remains as to what prevented the Muslim religious establishment in northern Nigeria, which is mainly organised in the two umbrella organisations of *Jamāʿat Naṣr al-Islām* [Society for the support of Islam] (JNI) and the Nigerian Supreme Council for Islamic Affairs (NSCIA), from publicly opposing the manner in which Islamic criminal law was introduced and initially implemented. In this article, it is suggested that a lack of central authority in northern Nigerian Islam and the perceived need to maintain Muslim unity at all costs in the face of an alleged attempt by non-Muslims to dominate the state are two main factors which forced the Muslim establishment to respond to outside criticism of *sharīʿa* implementation, which often enough was clearly provocative and Islamophobic, in an apparently aggressive way. The incidents and intra-Muslim debates during the second half of 2002 AD, the period of the aborted Miss World contest and the "fatwa" against Isioma Daniel, illustrate—maybe better than any other episode of the country's recent past—the struggle for leadership and preservation of unity in northern Nigerian Islam.[420] It is a worthwhile endeavour, thus, to look at this period as a starting point for an analysis of the problem of religious authority in present-day northern Nigeria.

## The Miss World riots and the "fatwa" against Isioma Daniel

After the Nigerian Agbani Darego won the 2001 Miss World contest in South Africa, Nigeria qualified for hosting the contest in 2002. Unusually for a beauty contest, the Nigerian federal government was heavily involved in the preparations, probably motivated by the wish to improve the country's international image after years of military rule and in light of the international controversy over the implementation of Islamic criminal law in northern Nigeria, in particular with regard to the stoning sentences of two unmarried mothers, Safiyya Hussaini and Amina Lawal, for alleged illicit sexual intercourse (Chapter Two). Safiyya Hussaini of Sokoto State was sentenced to death by stoning in October 2001. On 25 March 2002, the Sokoto State Sharīʿa Court of Appeal acquitted her for lack of evidence and quashed her stoning sentence (Peters 2006). Around the time of Hussaini's acquittal, Amina Lawal of Katsina State was sentenced to death by stoning for the same offence. Her sentence was confirmed on appeal before an upper *sharīʿa* court on 19 August 2002. Amina Lawal was finally acquitted in a second appeal before the

[420] This article does not primarily analyse the impact of the Miss World crisis on Muslim-Christian relations in Nigeria. These have been discussed elsewhere, e.g. in Weimann (forthcoming).

Katsina State Sharīʿa Court of Appeal on 25 September 2003, thus after the period under review.

The controversy about the implementation of the *sharīʿa* was fuelled further by the decision of the city of Rome (Italy) in September 2002 to grant honorary citizenship to Safiyya Hussaini. Muslim politicians, in particular state governors who had strongly advocated the implementation of the *sharīʿa*, were indignant. The governor of Safiyya Hussaini's home state of Sokoto, Attahiru Bafarawa, emphasised in an interview with the BBC that "Safiyat was charged for adultery and needed not to be honoured, it is unfortunate for the Italian government to honour an adulterer."[421] The governor of Zamfara State, Ahmad Sani, whose electoral campaign promise of "religious reforms" had triggered the movement for the introduction of the *sharīʿa*, declared that "[i]t was not surprising that she was taken to Rome because I have read long time ago that there are a lot of prostitutes in Rome," adding that he was ready to send more adulterers to the Italian capital.[422] But also JNI protested. In a statement signed by its secretary-general, Abdulkadir Orire, the organisation declared all those who collaborated in "smuggling out" Safiyya Hussaini to Italy "enemies of Allah":

> It is now an open secret that the enemies of Allah, i.e. the enemies of Sharia had surreptitiously smuggled Safiya Husseini out of Nigeria to Rome for what they considered to be honouring her and thereby ridiculing Islam. If any person is to be honoured, it should have been the sharia judge who freed her.[423]

At the time when the Miss World contest was approaching, sensitivities on both sides of the religious divide were thus already aroused. In spite of the tense situation, the Nigerian government, in its efforts to make the beauty contest a success, failed to avoid instances which would be readily interpreted by Muslims as symbols of the federal authorities' contempt for Islam. For example, the contest's final was initially scheduled to take place on 30 November 2002, or 25 Ramaḍān 1423.

Muslim organisations of all currents protested against the beauty contest. Frequently, they suspected a link between the holding of the pageant and the national and international protests against the introduction of the *sharīʿa*. Already in July 2002, the National Council of Muslim Youths (NACOMYO) announced that it would "use all constitutional means to disrupt" the contest.[424] The foundation of NACOMYO, an um-

---

[421] "Sokoto Governor queries Italy's honour for Safiyat," *The Guardian* (Nigeria), 10/09/2002, 96.

[422] "Yerima: 'A City of Adulterers'," *This Day*, 21/09/2002, 2.

[423] "Sultan chides sponsors of Safiya to Rome," *The Comet*, 16/09/2002, 3.

[424] "Muslim groups vow to disrupt Miss World contest," *This Day*, 26/07/2002.

brella organisation of Nigerian Muslim youth organisations, in 1987 was facilitated by the World Assembly of Muslim Youth (WAMY) (Loimeier and Reichmuth 1993: 67; Hock 1996: 68). Another group that sought to further its cause in the public by protesting against the Miss World contest was the Supreme Council for Sharia in Nigeria (SCSN), a pro-*sharīʿa* group established in 2000 whose main purpose has been the introduction of the *sharīʿa* on a national level. In a press release dated 19 September 2002 and signed by its secretary-general, Nafi'u Baba Ahmad, the SCSN not only condemned the "abduction of Safiyya Hussein to Rome" but also "frowned at the plan by the Federal Government to support the hosting of the miss World beauty pageant in Abuja, in the Month of Ramadan. It viewed this as an evident act of provocation to Muslims."[425] Such criticisms were echoed by the umbrella organisations. On 23 September 2002, the NSCIA protested against "the display of semi-naked female contestants" bodies during the last ten days of the month of Ramadan when Moslems are scheduled to be fasting and devoting all of themselves to Allah" before calling on "all Moslems, including government functionaries, not to participate in the proposed show of shame which is totally un-Islamic."[426]

Only after these protests, the final was postponed to 7 December 2002, after the end of Ramaḍān.[427] Nevertheless, on 11 November 2002, or 6 Ramaḍān 1423, 92 contestants arrived in Nigeria. The next day, 88 of them took part in a Christian prayer session at the chapel of the presidential villa in Abuja.[428] The extensive domestic media coverage of the events leading up to the final during the Muslim month of fasting was understood by many Muslims as a deliberate provocation.

The situation escalated a few days later. On 16 November 2002, the Nigerian privately owned, Lagos-based newspaper *This Day* published, in its arts pages, an article by Isioma Daniel, a young Christian journalist trained in the United Kingdom. Under the title "The World at their Feet," this article included the following passage:

> The Muslims thought it was immoral to bring ninety-two women to Nigeria and ask them to revel in vanity. What would Mohammed think? In all honesty, he would probably have chosen a wife from one of them.[429]

[425] Published, e.g., in *This Day*, 14/10/2002, 33.

[426] "Islamic Council asks Moslems to shun Miss World contest," *The Comet*, 24/09/2002, 3.

[427] "Miss World Beauty Pageant Postponed," *This Day*, 04/10/2002.

[428] "88 Miss World girls at Villa chapel," *The Comet*, 13/11/2002, 3.

[429] The article was deleted from *This Day*'s online archive. The text is available at <http://www.isioma.net/sds03002.html>. After the publication, Isioma Daniel fled the country.

It is unlikely that the author pursued a political goal with this article, and the quoted passage in particular. She probably aimed at satirising Muslim commentators and organisations for their criticism of the beauty pageant.

After the publication of the article, the newspaper tried to apologise—first in an editor's note on the front page, but as tensions grew by articles covering the whole front page in which the acceptance of the newspaper's apologies by Muslim representatives was highlighted and by placing the same articles in advertisements several pages long in major northern newspapers, such as *Weekly Trust*. However, this could not counterbalance the news of the alleged slander of the Prophet which was spreading rapidly among Muslims, particularly through text messages sent via mobile telephones (Human Rights Watch 2003: 7).

The mounting tensions finally escalated in Kaduna on 20 November 2002, when a group of Muslim adolescents destroyed and burnt *This Day*'s regional office. After this, they marched through Kaduna, demanding the death of the newspaper's editors for alleged slander of the Prophet. Already this death threat was called a "fatwa."[430] The three following days were marked by violent clashes between groups of Muslim and Christian youths, which left around 250 people dead (Human Rights Watch 2003: 2). On Friday, 22 September 2002, the riots spread to the federal capital Abuja: after the Friday prayer at the Abuja National Mosque, protesters stormed to Wuse market, attacking passers-by, destroying public and private buildings and burning cars. According to press reports, hoodlums had been brought in from Kaduna to instigate the crowd.[431] Under the impression of the riots, the Miss World contest was relocated to London on 23 September 2002.

This was not the end of the crisis. A second possibly inconsiderate, possibly well-considered statement, this time on the Muslim side, was going to inflame the debate further. On 25 November 2002, the then deputy governor of Zamfara State, Mamuda Aliyu Shinkafi,[432] spoke at a public gathering to representatives of 21 Muslim youth organisations.[433] The English-speaking press reported his central statement as follows:

---

She was granted political asylum in Norway, where she works as a journalist. See "Isioma Daniel: Blessings of a fatwa," *Punch*, 18/09/2008.

[430] "Moslems protest Miss Worldcontest, torch Thisday office," *The Guardian* (Nigeria), 21/11/2002.

[431] "The Miss World Tragedy," *Tell*, 09/12/2002, 31.

[432] In the April 2007 gubernatorial elections, Mamuda Aliyu Shinkafi succeeded Ahmad Sani as governor of Zamfara State. In 2009, he "decamped" the ANPP, the dominant party in the north after 1999 alleged to be pro-Muslim, to join the PDP, the very party that has been in power on the federal level since 1999.

[433] "Controversy over Nigerian fatwa," BBC News, 27/11/2002.

> Like Salman Rushdie, the blood of Isioma Daniel can be shed. [...] It is binding on all Moslems wherever they are, to consider the killing of the writer as a religious duty.[434]

It is not certain that Shinkafi used the word "fatwa" in his speech. Subsequently, however, a Zamfara State government spokesman described Shinkafi's statement as follows: "It's a Fatwa. It is based on the request of the people. [...] Being a leader, you can pass a Fatwa." He explained that a number of Islamic associations in Zamfara State had asked the state government to take action.[435]

As was to be expected, in parallel to the *fatwā* issued against Salman Rushdie by Ayatollah Khomeini in 1989, the Nigerian media, non-Muslim intellectuals such as Nigerian Nobel laureate Wole Soyinka and Christian leaders interpreted Shinkafi's statements as an appeal for murder (Weimann forthcoming). On the Muslim side, the debate centred on two questions: whether death is the appropriate punishment for a non-Muslim journalist who slandered the Prophet; and whether Shinkafi's "fatwa" was a *fatwā* in the sense of an Islamic legal opinion and who in Nigeria is entitled to issue *fatwās*.

With regard to the appropriate punishment, the secretary-general of the NSCIA, Dr. Lateef Adegbite, immediately excluded the death penalty on the grounds that the journalist was not a Muslim and that the newspaper had distanced itself from the article and had publicly apologised.[436] Leading Tijāniyya shaykh Dahiru Bauchi explained that the Muslim *umma* had a right to consider an apology from one who offended them or their religion in as much as such an apology was genuine. He stressed that repentance was a virtue of the believers and anyone who repents after sin.[437]

Other groups thought the death penalty was appropriate. The Muslim Student Society (MSS)[438] published a statement in which it condemned the article in *This Day* which it said had caused the crisis and declared its support for the death penalty passed on Isioma Daniel, insisting that "Muslim youths of this nation accept only the provisions of the Sharia on this matter. We are in full support of the declaration by the Zamfara State government to this effect."[439] Ja'far Mahmud Adam, a leading rep-

---

[434] See, e.g., "*Miss World*: Govt opposes 'death sentence' on journalist," *The Guardian* (Nigeria), 27/11/2002, 1-2. Shinkafi might have spoken in Hausa. Unfortunately, I am not in possession of the original text of the speech.

[435] "*Fatwa*: Saudi, Adegbite, FG Fault Zamfara Govt," *This Day*, 27/11/2002, 1-2.

[436] Ibid.

[437] "Zamfara's *Fatwa* dilemma," *Weekly Trust*, 13-19/12/2002, 19.

[438] On the foundation and the development of the MSS into a national Muslim organisation, see Loimeier and Reichmuth (1993: 65).

[439] "JNI seeks help for Kaduna victims," *Weekly Trust*, 06-12/12/2002, 6.

resentative of the Ahl al-Sunna movement in Kano and strong supporter of *sharīʿa* implementation, stated that if a slanderer repents he will be rewarded for his repentance in the hereafter. In this world, while some scholars are of the opinion that the slanderer should be pardoned, according to a dominant opinion among Muslim scholars, he must be punished to serve as a deterrent.[440]

Some Muslim leaders made a pardon conditional on a public apology by the offender. At a press conference in Ibadan, the first national vice president of the SCSN, Abdir-Rasheed Nadiyatullah, stated that the death sentence was the appropriate punishment for blasphemy against the Prophet. However, the author of the article may be spared if she tendered an unreserved apology.[441] Another influential Ahl al-Sunna leader, Yakubu Musa, criticised that Isioma Daniel had not apologised, as *This Day* had done. He interpreted this as an indication that the affair was "planned, calculated and executed by anti-Sharia forces from within and without."[442]

Concerning the validity of Shinkafi's "fatwa," many Nigerian Muslim scholars appeared astonished, at best, at the action taken by the Zamfara State government, arguing that public pressure on the government was no manner to achieve an acceptable *fatwā*. In a statement issued on 28 November 2008, JNI declared that the Zamfara State government "has no authority to issue *fatwa* and the *fatwa* issued by it should be ignored."[443] The statement also claimed that a *fatwā* can only be issued by JNI and the NSCIA, both of which are headed by the Sultan of Sokoto—"the recognised spiritual leader of Muslims in the country"—who already asked the NSCIA's *fatwā* committee to look into the issue. The following day, 29 November 2002, the NSCIA officially invalidated the "fatwa" by the Zamfara state government.[444] It was announced that the NSCIA's *fatwā* commission, headed by influential Tijāniyya shaykh Ibrahim Salih, had considered the issue, including the apologies offered by Isioma Daniel, and decided that they were sufficient to pardon her. The commission warned of decisions based on individual judgments (*al-ijtihādāt al-fardiyya*) with respect to "important *fatwā*s which might lead to confusion and disorder in the country." The NSCIA reiterated the claim that itself and JNI were

---

[440] "Zamfara's *Fatwa* dilemma," *Weekly Trust*, 13-19/12/2002, 19.

[441] "Soyinka condemns *fatwa*, asks Obasanjo to defend Constitution," *The Guardian* (Nigeria), 28/11/2002, 1-2.

[442] "Zamfara's *Fatwa* dilemma," *Weekly Trust*, 13-19/12/2002, 19.

[443] "JNI Cancels *Fatwa* on Daniel," *New Nigerian Newspaper*, 29/11/2009, 1; and "Islamic body says Zamfara can't pronounce *fatwa*," *The Guardian* (Nigeria), 29/11/2002, 80.

[444] "al-Majlis al-Islāmī al-Nayjīrī yulġī fatwā ihdār al-dam" [The Nigerian Islamic Council nullifies the *fatwā* of impunity for shedding blood], IslamOnline.net, 29/11/2002.

the only entities competent on the national level to issue *fatwās* of a public and general character.

The Abuja-based Muslim organisation Assembly of Muslims in Nigeria (AMIN) issued a statement signed by its executive secretary Dr. Siraj Abdulkarim. The organisation called upon Muslim scholars to educate Nigerians about Islam and to "alert our Muslim brethren on the dangers of issuing *fatwa* without due process as required by scholarship." The statement continued that the riots—the "unIslamic reactions of the youth"—were a result of the frustration born out of poverty and idleness caused by the alarming rise in unemployment in the country.[445] AMIN is chaired by Ibrahim Salih and, therefore, it is fair to assume that this statement reflects his personal views (see Chapter Four, p. 123).

The claim of the two umbrella organisations to being the supreme Islamic authority in Nigeria did not remain unchallenged. Ja'far Mahmud Adam stated that the position of JNI and the NSCIA had no basis in the Qur'ān or the prophetic traditions (*ḥadīth*). In his view, anyone well-versed and learned in Islamic jurisprudence can issue a *fatwā* on issues that affect the lives of Muslims. In a Muslim society, the authority to issue *fatwās* is not limited to one person or authority. Therefore, instead of annulling the Zamfara State government's "fatwa" on the grounds that the issuing instance had no authority to do so, JNI and the NSCIA should have assessed the position taken by the Zamfara State government in order to ascertain whether or not it was at variance with the *sharīʿa*.[446]

In the face of continued criticism of Shinkafi's actions, the Zamfara State government spokesman declared that the position of the government remained unchanged. The government had only specified the appropriate punishment for blasphemy in accordance with the *sunna* and the consensus of the scholars (*ijmāʿ*), adding that "we did not direct anybody to go and execute that lady but what we did was to ensure peace is maintained in our state." The execution of such a *fatwā*, he added, rested on the shoulders of the Muslim authority or, if there is none, the entire Muslim *umma*.[447] This insistence notwithstanding, the governor of Zamfara State, Ahmad Sani, declared in January 2003 in an interview with the BBC that the deputy governor had not issued a real *fatwā*:

> The fact is that the fatwa was not really a fatwa per se, the deputy governor was misquoted because he was simply trying to state the position of Islam as regards making derogatory remarks about

---

[445] "AMIN cautions on the dangers of *fatwa*," *Daily Trust*, 02/12/2002, 18.
[446] "Zamfara's *Fatwa* dilemma," *Weekly Trust*, 13-19/12/2002, 19.
[447] Ibid.

Prophet Mohammed. Therefore, I can say that he did not pass a death sentence on Isioma.[448]

This, one could have thought, closed the affair: JNI and the NSCIA had shown leadership, while critical comments were restricted to technicalities. The politicians had to surrender to the religious authorities. However, the issue came up again several months later. On 22 July 2003, a committee established by JNI to study the matter under the chairmanship of JNI's secretary-general, Abdulkadir Orire, presented its report at JNI's annual meeting in Kaduna. JNI confirmed that the statement of Deputy Governor Shinkafi was "an evident, unavoidable *fatwā*" (*fatwā thābita lā ḥayda ʿanhā*).[449] The committee concluded that Daniel insulted the Prophet and confirmed the decision that her life may be taken (*ihdār al-dam*), based on the consensus of the scholars of all schools and currents according to which any person—Muslim or non-Muslim—who insults the Prophet needs to be put to death and a pardon is not acceptable (*al-ʿafw lā yuqbal*). However, the death sentence can be carried out only by an independent body authorised by the state to do so.

This last condition is key to understanding the message. It is inconceivable that the secular Nigerian state empower a group of people to carry out such a *fatwā*. This must have been clear to all members of the committee. In this way, JNI affirmed the validity of the contents of the "fatwa" but subjected its execution to conditions impossible to fulfil. The statement, which was followed by protests of Christian groups threatening chaos if the sentence was executed,[450] was an attempt to embrace the critics of JNI's earlier statements, such as Ja'far Mahmud Adam. Nevertheless, JNI's conclusion, even if it had no practical consequences, was a reversal of the position expressed by the NSCIA's *fatwā* committee.

## *Fragmentation of authority*

This reversal of earlier held positions was surely done in an effort by the religious establishment, as organised in JNI and the NSCIA, to maintain its authority, which is built on being accepted as a representation of the greatest number of currents and factions in Nigerian Islam. Both JNI and the NSCIA were founded with the aim of giving Islam a unified voice—across all regional and dogmatic divisions—within the Nigerian state.

The regional focus of JNI, the older of the two organisations, has been northern Nigeria, its president being the Sultan of Sokoto. It was founded in 1962 in a bid to gain the support of religious scholars, par-

[448] "Fatwa: My Deputy was Misquoted, Says Zamfara Gov," *This Day*, 22/01/2003, 3.
[449] "Fatwā tuthīr intiqādāt fī Nayjīriyā" [*Fatwā* stirs up criticism in Nigeria], IslamOnline.net, 23/07/2003.
[450] Ibid.

ticularly of the *ṣūfī* brotherhoods, for the policies of the government of the then Northern Region (Loimeier and Reichmuth 1993: 47). The NSCIA was founded, in a very different political context, in 1973 by JNI and Muslim organisations from south-western Nigeria with the aim of achieving a national consensus in matters pertaining to the development of Islam in Nigeria (ibid.: 61). From the beginning, it was the NSCIA's intention "to serve as the only channel of contact on Islamic matters" (Hock 1996: 59). The president of the NSCIA is the Sultan of Sokoto, his deputy is the Shehu of Borno, while its secretary-general is a Yoruba Muslim. Based on this representation of all three major components of Nigerian Islam, the NSCIA claims to be the supreme body representing Muslims in Nigeria. Neither of the two organisations, however, is officially recognised, nor has their leadership been appointed by the Nigerian state. Their authority among Muslims is solely based on their ability to win the support of their constituencies, that is—at least in theory—all Muslims in Nigeria. A brief look on the development of religious authority in Islam in northern Nigeria will illustrate the scale of this task.

The region which is now covered by northern Nigeria has never been united under one single Muslim religious authority. During the nineteenth century AD, most of the region was part of the Sokoto Caliphate, an Islamic state established by a Muslim reform movement led by Usman ɗan Fodio. Only in the north-eastern corner, the Muslim empire of Bornu[451] remained independent, despite several attempts by Sokoto to conquer it. Sokoto and Bornu were not only political enemies but disputed also each other's claim to religious leadership. In a famous correspondence with the leaders of the Sokoto Caliphate, the later Shehu of Bornu Muḥammad al-Amīn al-Kanemi disputed the religious legitimacy of Sokoto's fight against fellow Muslims (Hiskett 1973: 109-10; Brenner 1973: 40-2). The challenge to Sokoto's religious authority triggered a voluminous intellectual production in Sokoto in an attempt to justify its aggressive stance towards its Muslim rival (Brenner 1973: 42). Eventually, a prevailing opinion in Sokoto emerged that all those who were not with Muslims, as understood in Sokoto, were against Muslims, and that all those against Muslims were non-Muslims (Last 1967: 58n).

The Sokoto Caliphate's elite belonged to the Qādiriyya, which for some time remained the predominant *ṣūfī* brotherhood (*ṭarīqa*) in the region. In the course of the nineteenth century AD, however, another *ṣūfī* brotherhood, the Tijāniyya, began to attract people discontented with what they saw as the reintroduction of pagan practices in the Ca-

[451] The spelling Bornu refers to the Bornu empire, while Borno is a state of the present Nigerian federation.

liphate's governance. After the British conquest, affiliation with the Tijāniyya was soon viewed as a symbol of resistance again (Umar 2006: 35-40). But brotherhoods are not monolithic blocks but are rather split up in a multitude of different networks coexisting and competing with each other, each grouped around a number of spiritually, politically and economically influential religious scholars. Whereas in earlier times the membership of *ṣūfī* brotherhoods was restricted to disciples initiated by recognised *ṣūfī* shaykhs, starting in the 1940s, the authority of the leading networks within the Nigerian *ṣūfī* brotherhoods was challenged by the success of the Tijāniyya-Ibrāhīmiyya and the Qādiriyya-Nāṣiriyya, respectively, networks led by a new generation of shaykhs who aimed at converting the *ṣūfī* brotherhoods into mass movements (Loimeier 1997: 15).

On the political level, during most of the colonial period, northern Nigeria, under the system known as indirect rule, remained dominated by the former aristocracies of Sokoto and Bornu. The British did not question the existing socio-political systems but attempted to modernise them along existing lines (Loimeier 1997: 5). The emirs' judicial powers were gradually subjected to the provisions of English law, in particular with regard to the offence of homicide (Chapter Three). Most emirs seem to have perceived the colonial situation as a challenge to their Islamic authority, which was based on the enforcement of Islamic law.[452] Eventually, on the eve of independence on 1 October 1960, the Penal Code for the Northern Region was adopted, which put an end to the application of uncodified Islamic criminal law in northern Nigeria. The Penal Code was drafted by an international Panel of Jurists after widespread consultations with political and religious leaders in northern Nigeria.[453] Since its adoption, the application of uncodified Islamic law has been restricted to personal matters. Eventually, the judicial powers of the emirs were completely abolished in 1968 (Ostien 2006: 228).

After independence in 1960, the Premier of the Northern Region, Ahmadu Bello, pursued a policy of political and religious unity in order to ensure the north's domination within the Nigerian federation.[454] One element of this policy was the foundation of JNI. Bello's major ally in the struggle for religious unity—and, one might add, control and leadership—in northern Nigeria was the reform-oriented, anti-*ṣūfī* scholar Abubakar Gumi (1922-1992). Gumi had made a rapid career in the northern Nigerian judicial system and was appointed Grand Qāḍī of the

[452] See Umar (2006: 104-56) for the emirs' responses to this challenge.

[453] For an extensive documentation on the composition, activities, discussions and recommendations of the Panel of Jurists, see Ostien (2007, vol. 1; 2006: 225-6).

[454] At independence, Nigeria comprised three regions, by far the biggest of which in both area and population was the Northern Region.

Northern Region in 1962. His close links to Saudi Arabia were based on his seat in the Muslim World League, founded in Mecca in 1962, which was delegated to him by Bello (Loimeier 1997: 156).

Gumi tried to use his appointment as the Grand Qāḍī to achieve a position of authority in northern Nigerian Islam. He submitted a memorandum to the Panel of Jurists during its second session of May/June 1962, in which the Panel reviewed the implementation of the Penal Code and accompanying legislation.[455] Among his proposals to the panel was the idea that, after the example of the system followed in the Sudan, the Grand Qāḍī of the Northern Region be vested with the power to issue *fatwās* that would be binding on *sharīʿa* courts in an effort to "unify the work of the courts" (Ostien 2007: 1:110). However, the Panel of Jurists did not follow the advice given by Gumi. In its report, which was submitted to the Minister of Justice of the Northern Region on 4 June 1962 (Ostien 2007: 134-56), it was recommended that necessary reforms of the law be introduced through legislation, rather than judicial circulars or memoranda. By way of compromise, the Panel proposed that such legislation be suggested by a committee of which the Grand Qāḍī is an *ex officio* member (Ostien 2007: 1:145). It is obvious that the Panel of Jurists tried to avoid creating an office that would have the authority to determine the interpretation of Islamic law to be administered in northern Nigerian courts. This attitude probably reflects the Panel's awareness of the already lingering conflict between Gumi and the *ṣūfī* brotherhoods.

Ahmadu Bello was assassinated in 1966 during the first of Nigeria's successive military coups. The following year, the three regions, into which the Nigerian federation was divided at independence, were replaced by smaller states. Muslim northern Nigeria lost its political unity. Each of the new states had its own Grand Qāḍī. Thus, once more the issue of leadership in northern Nigerian politics and religion was an open question. In the absence of Bello's iron-fist approach towards dissenting opinions, the superficial unity in the northern religious sphere that had been maintained with great difficulties by Bello rapidly disintegrated. The *ṣūfī* brotherhoods managed to prevent the takeover of JNI by Gumi and his followers. As a result, JNI disintegrated into a number of regional factions which were controlled by different networks (Loimeier 1997: 145).

Immediately after Bello's death, Abubakar Gumi began to attack the *ṣūfī* brotherhoods as carriers of corrupting innovations (*bidaʿ*) in Islam. He initiated an ambitious campaign to reform Islam in Nigeria with an aim, among others, of destroying the *ṭarīqas*. In reaction, Gumi and his followers have been labelled as Wahhābīs by their *ṣūfī* opponents

455 For the text of the memorandum, see Ostien (2007: 1:109-12).

(Seesemann 2000: 145). *Tafsīr* sessions, in particular during Ramaḍān, which were broadcast by radio, became an important tool in the ideological struggle (Brigaglia 2007). Gumi and Nasiru Kabara, the leading authority of the Qādiriyya in Kano at the time, published competing translations of the Qur'ān into Hausa. In these translations, both authors tried to substantiate their dogmatic position (Brigaglia 2005). In this situation, the foundation in 1973 of the NSCIA aimed at overcoming the escalating conflict between traditionalists and reformers. However, like in the case of JNI, the conflict between the two camps also largely paralysed the activities of the NSCIA for a long time (Loimeier 1997: 291-2).

After the ousting of the Christian military head of state Yakubu Gowon (1966-75), Abubakar Gumi found a strong supporter in his successor, Murtala Muhammad. Under his short-lived rule, Gumi became the official adviser on religious affairs to the government and was entrusted with the preparation of Nigeria's accession to the Organisation of the Islamic Conference (OIC) (Loimeier 1997: 164). Murtala Muhammad had plans to establish a federal *sharī'a* court of appeal[456] and already appointed Gumi to serve as the Grand Muftī. However, after Murtala Muhammad was killed in February 1976, his successor, Olusegun Obasanjo, a Yoruba Christian, shelved the project of a federal *sharī'a* court of appeal and the accession to the OIC. Gumi continued to receive the salary of a Grand Muftī but had no office and finally retired from civil service in 1986 (Loimeier 1997: 164).

Obasanjo's reluctance to continue his predecessor's project was not so much the result of Christian-Muslim tensions than of pressure exerted by Gumi's Muslim opponents. The Tijāniyya shaykh Dahiru Bauchi had successfully rallied the other leaders of the *ṣūfī* brotherhoods and a number of emirs to oppose the proposal to make Gumi supreme head of the federal Islamic judicial system.[457] In the confrontation with the reform movement, Dahiru Bauchi was able to establish himself as the spokesman for the brotherhoods, and in particular the Tijāniyya (Loimeier 1993: 153). Under the pressure of Gumi's attacks, the *ṭarīqa*s stopped their internal quarrels and in the late 1970s formed a common front against Gumi and his supporters.

After he realised that the brotherhoods were blocking his career in the national judicial system, Abubakar Gumi adopted a strategy of mass mobilisation (Loimeier 1993b: 141-2). Starting in the late 1970s, Gumi made a series of public pronouncements of *takfīr*, thus declaring as unbe-

[456] The controversy about the creation of a federal *sharī'a* court of appeal dominated the deliberations of the constituent assemblies of 1977-78 and 1988. On these debates, see Abun-Nasr (1988) and Ostien (2006).
[457] Loimeier (1997: 165). See also Gumi's autobiography (1994: 206).

lievers the followers of the *ṭarīqas*, particularly the Tijāniyya (Brigaglia 2005: 430). In 1978, Gumi's supporters established an organisation of their own, *Jamāʿat izālat al-bidʿa wa-iqāmat al-sunna* [The Society for the removal of innovation and the instatement of tradition] (Hausa: 'Yan Izala) in order to transfer the struggle against the *ṭarīqas* to the grassroot level.[458] The 'Yan Izala were extremely successful in mobilising a mostly young generation of Muslims in Nigeria and challenging the authority of the established *ṣūfī* brotherhoods. They introduced new forms of organisation and use of media and led the way in educating women. However, these efforts at modernisation did not secure the unity of the movement. In the 1980s, a number of disputes developed within the 'Yan Izala that led to the emergence to two competing factions in the early 1990s (Kane 2003: 217-26; Loimeier 2007: 54-5).

Neither the *ṣūfī* brotherhoods nor the reform movement aimed at directly changing the political system. The *ṣūfī* brotherhoods have a history of close relations with Muslim rulers in northern Nigeria. Their principal aim has been the propagation of Islam and their respective brotherhoods under the umbrella of a Muslim government. In general, the reform movement has aimed at social change, not at political overthrow. Its members expect the state to bring about this change and, thus, their strategy is political agitation and promotion of individual politicians whom they see as being in favour of Islamisation (Gwarzo 2003: 312).

In the aftermath of the 1979 Iranian revolution, however, the idea of an Islamic revolution in Nigeria appealed to many mostly young and educated Muslims in northern Nigeria, in particular members of the MSS. The most prominent representative of this revolutionary fundamentalist current has been Ibrahim al-Zakzaki and his Islamic Movement, also known as Muslim Brothers or 'Yan Brotha (O'Brien 2007: 52-3). Due to his political views and the massive support which he and his movement received from Iran, they have been labelled as *shīʿīs* by their adversaries and the media. In recent years, members of the Islamic Movement have openly converted to shīʿism, e.g. by celebrating *ʿāshūrāʾ* and Fatima's birthday (Loimeier 2007: 57). On its websites <www.islamicmovement.org> and <www.harkarmusulunci.org>, the Islamic Movement openly displays its adherence to *shīʿī* beliefs and the Iranian religious leadership.

Apart from Iran, also Libya tried to win supporters for its version of political Islam in Nigeria (Loimeier 1997: 289-91). In respect to the strong economic basis of the *ṭarīqas* as well as of the 'Yan Izala in Nigeria itself, however, it seems likely that external interests of foreign countries like

[458] On the 'Yan Izala, see Loimeier (1997) and Kane (2003).

Iran, Libya and Saudi Arabia are played off against each other by the Nigerian movements and instrumentalised for their own aims.[459]

## *Unity as a substitute for authority*

The strong competition between different Muslim movements, networks and personalities, accompanied and underscored by fundamental dogmatic rifts, have effectively thwarted all attempts by individual scholars or networks of scholars to be recognised as uncontested leaders in northern Nigerian Islam. Attempts to impose a canonical reading of the texts and a standardised religious practice have been met with counterattacks by opponents who, besides diverging understandings of the tenets of Islam, had to fear a loss of personal authority should they agree with the views of their peers. This dynamic has compromised the success of the umbrella organisations.

Since the late 1970s, however, an alternative strategy of building authority has proven to be more successful. This alternative consists not so much in acquiring a position allowing its holder to successfully propagate a particular interpretation of the religion than in advocating an interpretation of Islam broad enough to accommodate the different currents and allowing them to coexist under one umbrella. Thus, the claim of orthodoxy is replaced by a call for unity.

A scholar who has tried to provide dogmatic foundations for a compromise between the two camps is the Tijāniyya shaykh Ibrahim Salih of Maiduguri (Borno), born in 1939. His attempt to reformulate the doctrines of the Tijāniyya has generated internal disputes to the point of splitting the brotherhood (Seesemann 1998, 2000, 2009). Notwithstanding, or maybe for this reason, Ibrahim Salih has become—as noted above—the chairman of the *fatwā* committees of both JNI and the NSCIA. Contrary to Dahiru Bauchi, who defended the doctrines of the Tijāniyya without compromise, Ibrahim Salih's aim has been to reconcile the *ṣūfīs* with their opponents. This has been apparent in his approach to *sharīʿa* implementation: he stresses the need to educate Muslims to enable them to conform their behaviour to the *sharīʿa* without interference from the public authorities. Referring to a broad concept of the *sharīʿa* as a comprehensive code of conduct for Muslims in religious, private and public affairs, he has welcomed the commitment of the northern Nigerian states to the *sharīʿa* but criticised the implementation of the *ḥadd* punishments in the current situation (Chapter Four).

The strategy of advocating Muslim unity could develop and be successful in northern Nigeria because of two major developments. The first

---

[459] See Loimeier (1997: 291). During my time in Nigeria (2002-2004), I have gained a similar impression.

was the internal development in northern Nigerian Islam. A clear distinction between the major Muslim currents—the traditionalism of the *ṣūfī* brotherhoods, the modernism of the 'Yan Izala and the fundamentalism of the Islamic Movement—has become increasingly difficult over recent decades. While none of these currents has escaped internal fragmentation, they, or certain factions of them, seem to converge. The modernisation processes within the *ṭarīqa*s have brought them closer to the reform movement of the 'Yan Izala. At the same time, some parts of the reform movement have adopted revolutionary views, similar to those proposed by the Islamic Movement (Umar 2001). At the same time, the number of Western-educated Muslims, not affiliated with one of the existing religious movements, increased. This heterogeneous group comprises conservative bureaucrats and judges, but also young and radical Muslim intellectuals, mainly centred in high schools and universities of northern Nigeria, and finally dissidents from the conflicting parties of the *ṣūfī* brotherhoods and the 'Yan Izala (Loimeier 1997: 310-2). Since the 1990s, a younger generation of university-trained Muslim intellectuals have developed a Muslim political discourse in northern Nigeria that stresses the importance of the Sokoto Caliphate's legacy as a model for the development of Islam in Nigeria and emphasises international pan-Muslim solidarity, rather than regional affiliations to countries like Iran, Libya or Saudi Arabia (Loimeier 2007: 62-3).

The second factor was a rapid deterioration in the relations between Muslims and non-Muslims. Pentecostal and charismatic churches discovered northern Nigeria as an area for missionary activities. On the political level, Christians in the north have been represented by the northern branch of the national ecumenical Christian Association of Nigeria (CAN) (Kane 2003: 178-83; Loimeier 2007: 60). As a result of increasing efforts to convert northern communities to Christianity, many Muslims began to perceive an increasing threat to their religion from non-Muslims in Nigeria.[460] During the 1980s, Muslim-Christian tensions escalated and the intra-Muslim struggle for authority began to be relegated to a secondary position. The year 1987 was a turning point in Muslim-Christian relations. A number of events in this year made the unity of Muslims appear more urgent than the religious disputes among them. The Kafancan riots in March 1987, which started when a market was relocated from a Muslim quarter to a non-Muslim quarter of the city, were interpreted as a confrontation between religions. The results of the judicial probe that followed it were perceived as discriminatory to Muslims (Loimeier 1997: 295-7 and 304-5). Moreover, in the local government elections of 12 December 1987, Christian candidates in northern

[460] For mutual Muslim-Christian perceptions, see Hock (1996).

Nigeria succeeded even in majoritarily Muslim constituencies because several Muslim candidates were competing with each other (Loimeier 1997: 305-7). Sadly, the Kafancan riots were only the first of a long sequence of bloody inter-communal conflicts in Nigeria along sectarian divides.[461] Periodical outbursts of violence between Christians and Muslims have continued until today, including the *sharīʿa* riots in 2000 or recurrent outbursts of violence in and around the city of Jos, most recently in November 2008 (Ostien 2009) and January 2010. Most crises originate from local inter-communal tensions about access to resources and, in a second step, are interpreted as religiously motivated. The Miss World riots are a notable exception to this rule.

The energetic appearance of the supporters of Muslim unity led to a revitalisation of the Muslim umbrella organisations. The emirs, who dominated JNI and the NSCIA, came under pressure to act according to their political and religious demands (Loimeier 1997: 309). Since then, the two umbrella organisations have become active advocates of Muslim unity. Whereas the NSCIA represents mainly the national perspective, JNI, with its focus on northern Nigeria, has become the Muslim counterpart of the northern branch of CAN.

Eventually, a formal reconciliation between the *ṣūfī* brotherhoods and the reform movement took place in January 1988: in a public mass rally, the major opponents of both camps agreed to end their dispute. The formula of compromise was: "No one person could claim to know everything in Islam and should therefore restrict themselves to the areas of their specialisation."[462] This was a declaration of mutual tolerance, not acceptance. The result was a coalition of convenience (Loimeier 2007: 61), which has not alleviated, let alone resolved, the dogmatic discrepancies between the currents. Competition between the Muslim currents participating in this alliance has continued. Supporters of the brotherhoods and the reform movement have used issues apparently unrelated to religion, such as football, as alternative ideological battlegrounds (Loimeier 2000b). Nevertheless, since 1988, violence between Muslim groups has diminished significantly. Some violent disputes involve currents not bound by the 1988 agreement, such as revolutionary fundamentalist groups like the Islamic Movement. An example of such clashes is the confrontation between "Shi'ites" and "Sunnis" in Sokoto in 2006-7 culminating in the assassination on 19 July 2007 of a noted "Sunni" preacher, Umaru Hamza Dan Maishayi (Last 2008: 59).

The alliance between the *ṣūfī* brotherhoods and the reform movement, superficial as it may be, allowed their followers to dominate the

[461] For an overview of religious crises in the 1980s and 1990s, see Kane (2003: 179-206).
[462] Quoted in Loimeier (1997: 308).

religious scene in northern Nigeria, in which they have tended to share important positions among themselves.[463] This *entente cordiale* was based on a mutual recognition of religious qualifications in the 1988 compromise. Already in the late 1970s, in an attempt to settle the conflict between *ṣūfīs* and reformers, the activities of Muslim preachers were regulated. Since then, preaching permits have been issued by emirs, based on certified religious qualifications (Kane 2003: 102-3). Groups which do not have officially recognised qualifications, such as students of the traditional Islamic education system (*almajirai*), which concentrates on memorising the Qur'ān and learning the Arabic script, are largely excluded from access to positions in the religious establishment. Marginalised, such groups can become vulnerable to radicalisation. This seems to have been an important factor in the emergence of the 'Yan Tatsine movement and the violent conflict between it and the Nigerian state between 1980 and 1984, which claimed thousands of lives (Kane 2003: 98-103). To all appearances, a similar constellation underlied the so-called "Boko Haram" or "Nigerian Taleban" riots in early 2004 and late July 2009, in which many hundreds were killed. Thus, the coalition of convenience of unlikely partners has, in effect, become a means of excluding Muslim currents beyond its scope.

Under the doctrine of Muslim unity and mutual tolerance, the different currents developed further. Now banned from openly combating the *ṣūfī* brotherhoods, the focus of the reform movement seems to have shifted to Islamising politics and the legal system with a view to eliminating Western influences, which are believed to be responsible for corruption, crime and all sorts of social vice. The 'Yan Izala recovered from their internal disputes in the late 1990s, when a new generation of 'Yan Izala adherents became eager supporters of the campaign for the introduction of Islamic criminal law in northern Nigeria. Particularly outspoken and active in this respect was the Ahl al-Sunna movement, which was formed by young, radical Muslims who were socialised as members of the 'Yan Izala in the 1980s. Members of the Ahl al-Sunna movement still maintain some tenets of the 'Yan Izala, such as the struggle against *bidaʿ*, yet they are careful to stress the need for Muslim unity (Loimeier 2007: 69).

An outspoken member of the Ahl al-Sunna movement is Ibrahim Datti Ahmad, president of the SCSN, which criticises JNI and the NSCIA for their passivity in the *sharīʿa* issue and their alleged proximity to the Nigerian federal government (Human Rights Watch 2003: 26n99). Born in 1962, Ahmad is a medical doctor and the imam of the Bayero Univer-

[463] For an illustration of how this cooperation has worked with regard to *sharīʿa* implementation in Kano, see O'Brien (2007).

sity of Kano (BUK) Friday mosque. In the 1980s, he was a presidential candidate (Loimeier 2007: 72n23). However, possibly more influential than Datti Ahmad—on account of his religious qualifications—was another leading representative of the Ahl al-Sunna movement in Kano, Ja'far Mahmud Adam (Loimeier 2007: 69). After memorising the Qur'ān, Ja'far Mahmud Adam, who hailed from Maiduguri (Borno), continued his studies in Saudi Arabia. He returned to Nigeria in 1996, but left again to study in the Sudan. He finally established himself in both Maiduguri and Kano, where he became the Imam of the Dorayi mosque (Loimeier 2007: 72n23). He was assassinated in his mosque on 13 April 2007. O'Brien (2007: 59n38), argues that the circumstances of the murder and Ja'far Adam's close ties with the former governor of Kano, Rabi'u Musa Kwankwaso, and his People's Democratic Party (PDP) point to a political murder. There have been rumours that this assassination was instigated by the governor of Kano State, Ibrahim Shekarau, over Ja'far Adam's criticism of the way in which the *sharīʿa* was implemented in Kano. In July 2009, as a result of their investigations, the Nigerian police exonerated the state government.[464]

Ja'far Adam combined his support for the introduction of the *sharīʿa* with a social agenda. He headed the Usman Bin Affan Islamic Association, a Muslim organisation advocating good governance, transparency and the accountability of public officers (Gwarzo 2003: 302). When in November 2000 the Kano State House of Assembly debated the draft *sharīʿa* penal code, Ja'far Adam was among scholars who—in defiance of classical Islamic legal doctrine—supported the proposition that embezzlement of public funds be associated to the *ḥadd* offence of theft (*sariqa*) and made punishable with amputation (Sada 2007: 31). The provision has been included in the *sharīʿa* penal code but, it seems, never applied (see Chapter Three, p. 99). After the introduction of the *sharīʿa*, Ja'far Adam was appointed head of the *sharīʿa* commission of Kano State (O'Brien 2007: 58). Adam was an example of a younger generation of radical scholars who are pragmatic in that they cooperate with the authorities and even other Muslim currents on specific issues but are ready to defy these authorities if their actions are at odds with their own convictions.

When Nigeria returned to civilian rule in 1999, Muslim reform groups in northern Nigeria were already advocating the introduction of the *sharīʿa*. They were not revolutionaries but radicals exerting pressure on politicians to implement Islamic law and customs as they perceived it. At least some were motivated not only by dogmatic arguments or the opposition to perceived anti-Muslim federal policies, but also by a social

[464] "Sheik Ja'afar's murder: Shekarau, Kano Emirate, Freedom Radio cleared," *Daily Trust*, 03/07/2009.

agenda including transparent and accountable government and economic empowerment. The fact that these advocates of *sharīʿa* were subscribing to the ideal of Muslim unity across ideological divides prevented the Muslim religious establishment from opposing their initiatives directly. What is more, the umbrella organisations were forced to defend the activities of such groups, at least verbally, against any criticism from the outside and, when trying to find an accommodation with the rest of the country, had to take their views into account. This constellation largely determined the Muslim establishment's reactions to outside criticism of the introduction of Islamic criminal law after 1999.

Immediately after the introduction of Islamic criminal law in some northern states, harsh sentences, in particular stoning to death for illicit sexual intercourse and amputation of the right hand for theft, started to be handed down. When such sentences were pronounced by *sharīʿa* courts, Nigeria's non Muslims, national and international human rights groups and Western countries protested strongly. International protests and expressions of concern by non-Muslims over the implementation of Islamic criminal law increased the perceived urgency of unity among Muslims. Thus, most Muslim reactions to the introduction of Islamic criminal law in northern Nigeria emphasised Muslim unity, even at the risk of aggravating the Muslim-Christian antagonism. Few Nigerian Muslim scholars publicly opposed the way in which Islamic criminal law was introduced and implemented. Many of those who did were personalities outside the Muslim religious establishment. Ibrahim al-Zakzaki, for one, held that the *sharīʿa* could be implemented in an appropriate way exclusively by a just Islamic state in an Islamic society. Otherwise, it would become a mere instrument of oppression of the masses (O'Brien 2007: 53-4). Some Muslim intellectuals, such as Sanusi Lamido Sanusi, a member of the Fulani aristocracy of Kano and prominent banker,[465] spoke out against the way in which Islamic criminal law was administered. Also some factions of the *ṣūfī* brotherhoods protested. In Kano, the introduction of the *sharīʿa* was heavily criticised by the local *ṣūfī* leaders as being "Izala *sharīʿa*" (Gwarzo 2003: 313). Like al-Zakzaki, Dahiru Bauchi argued that, inasmuch as it was politically motivated and not introduced in a proper Islamic way, the introduction of the *sharīʿa* was illegal (Loimeier 2007: 65).

By contrast, the umbrella organisations did not openly criticise the introduction of Islamic criminal law. To the contrary, in the face of na-

[465] A selection of his articles is available at <http://www.gamji.com/sanusi/sanusi.htm>. In April 2009, he was appointed governor of Nigeria's Central Bank and embarked on an unprecedented campaign of fighting corruption and mismanagement in the Nigerian banking system.

tional and international protests and after remarks by the federal government implying that the adoption of the *sharīʿa* in twelve northern states had discouraged foreign investment, JNI issued a statement in which it encouraged the *sharīʿa*-implementing states to withstand the external pressure:

> In the face of such attempts aimed at misrepresenting or blackmailing moslems, the JNI wishes to commend the twelve northern states which have adopted *Sharia*, for standing firmly by their decision. We pray that their firm stance will serve as an inspiration for all the states in the country where moslems now demand the implementation of *Sharia* as a constitutionally guaranteed right.[466]

The ambiguity of the term *sharīʿa*, which not only covers Islamic criminal law but—in a larger sense—religious practice, personal behaviour and any kind of social interaction in conformity with Islam, allows virtually all Muslim factions to identify with this statement. To the non-Muslim observer, in contrast, the phrasing appears to be a public expression of support for the implementation of harsh penalties. It suggests a homogeneous Muslim front calling for the implementation of Islamic criminal law nationwide. Verbal Muslim unity, achieved only through rhetorical means, takes precedence over interreligious compromise. Thus, the stage was set for the Miss World crisis.

There can be no doubt that the crisis was triggered by the Nigerian federal government's approach to the Miss World contest. The government's disproportionate involvement in the preparation and organisation of the contest converted it into a political event. The beauty pageant, which is far from having been unanimously supported among non-Muslims in and outside Nigeria, became the symbol of a Western lifestyle, which in the Muslim discourse of northern Nigeria often is equalled to moral decay and political corruption. This perception was the link between the Miss World contest and the introduction of the *sharīʿa*: supporters of the *sharīʿa* saw the implementation of Islamic criminal law and measures related to public morals as a way of ridding society of destructive Western influences and, consequently, interpreted the selection of Nigeria as the location for the 2002 Miss World contest as a deliberate choice to thwart the project of returning northern Nigeria to its former Muslim glory. Subsequent events such as the bestowing of the honorary citizenship of Rome to Safiyya Hussaini only confirmed this perception. Isioma Daniel's article in *This Day* was considered to be part of an orchestrated media campaign aimed at humiliating Muslims. It is not surprising, thus, that many Muslim commentators portrayed

---

[466] "*Ja'amatu* [sic] Islam condemns *Sharia*'s critics," *The Comet*, 09/09/2002, 40.

the Miss World riots in Kaduna and Abuja as a reaction to continued provocation and blamed the federal government for not taking decisive steps in defence of Muslims (Weimann forthcoming).

It was probably the pressure from Muslim groups that triggered Shinkafi's polemical remarks about Isioma Daniels, which came to be known as a "fatwa." Immediately, the Muslim establishment attempted to appease the situation by declaring that the Zamfara State government had no right to issue *fatwās*. In the beginning, it seemed that the two umbrella organisations were successful in showing leadership in religious matters: they seemed to prevail over populist politics and to have found an interpretation that solved the crisis and was adapted to the secular political dispensation and multi-religious character of the Nigerian state.

However, their efforts were thwarted when dissenting currents from within questioned the organisations' prerogative of interpretation of the religion. In conformity with the claim of being the voice of Islam in Nigeria, the Muslim establishment had to embrace the critics. By recognising the validity of Shinkafi's "fatwa," the umbrella organisations renounced the claim to be the only instances competent of issuing *fatwās* of national importance. Paradoxically, in order to retain authority and safeguard the unity of Muslims, the Muslim religious establishment had to acquiesce in the demands of radical factions among its constituencies which challenged this very authority.

To avoid the execution of the "fatwa," the Muslim religious establishment had to find a formula of compromise which affirmed its contents but made its implementation impossible in the present situation. Tasking the Nigerian state to appoint a committee to carry out such a verdict was a rhetorical means by which JNI tried to prevent the murder of Isioma Daniel. The execution of the "fatwa" would only be possible under an Islamic state, not under the Nigerian Constitution. Probably the most important goal for JNI in choosing this formula was to appease the lingering conflicts in the Muslim camp. At the same time, however, while accommodating the greatest number of Muslim factions, this wording had to be understood as a provocation by non-Muslims, in particular in light of earlier, more conciliatory statements. In the last resort, the Nigerian Muslim religious establishment, organised in JNI and the NSCIA, assesses the unity of Muslims to be of a higher priority than safeguarding peaceful relations with non-Muslims in Nigeria.

## Conclusion

The Miss World controversy and the "fatwa" against Isioma Daniel illustrate some of the long-term effects which the perceived confrontation with non-Muslims in the country has had on the development of Islam in northern Nigeria.

The umbrella organisations' self-declared mission is to establish a national consensus and serve as the single point of contact for all matters pertaining to Islam in Nigeria. This united Muslim voice is to compensate, on the national level, the loss of the political unity of northern Nigerian Muslims through the dissolution of the Northern Region in 1966. In this regard, JNI and the NSCIA are political organisations, representing groups that are willing to cooperate with the Nigerian state. But the Muslim religious establishment in Nigeria is faced with a dilemma. Most of its members are in favour of peaceful relations with the Nigerian state and their non-Muslim fellow countrymen. However, the umbrella organisations cannot lead their constituencies through direct guidance, for example by issuing binding *fatwās*. Rather, their leadership is restricted to mediating between the competing currents and factions which they claim to represent.

As a result of its position, the Muslim religious establishment has been unable to counter the appropriation of the religious discourse by populist politicians and radical preachers. To the contrary, for fear of antagonising parts of their constituencies in public statements, the organisations have tended to support, at least verbally, positions that satisfy the radical factions, while the subtleties of the formulations have been difficult to detect for outside observers. This has been obvious in the public discussions on *sharīʿa* implementation in northern Nigeria after 1999. Members of the Muslim religious establishment in northern Nigeria, who disagreed with the manner in which Islamic criminal law was introduced and initially implemented in northern Nigeria, were reluctant to voice their criticism in public. The result was that non-Muslims in Nigeria and abroad frequently had the impression of a united Muslim front aiming at an Islamisation of the Nigerian state.

In effect, the agreement on mutual tolerance, conceived as a means to achieve Muslim unity in the face of an alleged Christian threat, has made it impossible for religious leaders to contain more radical Muslim voices aiming at, or willingly accepting, further deterioration of interreligious relations. In a way, the principle of leadership through safeguarding Muslim unity, symbolised by the umbrella organisations' claim to be the only bodies competent to issue *fatwās* of national importance, has turned into a beast. The Muslim religious leadership must tell their followers what they want to hear, trying not to offend any of its constituencies by choosing vague, ambiguous terms. Populist politicians and radical Muslim groups can influence, if not the agenda, then at least the rhetoric of the mainstream. The effect has been a general radicalisation of the public discourse, which makes it increasingly difficult to mediate between the opposing sides.

# Conclusion

The studies contained in this volume aim at analysing judicial practice in Islamic criminal law in northern Nigeria after 1999 in the region's historical, cultural, political and religious context. Some general conclusions may be drawn.

The information collected indicates that Islamic criminal law has not been enforced everywhere to the same extent. In the north-western states that constitute the core of the former Sokoto Caliphate, Islamic criminal law was applied with much greater emphasis than in the north-eastern states, where the legislation mainly remained a dead letter. In religiously mixed states, the bid to introduce the *sharīʿa* became part of religious groups' competition for hegemony and access to public resources, which often enough led to violent conflict.

Politically, the implementation of Islamic criminal law has been controversial even among Muslims. Many state governors introduced Islamic criminal law reluctantly and without conviction. They were caught between popular demands for the introduction of the *sharīʿa* and the exigencies of their office, established by the secular Nigerian Constitution. Unable to find a sustainable solution to this problem, they have opted for delaying tactics. Severe punishments, such as death penalties, amputation or retaliation, cannot be executed without prior confirmation of the state governor. In most cases, the governors have simply refused to assent to controversial sentences such as amputations, thereby preventing their execution.

By contrast, Muslim reform groups supported the introduction of Islamic criminal law because they saw it as an opportunity to impose *sharīʿa*-compliant behaviour on Muslims. These groups have put particular emphasis on illicit sexual relations (*zinā*) with a view to eradicate certain forms of extramarital sexuality that in spite of the long history of Islam in northern Nigeria have continued to be socially accepted. This strategy can be considered to have largely failed. Judicial practice has confirmed the privacy of the family compound and traditional conflict resolution through mediation. Thus, infractions of Islamic criminal law as regards sexuality, to the extent that the parties involved reach a settlement, are effectively withdrawn from the control of the courts.

This mitigating role of judicial practice can be attributed to a substantial part to resistance from influential Muslim scholars. In light of the existing tensions between Muslims and Christians in the country, they could not criticise the introduction of Islamic criminal law directly, as this would have exposed them to the accusation of going against the interests of Muslims. In the face of an alleged Christian threat, they had to emphasise Muslim unity in order to retain their authority. As a result, whereas publicly the Muslim religious establishment supported the introduction of the *sharīʿa*, their attitude was nothing but the attempt to prevent intra-Muslim dissent at all costs, even at the price of a further aggravation of the Muslim-Christian antagonism. Instead of public criticism, Muslim scholars exerted their influence on the Islamic judiciary and formulated alternative visions of *sharīʿa* implementation emphasising education of Muslims and an Islamisation of northern Nigerian society while relegating the enforcement of Islamic criminal law to the almost utopian state of an ideal Muslim community.

The expectations which many Muslims attached to the introduction of the *sharīʿa* were inflated. Quickly, it became clear that the impact of Islamic criminal law on the living conditions of the population would remain minimal. Nowadays, Nigerian Muslims continue to support a greater role of the *sharīʿa* as a comprehensive code of conduct in northern Nigerian public life but seem largely to reject the misuse of religion by politicians.

# Appendix: Identified trials under Islamic criminal law

In this overview, the states in which the trials took place are abbreviated as follows: *Bau.* Bauchi; *Jig.* Jigawa; *Kad.* Kaduna; *Kan.* Kano; *Kat.* Katsina; *Keb.* Kebbi; *Nig.* Niger; *Sok.* Sokoto; *Zam.* Zamfara. Articles for which no page numbers are specified were accessed through the Internet. Names are spelt as mentioned in the articles or in the way most frequently encountered. Unless specified otherwise, flogging sentences can be assumed to have been carried out immediately after the trial.

## *Rape*

1. Abubakar Aliyu (*Sok.*), sentenced in July 2001 to 100 strokes of the cane and one year's imprisonment after being caught having sexual intercourse with a mentally deranged woman.
   - "Man Sentenced for Committing Adultery with Lunatic," *This Day*, 14/07/2001.

2. Ado Baranda or Sarimu Muhammad (*Jig.*), sentenced in May 2002 to death by stoning for raping a four-year-old girl, acquitted in August 2003 on grounds of insanity.
   - "Sharia: Man to Die for Raping 9-year Girl," *This Day*, 10/05/2002.
   - "Sharia: Male convict to die by stoning," *Daily Champion*, 27/08/2002, 1-2.
   - "All Set for Sarimu's Public Stoning in Jigawa," *This Day*, 02/09/2002.
   - "Sharia: Stoning Verdict on Alleged Rapist Quashed," *This Day*, 20/08/2003, 4.

3. Dalha Danbako, Ibrahim White, Nura Garba, Sha'aibu Muhammed and Sule Jubril (*Jig.*), sentenced in September 2002 to five months in prison and fine for sexually assaulting an eleven-year-old girl.
   - "For rape, sharia court passes death, fines others," *The Guardian* (Nigeria), 03/09/2002, 7.

4. Aminu Ruwa (*Nig.*), sentenced in November 2002 to 100 lashes and paying the medical bill of the victim for raping a six-year-old girl.
   - "Man gets 100 strokes for indecency," *The Guardian* (Nigeria), 20/11/2002, 16; also published in *The Comet*, 20/11/2002, 6.

5. Ibrahim Ayuba and Mohammed Ibrahim (*Kat.*), apparently indicted summarily in January 2003 for raping a 4 and 3.5-year-old girl, respectively.
   - "Two Charged with Raping Minors," *This Day*, 27/01/2003.

6. Hamisu Suleiman (*Kan.*), sentenced in August 2003 to eighteen months in prison and a 15,000 Naira fine for rape.
   - "Rape suspect bags 18 months jail term," *Daily Trust*, 21/08/2003, 23.

7. Tukur Aliyu (*Zam.*), sentenced in October 2003 to 40 strokes of the cane and fine for raping a four-year-old girl who was his pupil.
   - "Man, 45, gets 40 lashes for raping four-year-old girl," *Daily Independent*, 20/10/2003.

8. Adamu Jugga (*Bau.*), charged with rape in October 2003.
   - "Alleged rape victim, 35, offers to swear by Qur'an," *Weekly Trust*, 04-10/10/2003, 17.

9. Selah Dabo (*Bau.*), sentenced in September 2004 to death by stoning for rape.
   - "Sharia: Legal Aid Council to appeal against 30 convictions," *Vanguard*, 17/11/2004.
   - Amnesty International Annual Report 2005.

10. Ade Debo (*Bau.*), sentenced in May 2007 to death by stoning for raping two teenage girls. His accomplice Shagari Abubakar received six months in prison.
   - "Sharia stoning for Nigerian man," BBC News, 17/05/2007.
   - "Sharia court sentences man to death by stoning," *The Guardian* (Nigeria), 18/05/2007.

## *Sodomy*

1. Attahiru Umar (*Keb.*), sentenced in September 2001 to death by stoning for sexual abuse of a seven-year-old boy.
   - "Sharia Court Sentences Man to Death by Stoning," *This Day*, 14/09/2001.
   - "Nigerian sentenced to stoning," *BBC News*, 14/09/2001.
   - "Obasanjo visits Zamfara, cautions on *Sharia*," *The Guardian* (Nigeria), 14/09/2001, print edition.

2. Abdullahi Barkeji (*Zam.*), sentenced in February 2002 to 100 strokes of the cane and one year's imprisonment for sodomy.
   - "Man Gets 100 Strokes, One-Year Jail for Sodomy," *This Day*, 28/02/2002, 5.

3. Jibrin Babaji (*Bau.*), sentenced in September 2003 to death by stoning for intercourse with three boys aged 10 and 13, acquitted in March 2004 on grounds of insanity.
   - "*Sodomy*: *Sharia* court sentences man to death by stoning," *Daily Trust*, 25/09/2003.
   - "*Sodomy*: Convict appeals against death sentence," *Daily Trust*, 24/10/2003.
   - "*Sodomy*: Convict alleges unfair trial," *Daily Trust*, 18/12/2003.
   - "Lawyer seeks retrial of sodomy case," *Daily Trust*, 02/01/2004.
   - "*Sodomy*: Judge to pay N3000 for wrongful conviction," *Daily Trust*, 23/03/2004, 5.
   - "Wrongful conviction: Lower Sharia court judge ordered to apologise," *New Nigerian Newspaper*, 24/03/2004, 21.
   - "Sodomy: Sharia appeal court rules against conviction of Babaji," *Vanguard*, 25/03/2004, 11.

## *Incest*

1. Umaru Tori (*Bau.*), sentenced in December 2003 to death by stoning for incest with his step-daughter, acquitted on appeal in May 2005. Fifteen-year-old Altine Tori was sentenced to 100 strokes of the cane to be administered after the delivery of her baby. She appealed the verdict.
   - "Incest: Sharia Court sentences man to death by stoning," *Daily Trust*, 06/01/2004, 1-2.
   - "Sharia: Man to die by stoning for impregnating step-daughter in Bauchi," *The Guardian* (Nigeria), 06/01/2004.
   - "Nigerian man faces stoning death," BBC News, 06/01/2004.
   - "NIGERIA: Man sentenced to stoning for sex with step-daughter," IRIN, 06/01/2004.
   - "MAN, 45, SENTENCED TO DEATH BY STONING," *New Nigerian Newspaper*, 07/01/2004, 28.
   - "Sharia Court rules on convicted teenager Dec. 7," *Daily Independent*, 19/11/2004.
   - "Shariah Court Entertains 11-Month-Old Appeal," *Weekly Trust*, 30/11/2004.
   - Amnesty International Annual Report 2006.

2. Umar Isa Zurena (*Jig.*), charged in November 2003 with incest for allegedly impregnating his niece.
   - "Man, 20, in court for impregnating niece," *Weekly Trust*, 22/11/2003.

## *Consensual unlawful sexual intercourse* (zinā)

1. Zuweira Aliyu and Sani Mamman (*Zam.*), sentenced in February 2000 to 100 lashes, in addition to one year's imprisonment for Mamman, for premarital relations.
   - "Nigerian flogged for having sex," BBC News, 17/02/2000.
   - "Sharia: Fornicator gets 100 lashes," *The Comet*, 18/02/2000, print edition.

2. Bariya Ibrahim Maguza (*Zam.*), sentenced in September 2000 to 180 strokes of the cane—later reduced to 100—after being found pregnant out of wedlock, publicly flogged in January 2001.
   - "Sharia sentence for pregnant teenager," BBC News, 14/09/2000.
   - "Nigerian girl gives birth and faces 180 lashes," AFP, 29/12/2000.
   - "180 lashes for Nigerian teen mum to go ahead: governor," AFP, 03/01/2001.
   - "NIGERIA: Caning for premarital sex to go on," IRIN, 05/01/2001.
   - "NIGERIA: Flogging sentence reduced, deferred," IRIN, 11/01/2001.
   - "Nigerian girl's lashing sentence cut," BBC News, 13/01/2001.
   - "Islamic court postpones flogging of child-mother, cuts sentence," AFP, 13/01/2001.
   - "Nigerian child-mother accepts 'guilt', as sentence eased," AFP, 14/01/2001.
   - "Nigerian single mother flogged," BBC News, 22/01/2001.
   - "NIGERIA: Teenage girl lashed for premarital sex," IRIN, 22/01/2001.
   - "In Nigeria, teenage mother receives 100 lashes," AFP, 22/01/2001.
   - "Sharia: Single Mum Flogged in Zamfara," *This Day*, 23/01/2001.

- "Sharia: Teenage mother gets 100 lashes in Zamfara," *The Comet*, 24/01/2001, 1 and 7.
- BAOBAB (2003: 10).

3. Attine Tanko and Lawal Sada (*Kat.*), sentenced in November 2000 to 100 lashes, in addition to one year's imprisonment for Sada, for premarital relations.
   - "Second teen mum in Nigeria awaits flogging for pre-marital sex," AFP, 11/01/2001.
   - "Another girl faces flogging for sex," IRIN, 12/01/2001.

4. Hajo Poki (*Bau.*), sentenced in 2001 to 100 strokes of the cane, flogged while still pregnant.
   - "Sharia court orders amputation of hands, legs in Sokoto," *The Guardian* (Nigeria), 20/12/2001, print edition.
   - "Niger sharia court sentences two to death by stoning," *The Guardian* (Nigeria), 29/08/2002, 1-2.

5. Aisha Musa (*Sok.*), sentenced in 2001 to 100 strokes of cane and one year's imprisonment on the basis of pregnancy out of wedlock, released on bail.
   - BAOBAB (2003: 12).

6. Hawa'u Garba and Hussaini Mamman (*Sok.*), charged in June 2001 after Hawa'u gave birth to a child out of wedlock in May 2001.
   - "Nigerian couple arraigned in Islamic court on adultery charge," AFP, 18/06/2001.

7. Amina Abdullahi (*Zam.*), sentenced in August 2001 to 100 lashes for premarital sex.
   - "Nigerian woman sentenced to 100 lashes," BBC News, 13/08/2001.

8. Safiyya Yakubu Hussaini (*Sok.*), sentenced in October 2001 to death by stoning, acquitted on appeal in March 2002. Selected sources:
   - "Nigerian appeals Sharia sentence," BBC News, 19/10/2001.
   - "My judgement is fair—Sharia judge," *Weekly Trust*, 02/11/2001.
   - "Sokoto adulteress appeals against death sentence," *Daily Trust*, 05/11/2001.
   - "The travails of convict Safiyatu," *The Comet*, 24/11/2001, 8-9.
   - "Sokoto Sharia court of appeal suspends stonning [sic] sentence," *Sunday Triumph*, 25/11/2001.
   - "Safiya Gets Reprieve at Appeal Court," *This Day*, 30/11/2001, print edition.
   - "Living on Nigeria's death row," BBC News, 05/12/2001.
   - "Give me justice, says Nigerian woman facing death by stoning," AFP, 13/01/2002.
   - "NIGERIA: Lawyers team up against the death penalty," IRIN, 15/01/2002.
   - "*Shari'a* court resumes hearing on Safiya's appeal," *New Nigerian Newspaper*, 20/01/2002, print version.
   - "NIGERIA: Islamic court frees woman from death by stoning," IRIN, 25/03/2002.
   - "Sharia court frees Nigerian woman," BBC News, 25/03/2002.
   - "Court saves Safiyat from death by stoning," *The Guardian* (Nigeria), 26/03/2002, 1 and 2.

- "Sharia Appeal Court Frees Safiya," *This Day*, 26/03/2002.
- Peters (2006); Ostien (2007: 5:17-51); Yawuri (2004, 2007).

9. Hafsatu Abubakar (*Sok.*), indicted in January 2002 for extramarital relations on the grounds of childbirth out of wedlock, acquitted in January 2002. Selected sources:
   - "Another Woman Faces Trial for Adultery in Sokoto," *This Day*, 07/01/2002.
   - "Second woman could face stoning in Nigeria," AFP, 07/01/2002.
   - "Mother of 2-week Baby on Capital Offence Charge," *This Day*, 11/01/2002.
   - "Nigerian Islamic court frees woman on sex-related charges," AFP, 23/01/2002.
   - "NIGERIA: Sharia court frees woman charged with adultery," IRIN, 24/01/2002.
   - "Sharia Court Acquits Hafsatu of Adultery," *This Day*, 24/01/2002.
   - "Sharia court acquits Hafsatu of adultery," *The Comet*, 24/01/2002, 1 and 2.

10. Amina Lawal (*Kat.*), sentenced in March 2002 to death by stoning, acquitted on appeal in September 2003. Selected sources:
    - "Nigerian woman who faced stoning to death is acquitted," AFP, 25/03/2002.
    - "Sharia court frees Nigerian woman," BBC News, 25/03/2002.
    - "... As another woman gets stoning sentence in Katsina," *The Triumph*, 26/03/2002.
    - "I was not given fair hearing—*Katsina adulteress*," *Daily Trust*, 27/03/2002, 1-2.
    - "Nigeria's stoning appeal fails," BBC News, 19/08/2002.
    - "NIGERIA: Islamic court upholds death-by-stoning sentence," IRIN, 19/08/2002.
    - "Sharia: Woman to Die by Stoning," *This Day*, 20/08/2002, 1 and 6.
    - "Katsina Sharia Court affirms death by stoning on nursing mother," *The Guardian* (Nigeria), 20/08/2002, 1-2.
    - "*Amina Lawal: Sharia* court begins hearing of appeal," *Daily Trust*, 29/08/2003.
    - "Sharia court quashes sentence, frees Amina Lawal," *The Guardian* (Nigeria), 26/09/2003.
    - "Sharia Court frees Amina Lawal," *Daily Trust*, 26/09/2003.
    - "Adultery: Sharia Appeal Court frees Amina," *New Nigerian Newspaper*, 26/09/2003, 1-2.
    - "Amina Lawal: Court Quashes Death Sentence," *This Day*, 26/09/2003.
    - "Appeal Court quashes death verdict on Amina Lawal," *Vanguard*, 26/09/2003.
    - Yawuri (2004, 2007); Ostien (2007: 5:52-107).

11. Adama Yunusa (*Bau.*), sentenced in 2002 to 100 strokes of the cane and banishment. Banishment lifted on appeal in May 2002.
    - "Sharia: Woman Gets 100 Strokes over Pregnancy," *This Day*, 06/05/2002.

12. Yunusa Chiyawa (*Bau.*), sentenced in June 2002 to death by stoning, acquitted on appeal in November 2003.
    - "Nigerian man faces death for adultery," BBC News, 27/06/2002.
    - "NIGERIA: Sharia court sentences man to death for adultery," IRIN, 01/07/2002.
    - HRW (2004: 32).

13. Fatima Usman and Ahmadu Ibrahim (*Nig.*), sentenced in August 2002 to death by stoning. Appeal filed; released on bail. Selected sources:
    - "Sharia: In Minna, Man, Lover to Die by Stoning," *This Day*, 29/08/2002.
    - "Niger sharia court sentences two to death by stoning," *The Guardian* (Nigeria), 29/08/2002, 1-2.

- "Nigeria's stoning couple freed," BBC News, 22/10/2002.
- "Two appeal against stoning to death in Minna," *Daily Trust*, 06/06/2003.
- HRW (2004: 25); Ibrahim and Lyman (2004: 20); Ostien and Dekker (2010: 604).

14. Maryam Abubakar Bodinga (*Sok.*), indicted in September 2002 for extramarital relations, acquitted in October 2002.
    - BAOBAB (2003: 13).

15. Zuwayra Shinkafi (*Zam.*), sentenced in March 2003 to thirty lashes, and Sani Yahaya, sentenced to eighty lashes and ten months' imprisonment for premarital relations (possibly identical with the case of March 2000).
    - HRW (2004: 62).

16. Hafsatu Idris and Ahmadu Haruna (*Kan.*), charged in March 2004 with consensual illicit relations. Idris alleged rape.
    - "Rape victim's father accuses police of changing FIR," *Daily Trust*, 24/03/2004, 29.

17. Daso Adamu (*Bau.*), sentenced in September 2004 to death by stoning, acquitted on appeal in December 2004.
    - "Sharia court grants convict bail," *Daily Trust*, 25/10/2004.
    - "Sharia Court Nullifies Death Penalty On Woman," *Vanguard*, 11/12/2004.

18. Hajara Ibrahim (*Bau.*), sentenced in October 2004 to death by stoning, acquitted on appeal in November 2004. Selected sources:
    - "Sharia court sentences woman to death by stoning," *Daily Trust*, 13/10/2004.
    - "Sharia : Woman to Die for Adultery," *This Day*, 13/10/2004.
    - "Sharia court sentences another woman to death over pregnancy," *Vanguard*, 13/10/2004.
    - "Sharia: Another woman faces death by stoning in Bauchi," *Daily Independent*, 13/10/2004.
    - "Hajara Ibrahim's family appeals against death sentence," *Vanguard*, 20/10/2004.
    - "Upper Sharia Court to rule in Hajara's appeal November 10," *Vanguard*, 28/10/2004.
    - "Nigeria court overturns stoning," BBC News, 10/11/2004.
    - "Islamic court overturns stoning sentence," *Independent Online* (South Africa), 10/11/2004.

## *Unfounded accusation of* zinā (qadhf)

1. An unidentified member of the State House of Assembly (*Zam.*), convicted in June 2000 of accusing his wife of adultery and sentenced to 80 lashes.
    - "Sharia flogging after adultery charge," BBC News, 04/07/2000.

2. Aishat and Haruna Dutsi (*Zam.*), sentenced in September 2000 to 80 lashes for accusing a village leader of having sexual relations with their daughter.
    - Amnesty International Annual Report 2000.

3. Gado Maradun (*Zam.*), sentenced in 2000 to 80 lashes for defaming a woman as a prostitute.
   - "Zamfara amputation: Raising the stakes of *Sharia* implementation," *The Guardian* (Nigeria), 29/03/2000, 8.

4. Ibrahim Na-Wurno (*Zam.*), sentenced in April 2001 to 80 lashes after he was unable to prove his allegation that his neighbour had committed sodomy.
   - "*Sharia*: Man earns 80 strokes of cane for false accusation," *Vanguard*, 19/04/2001, 10.

5. Hafsi Bakura, chairperson of the ANPP governing party in *Zam.* State, reported to court in January 2004 for having accused the ANPP chairperson in Gusau Local Government Area of extramarital relations. Unclear whether the tribunal admitted the complaint for trial.
   - "ANPP chieftains in Sharia court for alleged adultery," *Daily Independent*, 05/01/2004.

6. Halima Abdulkarim (*Kad.*), accused in May 2002 by her husband of committing *qadhf*.
   - "Woman Docked for Accusing Husband of Having an Affair with his Mother," *This Day*, 24/05/2002.

## *Homicide and bodily harm*

1. Dantanim Tsafe (*Zam.*), sentenced in February 2000 to paying "fine" or retaliation for knocking out his wife's front teeth. *Diya*: 157,933.70 Naira, later reduced to 50,000 Naira.
   - "*Sharia*: Farmer fined N158,000 for beating wife," *The Comet*, 15/02/2000, print edition.
   - "Zamfara amputation: Raising the stakes of Sharia implementation," *The Guardian* (Nigeria), 29/02/2000, 8.

2. Ahmadu Tijjani (*Kat.*), sentenced in May 2001 to retaliation or paying *diya* for blinding the plaintiff on the right side. *Diya*: 50 camels or 1.5 million Naira.
   - "In Katsina, it's an eye for an eye," *The Guardian* (Nigeria), 26/05/2001, 1-2.
   - "Plaintiff asks Nigerian Islamic court to pluck out a man's eye," AFP, 26/05/2001.
   - "Nigerian court orders 'eye-for-an-eye' ... literally," AFP, 06/06/2001.

3. Ado Bako (*Kan.*), sentenced in September 2001 to paying *diya* or six years' imprisonment for causing permanent damage to one of the plaintiff's eyes. *Diya*: 2,070,000 Naira. In April 2008, the Kano State government paid a compensation of 500,000 Naira to the plaintiff.
   - "Kano Govt Compensates Man for Losing Eye," *Leadership*, 11/04/2008.

4. Sani Yakubu Rodi (*Kat.*), sentenced in November 2001 to death by retaliation for stabbing to death a woman and her two children, hanged on 3 January 2002. Selected sources:
   - "*Sharia* court sentences man to death by knifing," *The Guardian* (Nigeria), 15/11/2001, print edition.
   - "Family will not appeal death sentence against Nigerian man," AFP, 22/11/2001.
   - "Sharia: Man to Be Hanged for Murder," *This Day*, 27/12/2001.
   - "Sharia: Katsina executes murder convict," *Vanguard*, 04/01/2002.
   - "Man Hanged for Murder," *This Day*, 04/01/2002.
   - "Katsina Executes First Shari'a Court Murder Convict," *This Day*, 04/01/2002.
   - "First Nigerian executed under Sharia laws," BBC News, 04/01/2002.
   - "Controversy over Sani Rodi's hanging," *New Nigerian Newspaper*, 16/01/2002, 14.
   - HRW (2004: 32).

5. Adamu Musa Hussaini Maidoya (*Bau.*), sentenced in January 2003 to amputation of the right leg for severing his wife's. Sentence upheld on appeal in August 2006. Selected sources:
   - "The Justice She Wants," *Newswatch*, 18/11/2002, 48-9.
   - "Man loses limb for amputating wife's leg," *New Nigerian Newspaper*, 06/01/2003, 30.
   - "Sharia Court of Appeal affirms first amputation in Bauchi," *Daily Trust*, 21/08/2006.

6. Sabo Sarki (*Bau.*), sentenced in March 2004 to paying *diya* for forcefully removing the plaintiff's eyes. Two accomplices were not convicted. *Diya*: 1000 dinar, 12000 dirham, 180 camels, 2000 cows, 2000 goats or sheep or 5.5 million Naira.
   - "Shariah court convicts man over ritual," *Daily Trust*, 30/03/2004, 5.
   - "Boy turns down N6m compensation for eyes," *Daily Trust*, 13/05/2004.

7. Luba Mainasara (*Zam.*), sentenced in April 2004 to 20 strokes of the cane and a 3,000 Naira fine for beating a fellow wife with a pestle, in addition to paying 50,000 Naira compensation to the fellow wife.
   - "Sharia Court Orders Housewife to Pay Mate N50,000," *Daily Trust*, 03/04/2002, print edition.

8. Isa Bello, Jamilu Nasiru and Yawale Muhammadu (*Sok.*), sentenced in 2007 to paying *diya* for forcefully removing the plaintiff's eyes. *Diya*: 11,160,000 Naira.
   - "Group Seeks Justice for Boy, 7," *This Day*, 16/05/2008.

## *Theft* (sariqa)

1. Buba Bello Jangebe (*Zam.*), sentenced in February 2000 to amputation of the right hand for stealing a cow. Amputation carried out on 22 March 2000. Selected sources:
   - "Nigerian Sharia court orders amputation," BBC News, 23/03/2000.
   - "Zamfara amputates man over theft," *The Guardian* (Nigeria), 24/03/2000, 1-2.

- "Zamfara amputes bicycle thief," *Punch*, 05/05/2001, 1-3.
- "Eyewitness: Nigeria's Sharia amputees," BBC News, 19/12/2002.
- HRW (2004: 37-9).

2. Nasiru Abba (*Kat.*), arraigned in August 2000 for stealing a radio worth 1,000 Naira.
   - "Man risks amputation in Katsina over alleged theft," *The Guardian* (Nigeria), 02/08/2000, print edition.

3. Kabiru Salisu (*Zam.*), sentenced in September 2000 to six months' imprisonment and 50 strokes of the cane for stealing a shirt worth 400 Naira.
   - "Two men flogged publicly in Nigeria for drinking, stealing," AFP, 25/09/2000.

4. Musa Gummi (*Zam.*), sentenced in September 2000 to amputation of "a limb" for stealing three bicycles.
   - "Nigerian man to lose leg for bicycle theft," AFP, 23/09/2000.

5. Lawali Isah (*Zam.*), nicknamed "Inchi Tara" (nine inches), sentenced in December 2000 to amputation of the hand for stealing three bicycles worth 9,500 Naira. Amputation carried out on 3 May 2001. Selected sources:
   - "Nigerian Islamic state amputates man's hand for stealing," AFP, 05/05/2001.
   - "Sharia: Man Loses Hand for Stealing Three Bicycles," *This Day*, 05/05/2001.
   - "Zamfara cuts another hand," *The Guardian* (Nigeria), 05/05/2001, 2.
   - "Zamfara amputes bicycle thief," *Punch*, 05/05/2001, 1-3.
   - "Eyewitness: Nigeria's Sharia amputees," BBC News, 19/12/2002.
   - HRW (2004: 37-9).

6. Adamu (*Kan.*), arraigned in 2000 or 2001 for stealing a cow.
   - "Sharia: Cow Thief to Get Judgement in Katsina," *This Day*, 08/01/2001.

7. Suleman Abdullahi and Isiyaku Sanni (*Kat.*), sentenced in January 2001 to amputation of the hand for stealing nine donkeys.
   - "NIGERIA: Two men face amputation for stealing," IRIN, 13/02/2001.

8. Dadin Duniya (*Zam.*), sentenced in April 2001 to amputation of the hand.
   - HRW (2004: 40).

9. Lawali Bello and Sani Mohammed (*Sok.*), sentenced in April 2001 to forty strokes of the cane and three months' imprisonment for stealing two goats and their kids worth 2,600 Naira.
   - "Two Kids Share 40 Lashes for Goat Theft," *This Day*, 25/04/2001.

10. Umaru Aliyu (*Sok.*), sentenced in April 2001 to amputation of the hand for stealing a sheep worth 3,000 Naira. Amputation carried out on 5 July 2001. Selected sources:
    - "Sharia: Man to Lose Hand for Stealing Sheep," *This Day*, 14/04/2001, 3.
    - "Sharia: Sokoto to Amputate Convict's Wrist," *This Day*, 06/07/2001, 5.
    - "Hand amputation in Nigeria," BBC News, 07/07/2001.

- "Nigerian state amputates man's hand for theft," AFP, 07/07/2001.
- "Amputee Gets N50,000 Govt Gift," *This Day*, 31/07/2001.
- "Nigerian state compensates Sharia criminal," BBC News, 01/08/2001.
- Peters (2003: 22).

11. Altine Mohammed (*Keb.*), sentenced in July 2001 to amputation of the hand.
    - HRW (2004: 20 and 46).

12. Lawali Garba (*Sok.*), sentenced in July 2001 to amputation of the hand for stealing car spare parts worth 17,000 Naira.
    - "Sharia Claims Another Victim in Sokoto," *This Day*, 13/07/2001.
    - "Nigerian state sentences spare parts thief to lose hand," AFP, 13/07/2001.

13. Danladi Dahiru (*Kan.*), sentenced in August 2001 to amputation of the hand for stealing several sewing machines worth up to 23,000 Naira.
    - "Two to be Amputated in Kano," *This Day*, 11/04/2002, print edition.
    - HRW (2004: 49 and 54).

14. Abubakar Aliyu (*Keb.*), sentenced in September 2001 to amputation of the hand for stealing 32,000 Naira cash. Sentence converted on appeal into flogging and one year in a children's remand home. Accomplices Kabiru Tukur and Umaru Shehu were sentenced to 50 lashes and 18 months in prison.
    - "Sharia court orders amputation of 15-year-old boy," *The Guardian* (Nigeria), 15/07/2001, last page.
    - "NIGERIA: Sharia Court orders amputation of 15-year-old," IRIN, 25/07/2001.
    - HRW (2004: 57).

15. Abubakar Mohammed (*Keb.*), sentenced in September 2001 to amputation of the hand for stealing a television and a video recorder.
    - HRW (2004: 48).

16. Musa Shu'aibu (*Zam.*), sentenced in September 2001 to amputation of the hand for stealing a ram worth 7,000 Naira.
    - "Sharia: Man's Wrist for Amputation over Ram Theft," *This Day*, 19/09/2001, print edition.

17. Aminu Bello (*Sok.*), sentenced in December 2001 to amputation of the hand for stealing property worth 65,000 Naira from a Christian woman. Appeal filed. His accomplice, Salisu Abdullahi, received 50 strokes of the cane and 3 years in prison.
    - "Another thief sentenced to hand amputation in Nigeria," AFP, 27/12/2001.
    - BAOBAB (2003: 17-8).

18. Mohammed Ali (*Sok.*), sentenced in December 2001 to 30 lashes and nine months' imprisonment for stealing kitchen goods worth "less than $8, or the price of a goat."
    - "Nigerian 'Christian' in Sharia court," BBC News, 11/12/2001.
    - "Hands-on sentence in Nigeria," BBC News, 13/12/2001.

- "Sharia court orders amputation of hands, legs in Sokoto," *The Guardian* (Nigeria), 20/12/2001, print edition.

19. Yahaya Kakale (*Keb.*), sentenced in December 2001 to amputation of the hand for stealing a video player, a television, a radio and CD player. Sentence confirmed on appeal. Second appeal filed at Federal Court of Justice.
    - HRW (2004: 42-44).
    - "Languishing in a Sharia jail," BBC News, 21/09/2004 (largely quoting the above).

20. Bawa Magaji and Altine Hassan (*Sok.*), sentenced in 2002 to amputation of the hand for shop breaking. Appeal filed.
    - BAOBAB (2003: 18-9).

21. Bello Garba (*Sok.*), sentenced in January 2002 to amputation of the hand for stealing a donkey worth 2,500 Naira. Appeal filed.
    - "Sharia: Man to lose hand for stealing donkey," *The Comet*, 24/01/2002, print edition.
    - BAOBAB (2003: 20).

22. Haruna Musa, Aminu Ahmed, and Ali Liman (*Kan.*), sentenced in January and February 2002 to amputation of the hand. Released on bail in May and June 2003.
    - HRW (2004: 40).

23. Lawal Garba and Bashir Alkali (*Sok.*), sentenced in 2002 to amputation of the hand. Acquitted on appeal in March 2002.
    - BAOBAB (2003: 17).

24. Malam Aliyu (*Sok.*), sentenced in 2002 to amputation of the hand.
    - BAOBAB (2003: 20).

25. Mohammed Bala and Abubakar Mohammed (*Kan.*), sentenced in January 2002 to amputation of the hand. Mohammed Bala's case ordered to be retried on appeal in December 2002. Bala released on bail in October 2003.
    - HRW (2004: 55-6).

26. Mohammed Sulaiman (*Sok.*), sentenced in 2002 to amputation of the hand for stealing a used air conditioner. Appeal filed.
    - BAOBAB (2003: 18).

27. Sirajo Idris (*Sok.*), sentenced in 2002 to amputation of the hand for stealing a television and a bag.
    - BAOBAB (2003: 19).

28. Two men (*Kat.*), sentenced in 2002 to amputation of the hand for stealing a bull. Appeal filed.
    - HRW (2004: 56).

29. Umaru Guda (*Sok.*), sentenced in 2002 to amputation of the hand for stealing personal effects. Appeal filed.
    - BAOBAB (2003: 19).

30. Abubakar Abdullahi (*Zam.*), sentenced in February 2002 to amputation of the hand for stealing nine bundles of textile and children's wear worth 30,500 Naira. His accomplice, Mustapha Ibrahim, was sentenced to six months in prison and thirty lashes.
    - "Sharia Court Orders Another Amputation," *This Day*, 19/02/2002.
    - HRW (2004: 48-9 and 56).

31. Usman Shehu and Umar Musa (*Ji.*), arraigned in March 2002 for stealing two goats worth 6,000 Naira.
    - "Sharia court adjourns for suspects to reconsider confession," *Daily Trust*, 27/03/2002, print edition.

32. Haruna Bayero of Gombe State (*Kan.*), sentenced in April 2002 to amputation of the hand for breaking into a shop and stealing property worth 17,500 Naira. Retrial ordered by appellate court in April 2004.
    - "Two to be Amputated in Kano," *This Day*, 11/04/2002, print edition.
    - HRW (2004: 53 and 56).

33. Abdul Jolly Hassan (*Bau.*), sentenced in June 2002 to one year's imprisonment and 40 strokes of the cane for stealing 18 sheep worth 50,000 Naira.
    - "Man Escapes Amputation over Theft of 18 Sheep," *This Day*, 24/06/2002.

34. Mustapha Abubakar (*Sok.*), arraigned in August 2002 for attempted theft.
    - "Man found in Security Van Charged to Court," *This Day*, 06/08/2002.

35. Musa Shuaibu (*Zam.*), sentenced in August 2002 to amputation of the hand. Acquitted on appeal in September 2002.
    - "Safiyat becomes honorary citizen of Rome," *The Guardian* (Nigeria), 06/09/2002, 56.

36. Abubakar Hamid (*Keb.*), sentenced in October 2002 to amputation of the hand for stealing motorbikes.
    - HRW (2004: 45-6).

37. Bello Mohammed and Mohammed Mansir (*Keb.*), sentenced in November 2002 to amputation of the hand.
    - HRW (2004: 41-2).

38. Abubakar Yusuf (*Zam.*), sentenced in April 2003 to amputation of the hand for stealing a video camera, a photo camera and a generator. Appeal filed.
    - HRW (2004: 51).

39. Sirajo Mohammed (*Zam.*), sentenced in April 2003 to amputation of the hand for stealing a sheep. Appeal filed.
    - HRW (2004: 47-8).

40. Abubakar Lawali and Lawali Na Umma (*Zam.*), sentenced in May 2003 to amputation of the hand for stealing provisions and money from a shop.
    - HRW (2004: 46-7).

41. Allassan Ibrahim and Hamza Abdullahi (*Kan.*), sentenced in June 2003 to amputation of the hand for stealing 20 cups of millet, dresses and a box of a total value of 6,000 Naira. Appeal filed.
    - "Kano Sharia court orders amputation of two men for theft," *The Guardian* (Nigeria), 24/06/2003, 3.
    - HRW (2004: 52).

42. Mustapha Hamza, Aminu Shehu, Bashir Ahmed, Aminu Haruna, Rabiu Turuku and Ahmadu Usman, known as the "Zaria 6" (*Kad.*), sentenced in August and September 2003 to amputation of the hand. Sentences set aside on appeal in May 2005. Selected sources:
    - "Sharia: 6 Await Amputation," *This Day*, 12/08/2004.
    - "Sharia appeal court to review conviction of six men," *Vanguard*, 17/08/2004.
    - "Sharia court grants bail to six convicts," *The Guardian* (Nigeria), 18/05/2005, 7.

43. Abubakar Sani and Masaudu Ibrahim (*Kat.*), sentenced in October 2003 to amputation of the hand for stealing food items and textile worth 45,000 Naira.
    - "Court orders amputation of limbs in Katsina," *Daily Independent*, 22/10/2003.

44. Ibrahim Sulaiman (*Zam.*), sentenced in December 2003 to amputation of the hand for breaking into a shop and stealing property worth thousands of Naira.
    - "Sharia court orders amputation," *New Nigerian Newspaper*, 28/01/2003, 30.

## *Armed robbery* (ḥirāba)

1. Garba Dandare and Sani Shehu (*Sok.*), sentenced in December 2001 to have their right hand and left foot amputated for armed robbery and stealing goods and cash.
    - "2 robbers face amputation in Sokoto," *Daily Trust*, 20/12/2001, 1.
    - "Sharia court orders amputation of hands, legs in Sokoto," *The Guardian* (Nigeria), 20/12/2001, print edition.

## *Intoxication* (shurb al-khamr)

1. Dahiru Sule (*Zam.*), sentenced in February 2000 to 80 lashes for drinking alcohol. Selected sources:
    - "Nigerian man flogged for drinking," BBC News, 11/02/2000.
    - "Sharia: Alcoholic gets 80 lashes," *The Guardian* (Nigeria), 12/02/2000, 1-2.

2. Nasiru Mohammed (*Kan.*), sentenced in July 2000 to flogging and imprisonment for "drunkenness and intentional insult of an innocent citizen under the influence of alcohol."
   - "Kano man to get 80 strokes for drinking alcohol," *The Guardian* (Nigeria), 05/07/2000, print edition.

3. Sule Sale (*Kat.*), sentenced in August 2000 to 86 lashes for drinking alcohol and stealing cigarettes.
   - Amnesty International Annual Report 2001.

4. Hassan Umoru (*Zam.*), sentenced in September 2000 to 80 lashes for drinking alcohol and one year's imprisonment for insulting an elderly man.
   - Amnesty International (2000: 7).

5. Lawali Jekada (*Zam.*), sentenced in September 2000 to 80 strokes of the cane for publicly consuming alcohol.
   - "Two men flogged publicly in Nigeria for drinking, stealing," AFP, 25/09/2000.
   - Amnesty International (2000: 7).

6. *Sharīʿa* court judge Muhammadu Na'ila (*Zam.*), sentenced in January 2001 to 80 strokes of the cane.
   - "In Nigeria, boozing Islamic court judge flogged for drinking," AFP, 20/01/2002.
   - "Sharia judge gets 80 lashes for taking alcohol," *The Punch*, 21/01/2002, print edition.
   - "Sharia judge flogged for boozing," BBC News, 21/01/2002.

7. Nuhu Abdullahi and Sa'adu Aminu (*Kan.*), sentenced in January 2001 to 80 strokes of the cane "on their bare backs."
   - "Crowd crams Nigerian court to watch boozers being flogged," AFP, 03/01/2001.
   - "Two Sharia Convicts Get 80 Lashes in Kano," *This Day*, 04/01/2001.

8. Umaru Bubeh (*Kat.*), sentenced in March 2001 to 80 lashes for drinking alcohol.
   - "Muslim flogged for drinking alcohol tells court he will not stop," AFP, 09/03/2001.
   - "Drama as *Sharia* convict dares judge with *Whisky* sachet," *Vanguard*, 09/03/2001, 1.

9. Umar Mohammed (*Sok.*), sentenced in April 2001 to 80 strokes of the cane for drinking beer.
   - "Two Kids Share 40 Lashes for Goat Theft," *This Day*, 25/04/2001.

10. Kabiru Yusuf, Salisu Danjuma and Rabiu Mohammed (*Kat.*), sentenced in May 2001 to 80 lashes each for drinking alcohol (based on a Funtua bye-law). Three other men were discharged and acquitted from the same offence.
   - "3 old men receive 80 lashes each for consuming alcohol," *Vanguard*, 12/05/2001, 2.

11. Bello Abdulkadir (*Jig.*), sentenced in February 2002 to 80 strokes of the cane for drunkenness.
    - "Man Receives 80 Lashes for Drunkenness," *This Day*, 01/03/2002.

12. Abdulkadir Garba (*Jig.*), sentenced in September 2002 to 80 strokes of the cane for drunkenness.
    - "Village Head, Tutor, Girlfriend Caned 240 Lashes," This Day, 25/09/2002.

13. Abdulsalam Garba and his girl friend Ladi Muhammad (*Jig.*), sentenced in September 2002 to 80 strokes of the cane for drunkenness.
    - "Village Head, Tutor, Girlfriend Caned 240 Lashes," This Day, 25/09/2002.

14. Abba Bashir (*Jig.*), a son of a senior member of the Dutse Emirate Council, sentenced on two occasions in December 2002 and January 2003 to 80 strokes of the cane for drunkenness.
    - "Man caned for drunkenness in Dutse," *New Nigerian Newspaper*, 03/01/2003, 24.
    - "20-Year-Old Prince Caned for Drunkenness," *Daily Trust*, 23/01/2003, print edition.
    - "Emirate declares war on Sharia police for caning ruler's son," *The Guardian* (Nigeria), 07/02/2003, 5.
    - "Emirate Council Dissolves Sharia Committee," *This Day*, 21/02/2003.
    - "Jigawa: Effective *Zakkat* system, poor sharia implementation," *Weekly Trust*, 26/07-01/08/2003, 7.

15. A man in his twenties (*Keb.*), sentenced in 2003 to flogging for intoxication.
    - HRW (2004: 61).

16. Garba Aliyu (*Zam.*), sentenced in July 2003 to 80 lashes for admitting drinking alcohol on earlier occasions.
    - HRW (2004: 59).

17. Ibrahim Musa (*Bau.*), sentenced in November 2004 to 80 strokes of the cane.
    - "Alcohol: Sharia Court Orders Man Caned 80 Strokes," *This Day*, 01/02/2005.

## *Other criminal offences*

1. Jafaru Isa and Maniru Abdullahi (*Zam.*), two of 200 arrested commercial motorcycle riders, sentenced in August 2000 to twenty lashes for carrying women to whom they were not married.
    - "Sharia lashings for motorbike taxi riders," BBC News, 10/08/2000.
    - "Sharia beating for motorcyclists," BBC News, 10/08/2000.

2. Garuba Bagobiri-Umguwar and Mohammadu Danige (*Zam.*), sentenced in September 2000 to 20 lashes for gambling.
    - "Islamic scholar jailed for preaching violence in Nigeria," AFP, 28/09/2000.
    - Amnesty International Annual Report 2001.

3. Militant preacher Mohammadu Sani Julijoka (*Zam.*), sentenced in September 2000 to one year in prison for inciting violence after he urged people to protest against the "lenient way" in which the *sharīʿa* was implemented in the state.
   - "Islamic scholar jailed for preaching violence in Nigeria," AFP, 28/09/2000.

4. More than forty-five women (*Kan.*), arraigned in late 2000 for prostitution.
   - "45 Prostitutes Face Kano Sharia Courts," *Post Express*, 16/12/2000, 94.

5. Emmanuel Oye and Femi Lasisi (*Sok.*), born Christians, sentenced in July 2001 to a 2,000 Naira fine or two months' imprisonment for "idleness" and "belonging to a group of thieves," insisted on being tried before a *sharīʿa* court.
   - "Sharia Court Convicts Two Christians," *This Day*, 01/08/2001.

6. Ten alleged prostitutes (*Kan.*), sentenced in February 2001 to two weeks' imprisonment, and twenty-six men, sentenced to one month's imprisonment, for participating in an "immoral gathering." They were among sixty people arrested in January 2001.
   - "Sharia Court Jails 10 Women in Kano," *This Day*, 16/02/2001.
   - "Sharia: Suspected prostitute dies in detention," *The Guardian* (Nigeria), 17/02/2001, 48.

7. Two policemen (*Kat.*), sentenced in 2001 to 100 strokes of the cane for illegal confiscation of petrol from fuel vendors.
   - "Sharia court orders amputation of hands, legs in Sokoto," *The Guardian* (Nigeria), 20/12/2001, print edition.

8. Dauda Maroki and Gambo Maibishi (*Kat.*), two traditional Hausa praise singers, sentenced in April 2001 to ten strokes of the cane.
   - "Sharia strokes for musicians," *The Comet*, 24/04/2001, print edition;
   - "Sharia: Musicians Caned for Playing at Wedding," *This Day*, 27/04/2001.

9. Sirajo Ashanlenle (*Kat.*), a traditional Hausa musician, indicted in April 2001 for performing music, pardoned after he promised never to play at weddings again.
   - "*Sharia* strokes for musicians," *The Comet*, 24/04/2001, print edition.
   - "Sharia: Musicians Caned for Playing at Wedding," *This Day*, 27/04/2001.

10. 107 alleged prostitutes (*Keb.*), sentenced in June 2001 to 20 lashes of the cane each for idleness and wandering.
    - "107 prostitutes, 20 gamblers caned in Kebbi," *Vanguard*, 16/06/2001, 3.

11. Four Muslims (*Sok.*), sentenced in July 2001 to lashing for smoking Marihuana.
    - "Sharia Court Convicts Two Christians," *This Day*, 01/08/2001.

12. Sani Mamman (*Sok.*), indicted in July 2001 for selling carrion.

- "Sharia Court Jails Man for Selling Dead Animal's Meat," *This Day*, 20/07/2001, 5.

13. Mohammed Jobi and Issa Abdullahi (*Sok.*), two officials of the state's branch of the National Orientation Agency, sentenced in August 2001 to corporal punishment and fine for embezzling the cash gratuity of an employee.
    - "Nigeria civil servants flogged under Sharia," BBC News, 15/08/2001.
    - "NOA Director, Accountant Get 80 Lashes for Cheating," *This Day*, 17/08/2001.

14. Yunusa Yargaba (*Jig.*), sentenced in August 2001 to 100 strokes of the cane for attempted rape of a blind woman.
    - "Man to Get 100 Lashes for Attempted Rape," *This Day*, 27/08/2001.

15. Traditional ruler Abba Ajiya (*Jig.*), sentenced in November 2001, together with his companion and an accomplice, to 40 strokes of the cane and one year's imprisonment for living with a woman to whom he was not married.
    - "Sharia: FG, Sokoto Fight Over Safiya," *This Day*, 18/11/2001, 1 and 4.
    - "Sharia court orders amputation of hands, legs in Sokoto," *The Guardian* (Nigeria), 20/12/2001, print edition.

16. Nagogo Kakumi (*Zam.*), accused in November 2001 of marrying more than four wives. It is unclear if this was treated as a criminal case.
    - "Man, 40, to Be Caned For Marrying 5 Wives," *Daily Trust*, 20/11/2001, print edition.

17. Abdulsalami Ahmed Asha (*Zam.*), a member of the State House of Assembly, indicted in November 2001 for selling his official car.
    - "Nigerian official faces Sharia court," BBC News, 25/05/2001.
    - "Sharia court orders amputation of hands, legs in Sokoto," *The Guardian* (Nigeria), 20/12/2001, print edition.

18. Hawa Yahaya, Umar Garba and Yaro (*Zam.*), indicted in February 2002 for conspiracy to robbery.
    - "Man Gets 100 Strokes, One-Year Jail for Sodomy," *This Day*, 28/02/2002, 5.

19. Two former Muslims (*Zam.*) who allegedly converted to Christianity, brought before a *sharīʿa* court in April 2002 on charges of apostasy. Case dismissed.
    - HRW (2004: 82).

20. Bus driver Tasi'u Saidu (*Kad.*), charged in June 2002 with injuring two women.
    - "Man Remanded for Assault on Pregnant Woman," *This Day*, 07/06/2002.

21. Seven alleged prostitutes (*Kat.*), sentenced in September 2002 to 15 strokes of the cane each for "loitering."
    - "Kebbi sacks Sharia court judge over financial scam," *The Guardian* (Nigeria), 10/09/2002, print edition.

22. Labaran Magayaki, Kwari, Shaibu and Kabiru (*Zam.*), sentenced in January 2003 to paying a fine and compensation to the complainant for criminal trespass.
    - HRW (2004: 69).

23. Saminu Abbas (*Kan.*), indicted in 2003 for "gross indecency" for raping a four-year-old girl.
    - "Man in Sharia court for raping 4-year-old girl," *Daily Trust*, 26/05/2003, 23.

24. Abdu Rabe (*Kat.*), sentenced in June 2003 to two years' imprisonment and 20 strokes of the cane for indecent behaviour after having entered in a female students' hostel, where he indecently touched a student.
    - "Sharia court jails 45-yr-old man," *Daily Trust*, 24/06/2003, print edition.

25. Mudansiru Abdulmumini (*Kan.*), sentenced in June 2003 to 20 lashes for dealing in intoxicants.
    - HRW (2004: 60).

26. Shafaiatu Tukur (*Zam.*), indicted in September 2003 for burning down her fellow wife's home.
    - "*Sharia* Court orders caning of woman," *The Guardian* (Nigeria), 02/10/2003.
    - "*Sharia* Court Orders Woman to Receive 30 Lashes for Arson," *Daily Trust*, 02/10/2003, print edition.

27. Four members of the governor's re-election campaign committee (*Zam.*), accused in October 2003 of diverting 374 motorcycles meant for the state's poverty alleviation programme.
    - "Sharia: Zamfara gov's campaign manager docked over theft," *Daily Independent*, 31/10/2003.

28. A wedding party (*Zam.*) comprising eight individuals, sentenced in December 2004 to 25 strokes of the cane and a fine of 5,000 Naira each for immoral acts after organising a picnic in honour of the groom.
    - "Wedding picnic: Sharia court sentences couples to 25 lashes," *Daily Trust*, 29/12/2004.

# Bibliography


Abun-Nasr, Jamil M. 1965. *The Tijaniyya: A Sufi Order in the Modern World.* London: Oxford University Press (Middle Eastern Monographs, volume 7).

———. 1988. "Zur politischen Bedeutung der Berufungsgerichte für die Muslime in Nigeria." *Die Welt des Islams*, 28:1, 38-61.

——— (ed.). 1993a. *Muslime in Nigeria: Religion und Gesellschaft im politischen Wandel seit den 50er Jahren*. Münster and Hamburg: Lit Verlag.

———. 1993b. "Islamisches Recht im nigerianischen Rechtssystem." In *Muslime in Nigeria*, ed. Jamil M. Abun-Nasr, 201-25. Münster and Hamburg: Lit Verlag.

Amnesty International. 2000. *Nigeria: Time for justice and accountability.* AFR 44/14/00.

Amnesty International and Legal Defence and Assistance Project (LEDAP). 2008. *Nigeria: 'Waiting for the Hangman'*. London and Lagos.

Anderson, J. N. D. 1957. "Conflict of Laws in Northern Nigeria." *Journal of African Law*, 1:2, 87-98.

Bambale, Yahaya Yunusa. 2003. *Crimes and punishments under Islamic law.* 2nd edn. Ikeja: Malthouse Press.

BAOBAB for Women's Human Rights. 2003. *Sharia Implementation in Nigeria: The Journey so far*. Lagos, available at <http://www.baobabwomen.org>.

Barkow, Jerome. 1971. "The Institution of Courtesanship in the Northern States of Nigeria." *Genève-Afrique*, 10:1, 59-73.

———. 1972. "Hausa Women and Islam." *Canadian Journal of African Studies / Revue Canadienne des Études Africaines*, 6:2, 317-28.

———. 1973. "Muslims and Maguzawa in North Central State, Nigeria: An Ethnographic Comparison." *Canadian Journal of African Studies / Revue Canadienne des Études Africaines*, 7:1, 59-76.

Blench, Roger; Selbut Longtau; Umar Hassan and Martin Walsh. 2006. *The Role of Traditional Rulers in Conflict Prevention and Mediation in Nigeria*. Study prepared for the United Kingdom's Department for International Development (DFID), Nigeria.

Bossaller, Anke. 1994. "Kwantacce, ‚schlafende' Schwangerschaft bei den Hausa." *curare*, 17:2, 171-80.

———. 2004. *'Schlafende Schwangerschaft' in islamischen Gesellschaften. Entstehung und soziale Implikationen einer weiblichen Fiktion*. Würzburg: Ergon.

Boyd, Jean, and Hamyat M. Maishanu. 1991. *Sultan Siddiq Abubakar III: Sarkin Musulmi*. Ibadan: Spectrum Books.

Brenner, Louis. 1973. *The Shehus of Kukawa: A History of the Al-Kanemi Dynasty of Bornu*. Oxford: Oxford University Press.

Brigaglia, Andrea. 2005. "Two Published Hausa Translations of the Qur'ān and their Doctrinal Background." *Journal of Religion in Africa*, 35: 4, 424-49.

———. 2007. "The Radio Kaduna Tafsīr (1978-1992) and the construction of public images of Muslim scholars in the Nigerian media." *Journal of Islamic Studies*, 27, 173-210.

Callaway, Barbara J. 1984. "Ambiguous Consequences of the Socialisation and Seclusion of Hausa Women." *Journal of Modern African Studies*, 22:3, 429-50.

Christelow, Allen [Allan]. 1994. *Thus Ruled Emir Abbas: Selected Cases from the Records of the Emir of Kano's Judicial Council*. East Lansing: Michigan State University Press.

Christelow, Allan. 2002. "Islamic Law and Judicial Practice: An Historical Perspective." *Journal of Muslim Minority Affairs*, 22:1, 186-204.

———. 2006. "Islamic Judicial Councils and their Sociopolitical Contexts: A Trans-Saharan Comparison." In *Dispensing Justice in Islam*, ed. Muhammad Khalid Masud et al., 299-319. Leiden and Boston: Brill.

Dekker, Albert, and Philip Ostien. 2009. "L'application du droit pénal islamique dans le Nord-Nigeria." *Afrique contemporaine*, 231, 245-64.

Garba, Ahmed S. 2006. "The Place Of Community Policing Under The Shari'ah And The Advent Of Hisbah." Electronic essay published at <http://www.gamji.com> in August 2006.

Gumi, Abubakar. 1994 (repr. 2001). *Where I Stand*. Ibadan: Spectrum Books.

Gwarzo, Tahir Haliru. 2003. "Activities of Islamic civic associations in the Northwest of Nigeria: with particular reference to Kano State." *africa spectrum*, 38:3, 289-318.

Hauck, Gerhard. 2001. *Gesellschaft und Staat in Afrika*. Frankfurt am Main: Brandes & Apsel.

Hiskett, Mervyn. 1973. *The Sword of Truth: the life and times of the Shehu Usuman Dan Fodio*. New York: Oxford University Press.

Hock, Klaus. 1996. *Der Islam-Komplex: Zur christlichen Wahrnehmung des Islams und der christlich-islamischen Beziehungen in Nordnigeria während der Militärherrschaft Babangidas*. Hamburg: Lit Verlag.

Hodges, Anthony (ed.). 2001. *Children's and Women's Rights in Nigeria: A Wake-up Call*. Joint report by UNICEF and the Nigerian National Planning Commission, Abuja.

Human Rights Watch. 2001. *Jos: A City Torn Apart*. 13:9 (A).

———. 2003. *The "Miss World Riots": Continued Impunity for Killings in Kaduna*. 15:13 (A).

———. 2004. *"Political Shari'a"? Human Rights and Islamic Law in Northern Nigeria*. 16:9 (A).

Hunwick, John O. 1995. *Arabic Literature of Africa, vol. II: The Writings of Central Sudanic Africa*. Leiden and Boston: Brill.

Ibn Farḥūn. 1995. *Tabṣirat al-ḥukkām fī uṣūl al-aqḍiya wa manāhij al-aḥkām*. 2 vols. Beirut: Dār al-kutub al-ʿilmiyya.

Ibrahim, Hauwa, and Princeton N. Lyman. 2004. *Reflections on the New Shari'a Law in Nigeria*. New York and Washington: Council on Foreign Relations.

Ibrahim, Jibrin. 2003. "Ethno-Religious Differences and the Politics of Tolerance in Nigeria." Paper presented at a Conference on State and Nation Making in Contemporary Africa and Asia, 17-19 February 2003, Pretoria, South Africa.

——— (ed.). 2004. *Sharia Penal and Family Laws in Nigeria and in the Muslim World: Rights Based Approach*. Zaria: Ahmadu Bello University Press.

Imam, Ayesha. 1991. "The Development of Women's Seclusion in Hausaland." *Dossier 9-10*, ed. Women living under Muslim laws (WLUML).

———. 2004. "Fighting the Political (Ab)Use of Religion in Nigeria: BAOBAB for Women's Human Rights, Allies and Others." In *Warning Signs of Fundamentalisms*, ed. Women living under Muslim laws (WLUML), 125-34.

International Crisis Group. 2006. *Nigeria: Want in the Midst of Plenty*. Africa Report No. 113.

Johansen, Baber. 2002. "Signs as Evidence: the doctrine of Ibn Taymiyya (1263-1328) and Ibn Qayyim al-Jawziyya (d. 1351) on proof." *Islamic Law and Society*, 9:2, 168-93.

Kane, Ousmane. 2003. *Muslim Modernity in Postcolonial Nigeria: A Study of the Society for the Removal of Innovation and Reinstatement of Tradition*. Leiden and Boston: Brill (Islam in Africa, volume 1).

Kirwin, Matthew. 2009. "Popular Perceptions of Shari'a Law in Nigeria." *Islam and Christian-Muslim Relations*, 20:2, 137-51.

Kleiner-Bossaller, Anke. 1993. "Zur Stellung der Frau in der Hausagesellschaft: Ein brüchig gewordener Konsens." In *Muslime in Nigeria*, ed. Jamil M. Abun-Nasr, 83-126. Münster and Hamburg: Lit Verlag.

Kogelmann, Franz. 2006. "The 'Sharia Factor' in Nigeria's 2003 Elections." In *Muslim-Christian Encounters in Africa*, ed. Benjamin F. Soares, 256-74. Leiden and Boston: Brill.

Ladan, Muhammad Tawfiq. 2004. "Legal Pluralism and the Development of the Rule of Law in Nigeria: Issues and Challenges in the Development and Application of the Sharia." In *Sharia Penal and Family Laws in Nigeria and in the Muslim World: Rights Based Approach*, ed. Jibrin Ibrahim, 57-113. Zaria: Ahmadu Bello University Press.

Last, Murray. 1967. *The Sokoto Caliphate*. London: Humanities Press.

———. 2000. "La charia dans le Nord-Nigeria." *Politique africaine*, 79, 141-52.

———. 2008. "The Search for Security in Muslim Northern Nigeria." *Africa*, 78:1, 41-63.

Layish, Aharon. 2004. "The Transformation of the *Sharīʿa* from Jurists' Law to Statutory Law in the Contemporary Muslim World." *Die Welt des Islams*, 44:1, 85-113.

Loimeier, Roman. 1993a. *Islamische Erneuerung und politischer Wandel in Nordnigeria*. Münster and Hamburg: Lit Verlag.

———. 1993b. "Auseinandersetzungen im islamischen Lager." In *Muslime in Nigeria*, ed. Jamil M. Abun-Nasr, 127-64. Münster and Hamburg: Lit Verlag.

———. 1997. *Islamic Reform and Political Change in Northern Nigeria*. Evanston, IL: Northwestern University Press.

——— (ed.). 2000a. *Die islamische Welt als Netzwerk: Möglichkeiten und Grenzen des Netzwerkansatzes im islamischen Kontext*. Würzburg: Ergon Verlag.

———. 2000b. "Ist Fußball unislamisch? Zur Tiefenstruktur des Banalen." In *Die islamische Welt als Netzwerk*, ed. Roman Loimeier, 101-19. Würzburg: Ergon Verlag.

———. 2007. "Nigeria: The Quest for a Viable Religious Option." In *Political Islam in West Africa*, ed. William F.S. Miles, 43-72. Boulder, CO: Lynne Rienner Publishers.

Loimeier, Roman, and Stefan Reichmuth. 1993. "Bemühungen der Muslime um Einheit und politische Geltung." In *Muslime in Nigeria*, ed. Jamil M. Abun-Nasr, 41-81. Münster and Hamburg: Lit Verlag.

Ludwig, Frieder. 2008. "Christian-Muslim Relations in Northern Nigeria since the Introduction of Shari'ah in 1999." *Journal of the American Academy of Religion*, 76:3, 602-37.

Marshall, Paul. 2002. *The Talibanisation of Nigeria: Sharia Law and Religious Freedom*. Washington: Freedom House.

Masud, Muhammad Khalid; Rudolph Peters and David S. Powers (eds.). 2006. *Dispensing Justice in Islam: Qadis and their judgments*. Leiden and Boston: Brill (Studies in Islamic Law and Society, volume 22).

Miles, William F.S. (ed.). 2007. *Political Islam in West Africa: State-Society Relations Transformed*. Boulder, CO: Lynne Rienner Publishers.

Mitchell, Richard P. 1969 (repr. 1993). *The Society of the Muslim Brothers*. New York: Oxford University Press.

Mohammed, Kyari. 2002. "Religion and Federalism in Nigeria, 1958-2002: Contextualizing the Shari'ah Project." Paper presented at an International Conference on Federalism and the State, University of Ibadan, Nigeria, 25-26 November 2002.

Nasir, Jamila M. 2007. "Sharia Implementation and Female Muslims in Nigeria's Sharia States." In *Sharia Implementation in Northern Nigeria 1999-2006*, ed. Philip Ostien, 3:76-118. Ibadan: Spectrum Books.

O'Brien, Susan M. 2007. "La charia contestée: démocractie, débat et diversité musulmane dans les « États charia » du Nigeria." *Politique africaine*, 106, 46-68.

Ostien, Philip. 2002. "Ten Good Things about the Implementation of Shari'a taking place in some States of Northern Nigeria." *Swedish Missiological Themes*, 90:2, 163-74.

———. 2006. "An Opportunity Missed by Nigeria's Christians: The 1976-78 Sharia Debate Revisited." In *Muslim-Christian Encounters in Africa*, ed. Benjamin F. Soares, 221-55. Leiden and Boston: Brill.

——— (comp. and ed.). 2007. *Sharia Implementation in Northern Nigeria 1999-2006: A Sourcebook*. 5 vols. Ibadan: Spectrum Books.
Vol. 1, *Historical Background*.
Vol. 2, *Sharia Implementation Committee Reports and Related White Papers*
Vol. 3, *Sanitizing Society*.
Vol. 4, *The Sharia Penal and Criminal Procedure Codes*.
Vol. 5, *Two Famous Cases*.

———. 2009. "Jonah Jang and the Jasawa: Ethno-Religious Conflict in Jos, Nigeria." *Muslim-Christian Relations in Africa* (www.sharia-in-africa.net).

Ostien, Philip, and Albert Dekker. 2010. "Sharia and National Law in Nigeria." In *Sharia incorporated: A Comparative Overview of the Legal Systems of Twelve Muslim Countries in Past and Present*, ed. J.M. Otto, 553-612. Leiden: Leiden University Press.

Ostien, Philip; Jamila M. Nasir and Franz Kogelmann (eds.). 2005. *Comparative Perspectives on Shari'ah in Nigeria*. Ibadan: Spectrum Books.

Ostien, Philip, and M.J. Umaru. 2007. "Changes in the Law in the Sharia States Aimed at Suppressing Social Vices." In *Sharia Implementation in Northern Nigeria 1999-2006*, ed. Philip Ostien, 3:9-75. Ibadan: Spectrum Books.

Otto, Jan Michiel (ed.). 2010. *Sharia incorporated: A Comparative Overview of the Legal Systems of Twelve Muslim Countries in Past and Present*. Leiden: Leiden University Press.

Paden, John N. 2005. *Muslim Civic Cultures and Conflict Resolution: The Challenge of Democratic Federalism in Nigeria*. Washington D.C.: Brookings Institution Press.

Paret, Rudi. 2001. *Der Koran: Kommentar und Konkordanz. 6. Auflage*. Stuttgart: Kohlhammer.

Pereira, Charmaine. 2005. "Zina and transgressive heterosexuality in northern Nigeria." *Feminist Africa*, 5, 52-79.

Pérouse de Montclos, Marc-Antoine. 2008. "Conversions to Islam and Modernity in Nigeria: A View from the Underworld." *Africa Today*, 54:4, 71-87.

Peters, Rudolph. 1994. "The Islamization of Criminal Law: a comparative analysis." *Die Welt des Islams*, 34:2, 246-74.

———. 2002a. "From Jurists' Law to Statute Law or What Happens When the Shariʿa is Codified." *Mediterranean Politics*, 7:3, 83-95.

———. 2002b. "Murder in Khaybar: Some Thoughts on the Origins of the *Qasāma* Procedure in Islamic Law." *Islamic Law and Society*, 9:2, 132-67.

Peters, Ruud [Rudolph]. 2003. *Islamic Criminal Law in Nigeria*. Ibadan: Spectrum Books.

Peters, Rudolph. 2005. *Crime and Punishment in Islamic Law: Theory and Practice from the Sixteenth to the Twenty-first Century*. Cambridge: Cambridge University Press.

———. 2006. "The Re-Islamization of Criminal Law in Northern Nigeria: The Safiyyatu Hussaini Case." In *Dispensing Justice in Islam: Qadis and their judgments*, ed. Muhammad Khalid Masud et al., 219-41. Leiden and Boston: Brill.

———. 2009. "Sharia and 'Natural Justice': The Implementation of Islamic Criminal Law in British India and Colonial Nigeria." In *Islamica: Studies in the memory of Holger Preißler (1943-2006)*. Oxford: Oxford University Press (Journal of Semitic Studies Book Supplement Series, issue 26), 127-150.

Raymond, Petra, and Harruna Attah. 2004. *Conflict: What has Religion got to do with it? An African-European Dialogue*. Accra: Goethe-Institut Accra and Woeli Publishing Services.

Reza, Sadiq. 2007. "Torture and Islamic Law." *Chicago Journal of International Law*, 8:1, 21-41.

Robson, Elsbeth. 2000. "Wife Seclusion and the Spatial Praxis of Gender Ideology in Nigerian Hausaland." *Gender, Place and Culture*, 7:2, 179-99.

Sada, Ibrahim Na'iya. 2002. "Death Penalty: The Islamic Perspective." Paper presented at a Consultation on Human Rights and Death Penalty in Nigeria, organised by the Nigerian National Human Rights Commission, Abuja, Nigeria, 10 October 2002.

———. 2007. "The Making of the Zamfara and Kano State Sharia Penal Codes." In *Sharia Implementation in Northern Nigeria 1999-2006*, ed. Philip Ostien, 4:22-32. Ibadan: Spectrum Books.

Sanusi, Sanusi Lamido. 2004. "Fundamentalist Groups and the Nigerian Legal System: Some Reflections." In *Warning Signs of Fundamentalisms*, ed. Women living under Muslim laws (WLUML), 79-82.

———. 2007. "Politics and Sharia in Northern Nigeria." In *Islam and Muslim Politics in Africa*, ed. Benjamin F. Soares and René Otayek, 177-88. New York: Palgrave Macmillan.

Schacht, Joseph. 1964. *An Introduction to Islamic Law*. Oxford: Clarendon Press.

Seesemann, Rüdiger. 1998. "The *Takfīr* Debate: Sources for the Study of a Contemporary Dispute among African Sufis, Part I: The Nigerian Arena." *Sudanic Africa*, 9, 39-70.

———. 2000. "Der lange Arm des Ibrāhīm Sāliḥ: Erfahrungen eines deutschen Forschers mit dem Netzwerk eines nigerianischen Gelehrten." In *Die islamische Welt als Netzwerk*, ed. Roman Loimeier, 135-61. Würzburg: Ergon Verlag.

———. 2009. "Three Ibrāhīms: Literary Production and the Remaking of the Tijāniyya Sufi Order in Twentieth-Century Sudanic Africa." *Die Welt des Islams*, 49:3-4, 299-333.

Soares, Benjamin F. (ed.). 2006. *Muslim-Christian Encounters in Africa*. Leiden and Boston: Brill (Islam in Africa, volume 6).

Soares, Benjamin F., and René Otayek (eds.). 2007. *Islam and Muslim Politics in Africa*. New York: Palgrave Macmillan.

Tabi'u, Muhammed. 2004, "An Overview of Sharia Law and Practice in Nigeria." In *Sharia Penal and Family Laws in Nigeria and in the Muslim World: Rights Based Approach*, ed. Jibrin Ibrahim, 115-127. Zaria: Ahmadu Bello University Press.

Tijani, Kyari. 2002. "Issues in the *Shari'a* debate—learning from Al-Kanemi (a political economy perspective)." *Borno Museum Society Newsletter*, 50-51, 7-31.

Umar, Muhammad S. 2001. "Education and Islamic Trends in Northern Nigeria: 1970s–1990s." *Africa Today*, 48:2, 126-50.

———. 2006. *Islam and Colonialism: Intellectual Responses of Muslims in Northern Nigeria to British Colonial Rule.* Leiden and Boston: Brill (Islam in Africa, volume 5).

United Nations, Committee on the Rights of the Child. 2004. "Second periodic reports of States parties due in 1998: Nigeria (17 September 2004)." CRC/C/70/Add.24.

Vikør, Knut S. 1999. *The History of Kawar, a Saharan Centre of Salt Production.* Bergen: Centre for Middle Eastern and Islamic Studies (Bergen Studies on the Middle East and Africa, volume 3).

Wall, L. Lewis. 1998. "Dead Mothers and Injured Wives: The Social Context of Maternal Morbidity and Mortality Among the Hausa of Northern Nigeria." *Studies in Family Planning*, 29:4, 341-359.

Weimann, Gunnar J. 2004. "Openness to Dialogue and the Limits of Intercultural Dialogue." In *Conflict: What has Religion got to do with it? An African-European Dialogue*, ed. Petra Raymond and Harruna Attah, 15-24. Accra: Goethe-Institut Accra and Woeli Publishing Services.

———. 2007. "Judicial Practice in Islamic Criminal Law in Nigeria—A tentative overview." *Islamic Law and Society*, 14:2, 240-86.

———. 2009. "Divine Law and Local Custom in Northern Nigerian *zinā* Trials." *Die Welt des Islams*, 49:3-4, 429-65.

———. 2010a. "An Alternative Vision of Shariʿa Application in Northern Nigeria: Ibrahim Salih's *Hadd Offences in the Shariʿa.*" *Journal of Religion in Africa*, 40:2, 192-221.

———. 2010b. "Islamic Law and Muslim Governance in Northern Nigeria: crimes against life, limb and property in *sharīʿa* judicial practice." *Islamic Law and Society*, 17:3-4.

———. Forthcoming. "Die Miss-World-Unruhen und die Beziehungen zwischen Muslimen und Christen in Nigeria." *Loccumer Protokoll 50/07* (proceedings of the VI. Interreligiöse Sommeruniversität "(Un-)Fähig zum Frieden? Juden, Christen, Muslime und ihre Rolle in Konflikten," Evangelische Akademie Loccum, Germany, 16-23 August 2007).

Werthmann, Katja. 1995. "Eingeschlossene Frauen? Seklusion in Nordnigeria: Ideologie und Alltagspraxis." In *Sprachkulturelle und historische Forschungen in Afrika. Beiträge zum 11. Afrikanistentag*, ed.

Axel Fleisch and Dirk Otten, 327-34. Cologne: Rüdiger Köppe Verlag.

———. 2000. "Hüterinnen der Tradition? Frauen und Islam in Afrika." *Journal of Religious Culture*, 41.

Wiedemann, Charlotte. 2006. "Zum Frieden verdammt." *Die Zeit*, 13/2006 (23 March 2006), 17.

Yadudu, Auwalu H. 1991. "Colonialism and the Transformation of the Substance and Form of Islamic Law in the Northern States of Nigeria." *Journal of Law and Religion*, 9:1, 17-47.

———. 2001. "Benefits of Shariah and Challenges of Reclaiming a Heritage." Paper presented at the Restoration of Shariah in Nigeria: Challenges and Benefits conference, organised by the Nigeria Muslim Forum, UK, London, 14 April 2001.

Yawuri, Aliyu Musa. 2004. "Issues in Defending Safiyyatu Husseini and Amina Lawal." In *Sharia Penal and Family Laws in Nigeria and in the Muslim World: Rights Based Approach*, ed. Jibrin Ibrahim, 183-204. Zaria: Ahmadu Bello University Press.

———. 2007. "On Defending Safiyatu Hussaini and Amina Lawal." In *Sharia Implementation in Northern Nigeria 1999-2006*, ed. Philip Ostien, 5:129-139. Ibadan: Spectrum Books.

Zakaria, Yakubu. 2001. "Entrepreneurs at Home: Secluded Muslim Women and Hidden Economic Activities in Northern Nigeria." *Nordic Journal of African Studies*, 10:1, 107-23.

# Summary

In 2000 and 2001, twelve northern states of the Federal Republic of Nigeria introduced Islamic criminal law by establishing *sharīʿa* courts and adopting *sharīʿa* penal codes which contained provisions on the *ḥadd* punishments and the Islamic law of homicide and bodily harm. The present thesis analyses available information on judicial practice in Islamic criminal law in northern Nigeria. Main sources on judicial practice have been media reports and non-governmental organisations.

The overall analysis shows that Islamic criminal law has not been implemented equally in every place and at any given time. Geographically, the new legislation has been applied more frequently in the north-west of the country, the core region of the former Sokoto Caliphate. Chronologically, it seems to have been applied with greater emphasis in the beginning, whereas for subsequent years the numbers of known trials rapidly decline.

In subsequent steps, judicial practice was analysed with regard to particular offences. The change in judicial practice is particularly visible in trials for extramarital sexual intercourse, some forms of which continue to be socially accepted in northern Nigeria. The prosecution of such offences was an attempt to enforce Islamic behaviour on Muslims. However, all sentences of stoning to death for unmarried mothers were revoked on appeal. Since 2004, no new indictments for consensual extramarital sexual relations have been reported. The courts have rejected accusations based on suspicion and confirmed the inviolability of the family compound.

With regard to crimes against life, limb and property, judicial practice does not present a clear picture. While the number of people prosecuted for violent offences has been small, a great number of sentences to amputation for theft have been handed down. However, not more than three amputations have taken place, all of them in the beginning of *sharīʿa* implementation. After 2001, no amputation has taken place in northern Nigeria. This finding attests to the fact that state governors, many of whom were forced by popular pressure to introduce Islamic criminal law, find it difficult to reconcile its implementation with their position in the secular Nigerian political system.

The findings concerning judicial practice in Islamic criminal law were put into context in the subsequent research. An alternative vision of *sharīʿa* application by an influential northern Nigerian Muslim scholar was analysed. His interpretation, which was clearly a response to the introduction of Islamic criminal law, emphasises the need to educate

Muslims and improve living standards. Only when a just Islamic society had become a reality would it be possible to implement Islamic criminal law. It is argued that such interpretations were at the root of the observed changes in judicial practice.

The existence of this counter-discourse promoted by one of the most influential scholars of northern Nigeria demonstrated that Muslims in northern Nigeria were far from unanimously supporting the implementation of Islamic criminal law. This raised the question as to the motives of the Nigerian Muslim religious establishment, represented in two umbrella organisations, for not challenging publicly the way in which Islamic criminal law was administered in the beginning. Based on an analysis of the public debates among Muslims with regard to the aborted 2002 Miss World contest in Nigeria, it is argued that the umbrella organisations' authority is built on their claim to represent Muslims in Nigeria on a political level and to unite them against the perceived threat from non-Muslims in the country. Had they criticised the introduction and implementation of Islamic criminal law in public, they would have risked damaging their position. Instead, the Muslim organisations supported the introduction of the *sharīʿa* in public statements, thereby contributing to a further aggravation of the Muslim-Christian antagonism.

# Samenvatting

In 2000 en 2001 hebben twaalf noordelijke staten van de Federale Republiek Nigeria het islamitisch strafrecht ingevoerd door *sharīʿa*-rechtbanken op te zetten en strafwetboeken volgens de *sharīʿa* aan te nemen met bepalingen over *ḥadd*-straffen en de islamitische wet betreffende moord en het toebrengen van lichamelijk letsel. In dit proefschrift wordt de beschikbare informatie geanalyseerd betreffende de juridische praktijk onder het islamitische strafrecht in het Noord-Nigeria. Als belangrijkste bronnen voor de juridische praktijk zijn rapporten uit de media en van niet-gouvernementele organisaties gebruikt.

De algemene analyse laat zien dat het islamitisch strafrecht niet overal en op elk moment in gelijke mate is toegepast. Geografisch gezien wordt de nieuwe wetgeving vaker in de praktijk gebracht in het noordwestelijke deel van het land, de kernregio van het voormalige Sokoto Caliphate. Chronologisch gezien schijnt deze vaker en nadrukkelijker te zijn toegepast in het begin, terwijl gedurende de daaropvolgende jaren voor zover bekend de aantallen rechtszaken snel afnamen.

Vervolgens is de juridische praktijk geanalyseerd met betrekking tot specifieke strafbare feiten. De verandering in de juridische praktijk is vooral zichtbaar bij rechtszaken wegens buitenechtelijke seksuele gemeenschap, waarvan sommige vormen nog altijd sociaal geaccepteerd zijn in Noord-Nigeria. Dergelijke strafbare feiten werden vervolgd in een poging om de moslims islamitisch gedrag op te dringen. Alle veroordelingen tot dood door steniging voor ongetrouwde moeders zijn in hoger beroep ingetrokken. Sinds 2004 zijn er geen nieuwe aanklachten meer gerapporteerd wegens vrijwillige buitenechtelijke seksuele relaties. De rechters hebben beschuldigingen op basis van verdenking verworpen en hebben de onschendbaarheid van de familienederzetting erkend.

Er blijkt geen duidelijk beeld uit de juridische praktijk met betrekking tot misdaden tegen lijf en goed. Terwijl het aantal mensen dat is vervolgd wegens geweldsmisdrijven klein is, zijn er veel veroordelingen tot amputatie wegens diefstal uitgesproken. Er zijn echter niet meer dan drie amputaties uitgevoerd, allemaal kort na invoering van de *sharīʿa*. Sinds 2001 zijn er geen amputaties meer uitgevoerd in Noord-Nigeria. Deze bevindingen bevestigen dat de lokale bestuurders, van wie velen door druk vanuit de bevolking gedwongen werden het islamitische strafrecht in te voeren, het moeilijk vinden de toepassing daarvan in overeenstemming te brengen met hun positie in het seculiere Nigeriaanse politieke systeem.

De bevindingen betreffende de juridische praktijk in het islamitische strafrecht zijn in hun context geplaatst in het vervolgonderzoek. Een alternatieve visie is geanalyseerd van een invloedrijke Noord-Nigeriaanse moslimgeleerde betreffende de toepassing van de *sharīʿa*. Zijn interpretatie was duidelijk een antwoord op de invoering van het islamitische strafrecht en benadrukte de noodzaak om moslims te ontwikkelen en hun levensstandaard te verbeteren. Pas als een rechtvaardige islamitische samenleving realiteit is geworden, is het mogelijk om het islamitisch strafrecht in te voeren. Gesteld wordt dat dergelijke interpretaties de aanzet hebben gegeven tot de waargenomen veranderingen in de juridische praktijk.

Het bestaan van deze tegenstroming, ondersteund door een van de meest invloedrijke geleerden van Noord-Nigeria, laat zien dat moslims in Noord-Nigeria bij lange na niet unaniem achter de invoering van het islamitisch strafrecht staan. Dit riep vragen op over de motieven van het religieuze moslim-establishment in Nigeria, vertegenwoordigd in twee koepelorganisaties, voor het niet in het openbaar protesteren tegen de manier waarop in het begin het islamitische strafrecht werd toegepast. Op basis van een analyse van de publieke debatten onder moslims met betrekking tot de afgeblazen Miss-Worldverkiezing in 2002, wordt gesteld dat het gezag van de koepelorganisaties steunt op hun bewering dat ze moslims in Nigeria vertegenwoordigen op politiek niveau en hen verenigen tegen de vermeende haat van niet-moslims in het land. Als ze de invoering en toepassing van het islamitisch strafrecht in het openbaar hadden bekritiseerd, zou dat afbreuk hebben kunnen doen aan hun positie. De moslim-organisaties hebben daarentegen de invoering van de *sharīʿa* in openbare verklaringen ondersteund en daardoor bijgedragen aan een verergering van de tegenstellingen tussen moslims en christenen.